R

Ex-Detective Chief Superintendent Roy Ranson investigated many of Britain's most infamous crimes in a thirty-three-year career as one of Scotland Yard's most senior detectives. In a distinguished police career, his many notable cases included the attempted kidnapping of Princess Anne; the theft of tax papers from former Prime Minister Harold Wilson; the Spaghetti House Siege in Knightsbridge; the foiling of a mass break-out of prisoners from Brixton Jail; and the attempted theft of the Stone of Scone from Westminster Abbey. None of his cases, however, captured the public imagination in the same way as the baffling 1974 disappearance of Richard John Bingham, the seventh Earl of Lucan.

After leaving the Metropolitan Police, Ranson became Chief Investigator for the BBC, uncovering corruption and theft among its thousands of staff. He lived in retirement with his wife Irene in Kent, but never retired from the Lucan inquiry. He died in December, 1994.

ROBERT STRANGE

As crime reporter for the *Evening Standard*, Robert Strange was one of the first journalists to report from the murder scene at the Lucan's Belgravia home. He has studied the case for twenty years, while graduating from Fleet Street newspapers to produce documentaries and current affairs programmes for all the major British television networks. He was the Executive Producer in 1994 of a major Channel Four *True Stories* documentary about the Lucan mystery. He lives in Kent with his wife Pamela and two children.

LOOKING FOR LUCAN
The Final Verdict

EX-DETECTIVE CHIEF SUPERINTENDENT
ROY RANSON
with Robert Strange

WARNER BOOKS

A *Warner* Book

First published in Great Britain in 1994 by
Smith Gryphon Limited

This edition published in 1995 by Warner Books

A CIP catalogue record for this book is
available from the British Library.

ISBN 0 7515 1143 9

Printed and bound in Great Britain by
Clays Ltd, St. Ives plc

Warner Books
A Division of
Little, Brown and Company (UK)
Brettenham House
Lancaster Place
London WC2E 7EN

CONTENTS

ACKNOWLEDGEMENTS

While writing this book I also worked with the Kilroy Television Company to produce a 'True Stories' documentary about the Lucan case for Channel Four. I would like to thank the entire production staff for their professionalism and help, not least for arranging my safe return from southern Africa. Among the team, my thanks in particular go to Susanna White, Robert Moore, Charlotte Desai, Tory Bridges and Sue Whiteley. For the illustrations in this book I would like to thank F. W. Strange and for taking many of the pictures, Byron Rees. On a personal level, my thanks to my agent Doreen Montgomery, to my son Charles Ranson for his help and advice, to Pamela, David and William Strange for understanding how much hard work a book can involve – and to my own wife, Irene, for putting up with both me and Lord Lucan for the past 20 years.

Plan of the basement at 46 Lower Belgrave Street

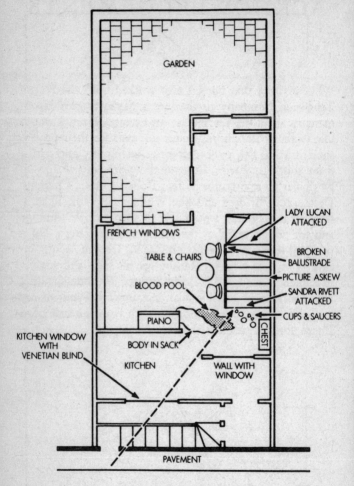

GARDEN

LADY LUCAN ATTACKED

BROKEN BALUSTRADE

PICTURE ASKEW

SANDRA RIVETT ATTACKED

CUPS & SAUCERS

FRENCH WINDOWS

TABLE & CHAIRS

BLOOD POOL

CHEST

PIANO

KITCHEN WINDOW WITH VENETIAN BLIND

BODY IN SACK

WALL WITH WINDOW

KITCHEN

PAVEMENT

Belgravia, London

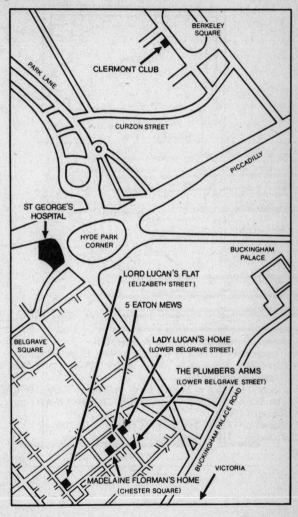

PARK LANE

BERKELEY SQUARE

CLERMONT CLUB

CURZON STREET

PICCADILLY

ST GEORGE'S HOSPITAL

HYDE PARK CORNER

BUCKINGHAM PALACE

LORD LUCAN'S FLAT
(ELIZABETH STREET)

5 EATON MEWS

BELGRAVE SQUARE

LADY LUCAN'S HOME
(LOWER BELGRAVE STREET)

THE PLUMBERS ARMS
(LOWER BELGRAVE STREET)

BUCKINGHAM PALACE ROAD

VICTORIA

MADELAINE FLORMAN'S HOME
(CHESTER SQUARE)

Sightings of Lord Lucan in Africa

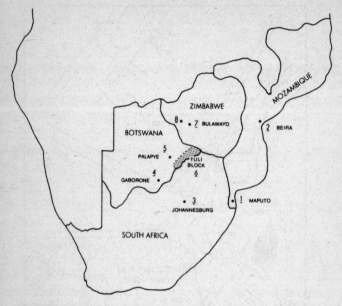

1. Maputo (formerly Lourenço Marques) – Dr Brian Hill sighting (1975)
2. Beira – David Hardy address book (1981)
3. Johannesburg – Home of Lucan's brother, Hugh Bingham
4. Gaborone – Sightings by Trevor Walton (1976), Janice Main and Brumpy Malan (1981)
5. Palapye – Named as Lucan's home by Trevor Walton (1976)
6. Tuli Block – Sightings investigated by Norman Chandler and Eric Ramsden (1981)
7. Bulawayo – Lucan bank account containing £15,000
8. Bulawayo – Lucan family farm

PREFACE

A degree of tact and an ability to get along with London's wealthiest and most influential residents is an essential qualification for police officers posted to Scotland Yard's 'A' Division in Westminster, central London. Those residents include Her Majesty The Queen at Buckingham Palace and the Royal Household at Windsor Castle, which, although outside London, is nevertheless under the protection of the Metropolitan Police.

Among my more unusual responsibilities, when I took over as the area's senior detective in 1973, was the transportation and protection of the British Crown Jewels. Normally housed in the impregnable Tower of London, some part of the collection of priceless jewels is occasionally required by the Queen on state ceremonial occasions. If Her Majesty wanted one of her crowns, it was my job to make sure it was safely delivered into her hands and subsequently returned intact to the Tower. One attempt had already been made to steal the Crown Jewels; but it was a little before my time, in 1671 to be precise, and it seemed unlikely that another attempt was imminent.

I therefore settled down to the busy routine of divisional police life, little expecting to find myself at the centre of headline news. That was the first of several wrong assumptions for, within a year, my new post was to make me the busiest detective in London.

The mayhem began on 20 March 1974, when a mentally ill gunman rammed one of the royal limousines near Buckingham Palace and tried to kidnap the Queen's only daughter, Her Royal Highness Princess Anne. The abduction, for which a £3 million ransom was to be demanded, was only foiled by the bravery of her police bodyguard, her chauffeur and two members of the public who were all shot in preventing the assailant's escape.

The would-be kidnapper, Ian Ball, had barely been sentenced when another lone fanatic attempted to steal a national treasure, the ancient Stone of Scone, from inside Westminster Abbey. The thief, a fanatical Scottish nationalist who wanted to return the Coronation stone to Scotland, was caught at the scene, but it took many weeks of investigations before I could be certain that no conspiracy was involved.

When, in October 1974, the then British Prime Minister, Harold Wilson, reported the theft of highly personal tax papers from his Whitehall home, I was once again thrust into the centre of a sensitive political inquiry. With the help of an informant I retrieved some of the missing documents, and two thieves were convicted. I thought that with this case my run of headline-making crimes must, at last, come to an end. Such thoughts were, however, simply tempting fate once again.

After such a hectic summer, I was grateful for a quiet evening on Thursday, 7 November 1974; a rare chance for an uninterrupted meal with my wife, Irene, and our children at our home in Kent. By 11 pm I was in bed for an early night and a deep and dreamless sleep.

My slumbers were rudely disturbed around midnight when the telephone rang. It was Dave Gerring, my Detective Chief-Inspector in charge of the Criminal Investigation Department (CID) at Gerald Road, one of the several local police stations under my command. Dave apologized for waking me but reported that he had been called out to a suspicious death.

The address was in the wealthy residential district of Belgravia. A woman's body had been found in a sack in the basement. He told me that the house, at 46 Lower Belgrave Street, was the home of Lord and Lady Lucan and that the Countess was in St George's Hospital, Hyde Park Corner, with serious head injuries. The dead woman was thought to be the children's nanny, and Lord Lucan had decamped from the scene. Dave thought the whole matter was an open-and-shut domestic murder that I could safely leave to him.

In my drowsy state I agreed to Dave Gerring's suggestion, but then, after first attempting to get back to sleep, I had what I can only describe as a premonition of just how important this 'open-and-shut' case would eventually prove to be. Starting bolt upright in bed, I woke my long-suffering wife again and told her I had to get off to work at once.

Irene was well used to a police officer's antisocial hours. While I showered and dressed, she threw a gown over her nightie and went outside to move her car out of the way, in order to drive mine out from the back of our garage. It was a wet and dismal November night, and as Irene shuttled cars back and forth she noticed a police panda car, parked in the street with two uniformed police officers observing, with some amazement, her early hours comings and goings. My wife was an unlikely criminal type, but it still took an explanation from me to satisfy the two conscientious officers that she should not become the very first suspect to be arrested in the course of the Lord Lucan inquiry.

I drove up to town through the shabby streets of South London and arrived at 46 Lower Belgrave Street soon after one o'clock in the morning. There, I took command of the investigation that proved to be the most fascinating case I was to deal with in my 33 years of police service. Because of it I extended my service with Scotland Yard beyond my expected retirement date. Since then, through a second career as an investigator with the BBC and into retirement, I have maintained my interest and have dug ever deeper into the mystery.

You could call it an obsession, you could call it a hobby, but either way it is very hard to escape from the missing Earl. The case returns to me with each of the constant references to Lucan in books, newspapers, cartoons and television programmes.

During these years I have been approached many times by journalists seeking an instant quote, or by authors anxious to push their own pet ideas about the

Lucan case. Until now I have avoided in-depth discussion of my own findings, preferring to sidestep the issue with a brief comment that Lucan could well be dead. I have found over the years that such a suggestion usually puts an end to further discussion.

But now an entire generation has grown up which knows little or nothing of this terrible crime; a murder mystery with a twist so unlikely that you would never believe it as a novel: *The Mystery of the Missing Earl*. In the absence of hard fact, rumour abounds, and such rumour and fiction are now in danger of obscuring the truth.

In the 20 years since that night, the case of Lord Lucan has taken on the mantle almost of a myth or legend. It has joined the ranks of a myriad other unsolved mysteries – but with one vital difference. The Lucan case is not an unsolved murder mystery. The crime was resolved to my satisfaction within days of its occurrence and to the satisfaction of a British coroner's jury a little while later. All that now remains is to bring the cold-blooded killer to justice. It is a wish that, for the past two decades, has kept me 'Looking for Lucan'.

CHAPTER 1

A MURDEROUS MISTAKE

The killer crouched low in the darkness at the side of the basement steps. Terrified by the enormity of the crime he was about to commit, yet driven by the certainty that brutal murder was his only solution. He was a ruined man anyway. Penniless and facing the unbearable shame of the bankruptcy courts; his beloved children in the hands of a woman he believed to be mad; his former life of luxury and wealth already but a fading memory. He had nothing left to lose.

By nature this killer was a gambling man. Addicted to the adrenalin surge that came with the turn of a card, the throw of the dice or the spin of a roulette wheel. That familiar adrenalin rush was with him tonight, in this, his highest stakes, life-or-death gamble. For he was a gambler by profession, as well as inclination. As with all of his bets, he had weighed up his chances most carefully. His plans had been laid – and the odds had been stacked in his favour.

The silent, waiting man heard, far above him, a murmur of conversation and, a few moments later, the first distant footsteps. He had chosen his evening carefully. The children's new nanny would be out tonight, leaving his wife and his children alone in the house. His wife was in the habit of descending to the basement kitchen at nine o'clock each night. She would make her cup of tea and take it upstairs to her room. After 11 years of marriage he knew her routine.

At the top of the basement stairs, the woman paused and flicked on the light switch. Her killer knew that the light would not work. The missing light bulb still lay on the chair, where he had placed it after reaching up with gloved hands to the ceiling socket. Darkness was his ally. Only the faintest light came from a distant street lamp, filtering through the half-closed venetian blinds and the tiny red glow of the power switch on the kitchen kettle.

Undaunted by the darkness, the woman trod slowly down the final flight of steps, careful not to drop the crockery she balanced in each hand. At the bottom she paused for an instant, suddenly aware of the terrible danger that was lying in wait. Then, as she started to turn towards a sudden movement, the murderer struck. Once . . . twice . . . three . . . four times, the heavy lead bludgeon came down with savage force. On the first sickening blow there was little blood; but with the second and third and fourth strikes, blood from the already open head wounds sprayed out across the room.

There was barely a sound and no more than a

reflex action from the victim to defend herself. She slumped to the floor amid a further frenzied rain of blows, her life-blood draining into the growing pool around her body.

The woman was dying from massive brain damage, but those injuries were not to kill her directly. Lying, deathly still, on the basement floor, the blood from internal injuries of her head and neck flowed into her throat and her lungs. She was too deeply unconscious to feel any pain; already too near death for the body's coughing reflexes to clear her air passage. Within the minute, she had choked quietly to death.

For the killer, panting with the maniacal effort that had gone into his blows, there was a moment of grim realization that the act had been done – he had murdered his wife. Then, his own survival instincts took over as, still working in the dark, he stooped over the tiny corpse.

He was a big man. It was a simple task to double the body up, into the waiting canvas mailsack lying ready and open on the basement floor. But the canvas proved an inadequate shroud. As he gathered the top together, one arm fell free, dangling grotesquely out of the sack and stubbornly resisting his efforts to tidy the body away. It may have been at this point, as he struggled in the dark with what he firmly believed was the still warm corpse of his wife, that the killer discovered his mistake. The body in the bag was not that of his wife of 11 years and the mother of his three children. It was his children's nanny; the same height and of similar build to his wife, but most definitely not her. He had murdered the wrong woman.

As in many walks of life, the art of criminal detection has its fads and its fashions. One such fashion, in recent years, has sought to uncover the root causes of adult criminal behaviour in the early years of childhood. The young mugger who beats up old ladies may himself have had a violent family history; the sex offender was abused as a child and so on. While a disturbed family background can never excuse such adult actions, it often is the case that criminal acts may spring from an unhappy and deprived upbringing. It would be hard, however, for anybody to put forward such a plea of mitigation for the seventh Earl of Lucan.

He was born, as Richard John Bingham, into a world of aristocratic privilege. A member of one of Britain's foremost noble families, a military family, with a proud record of service for their country. In material terms his childhood lacked for nothing. Yet, after two decades of studying his background, his motivations, the instincts that 'make him tick', I now believe that the key to Sandra Rivett's savage murder can be found in Lord Lucan's earliest days.

The Bingham family had received their earldom in 1795. It was Lucan's great-great-grandfather, the third Earl, who gave the fateful order for the Charge of the Light Brigade against the Russian guns in the Crimean War. The elder Lucan's actions arose from confusions in the orders he received. Nevertheless, he took more than his fair share of blame for this military disaster and returned to England with his reputation in ruins. Like his latter-day counterpart, the disgraced Earl steadfastly refused to accept any blame. Convinced of his innocence, he pleaded for the chance to restore his good name.

Lucan demanded to be court-martialled.

For the rest of his life Lord Lucan was obsessed with ever more frantic appeals for justice to both the army and the government. He was never granted the trial that he sought and died, without ever having had the opportunity to vindicate his name in public, in 1888. I have always felt it ironic that while the third Earl spent more than 20 years pleading to get into a British courtroom, the seventh Earl has spent an equal amount of time determined to stay out.

Although born into a family steeped in history, the seventh Earl was, most significantly, not born into a world of great wealth. In years gone by the silver spoon that fed Lord Lucan had been tarnished by a spendthrift ancestor. His great-grandfather, the fourth Earl of Lucan, had made substantial inroads into the family fortune. There was still money in family trusts and landholdings, enabling his descendants to maintain the style of a lord. But, by comparison with many of their contemporaries, the Lucans were not in the class of the seriously rich.

Born in London on 18 December 1934 at a nursing home at 19 Bentinck Street, Marylebone, the new baby's name was registered on the birth certificate as Richard John Bingham. The Christian name was then promptly adapted by the entire family to simply, John. Changing the name in that way was something of a family tradition. His father had been christened George Patrick but was known to family and friends as Pat.

The new baby John's father had not, at that time, yet succeeded to the earldom. He held the title Lord Bingham, rather than Earl of Lucan. Following in the family tradition of army service, Lord Bingham had been commissioned into the Coldstream Guards and was serving as a major. At the time of the birth he was based in the White Lodge officers' quarters in Colchester.

Baby John's mother was Kaitilin Bingham, the only daughter of a distinguished Royal Navy captain, the Honourable Edward Dawson. The couple had married in 1920, in a union regarded by both families as an excellent match. They were to stay deeply in love for more than 40 years, sharing important political careers and producing two sons and two daughters, before Pat's death in 1964.

With a modicum of inherited wealth and Lord Bingham's officer's salary, the family were able to afford a fashionable riverside home in Chelsea and nannies and nurserymaids for the growing young children. At the age of 3, after a family move just down the road to still more fashionable Belgravia, John started at the local preparatory school.

Even as he adapted to his new school environment, the near certainty of war with Germany was threatening imminent change. John's father, with his widespread political and military connections, was better placed than most to know just how poor were Britain's chances in the looming conflict. When war was declared, John's school was evacuated, like many others, to the Shire counties, but the Lucan family no longer wanted to risk their children's lives in Britain.

Both John's father and his mother, Kaitilin, were committed socialists who tried never to abuse their privileged social position. Their principles, however, meant little where the safety of their children was concerned. In April 1940, believing that a German invasion was impending, the family pulled all of their establishment strings and despatched their youngsters out of the country. John, his younger brother, Hugh, and their sisters, Sarah and Jane, were shipped off to North America.

The young family travelled with the family nanny to Canada, where they stayed briefly while long-term arrangements were made for their care. Within weeks all four of the children were moved on to the United States. Once there they were taken into the care of a friend of the family, the immensely wealthy American socialite, Marcia Brady Tucker.

Young John Bingham had led a comfortable and cosseted existence in England, but he had never before been exposed to great wealth. Now, at this impressionable age, the young boy was thrust suddenly into the world of the fabulously rich. Not only did Aunt Marcia have a beautiful house, with a children's paradise of apparently limitless acres of ground, but also she had several such homes all over America.

The Bingham children were based at the main family home in Westchester, New York State, but became frequent visitors to their other residences in Florida, in Washington and in New York City and to their smaller holiday cottage in Maine. At other times they were entertained on the Tucker family's ocean-going yacht for lazy holidays at sea.

Everywhere were servants to satisfy their slightest whim. The children even had their own separate house, complete with staff, in the grounds of Aunt Marcia's New York estate. John went to the local American preparatory school, commencing his privileged education among the sons of America's richest and most influential families.

Throughout his American years, the young John Bingham wanted for nothing in material terms but for much in terms of parental affection. True, the Brady family, in general, and Aunt Marcia, in particular, were loving and caring guardians. True, he had the companionship of his brother and sisters and the care of a loving nanny. What he did not have was the day-to-day love of his real mother and father.

Even had he stayed in England, John would have been looked after primarily by his nanny and, later, by boarding-school staff. But his parents would have been distanced only by traditional upper-class reserve rather than by the width of the Atlantic Ocean. For most of these formative years John's only contacts with his parents were his mother's emotional notes and his father's more formal letters. Communications from the sixth Earl of Lucan taught the young boy only about the conduct of a distant war and the politics of a barely remembered home country.

It was a country to which John and his brother and sisters returned only once victory was in sight, and their safety seemed assured. Their father reportedly felt guilty about their absence from England throughout the hostilities and so arranged for their return in the early months of 1945.

It must have been a rude awakening for John, then 11 years old, to return from the luxuries of Aunt Marcia's America to the bleak world of post-war Britain. Even with the family's privileged position, they still had to contend with food and clothing rationing and the after-effects of an economy ruined by war.

It is hardly surprising that John grew up during his five years in America expecting only the best. I believe that his experiences of unlimited wealth at this early stage of his development were to mark his character for the rest of his life. Even Lucan's staunchest defenders, his own family and friends, have spoken to me of his compulsion for only the best things in life. Over my many years of studying the man it has become clear that, for Lucan, only that would do.

I believe it was a character trait that was to play a crucial role in shaping his actions when, several decades later, his marital problems threatened to engulf him in the poverty he could never have faced. Lord Lucan needed money, not for its own sake, but because that was the only way of maintaining the lifestyle to which he had become accustomed at so tender an age. He wouldn't have known how to be poor.

For young John there was also now a confusing change of political loyalties among the adult role models in charge of his care. After the capitalist years of his American upbringing, he now found himself in a socialist household. John was too young to understand the politics involved, but old enough to see the difference in attitudes towards those less fortunate than himself. The sixth Earl and his wife were both committed members of the Labour Party with deeply held socialist principles. John's father, Patrick, shocked the rest of the family when he took the Labour whip in the House of Lords upon his succession to the title of sixth Earl in 1949.

Earlier he had served briefly as aide-de-camp to the governor-general of South Africa, a posting that was to give him a lifelong love of the country and a lasting political interest in Commonwealth affairs. This was to earn him ministerial promotion as Under-Secretary for Commonwealth Relations and subsequently as Chief Opposition Whip in the Lords.

His wife, Kaitilin, shared his lifelong Labour Party convictions, and her passionate support was instrumental in advancing his political career. Even after her husband's death in 1964, the then Dowager Countess was to continue her support for the party. She was a Labour member of St Marylebone Borough Council, and, as late as 1979, she was to be found canvassing votes for local Labour political candidates.

Despite the socialist sympathies of both of John's parents there was never any question that he was destined to follow in his father's footsteps to a school life at Eton. Despite the years of American education, the Eton new boy had little trouble in fitting into the routine of a British boarding-school.

He was not the wealthiest boy in the class, but he was impeccably well connected and would inherit an earldom one day. On top of those credentials, there is also no doubt that Lucan had a natural charm that quickly won him friends at the school. It was a charm that was to stand him in good stead throughout his adult life – and may well be helping him still. For, over the years, very many of his contemporaries have repeatedly described him to me as 'a charming man . . . the warmest of fellows . . . the nicest man I have known . . . the truest of friends'.

Even as a 13-year-old boy, though, John was already demonstrating something of the distaste for hard work that was to mark his adult life. There was no doubt he was both popular and bright, a good sportsman, who developed a keen appreciation of music, liked history and dabbled in photography as a hobby. It was his academic work that never quite lived up to expectations. The phrases 'could do better' and 'needs greater application' began to dog his school career. But his aristocratic and faintly old-fashioned air allowed him to rise above such minor schoolwork problems.

His closest Eton schoolfriend, Charles Benson, later wrote in the *Daily Express*: 'He was about six months older than me but then, and even more so later, when age is normally of little significance, he liked to emphasise his seniority. You could say he was born an old man.'

Benson, famous as racing tipster 'The Scout' in the *Express*, said that John was teased by schoolfriends about his claims to wisdom. He became known by nicknames such as 'Oldtimer' or 'The Relic'. They were nicknames that were destined to stick, and years later in the gaming clubs of Mayfair close friends would still refer to Lucan as the 'Old Fossil'.

Midway through Lucan's Eton schooldays, like many of his contemporaries, he became a gambler. With a school population drawn from the richest strata of society, many of the young scholars had gambling in their blood. They all too often followed in the footsteps of fathers who were themselves sporting men, keen students of the Turf, frequently the owners of thoroughbreds rather than simply the backers of racehorses.

In many Eton classrooms, racing form books were studied more assiduously than Latin grammar, and gambling odds were calculated more carefully than an approved mathematics curriculum. Most of the pupils had the money to indulge such whims, but money was limited for John since his return from the riches of America.

Within easy reach of school were the major British racecourses of Ascot, Sandown, Epsom, Kempton Park and Newbury. Just a few miles away was the smaller Windsor riverside course, the scene of midweek and evening meetings, which Eton boys had been known to frequent.

It was around the time of his sixteenth birthday that Lucan first got into trouble at school for slipping away to the races. He was soon reputed to have his own secret bank account to handle his growing gambling finances. For a while he ran his own gambling book, acting as bookmaker to the other boys and shading the odds to give a percentage in his favour.

There were cards and other gaming as well. Lucan became an accomplished bridge and poker player and an almost unrivalled opponent at the backgammon table. The money he raised helped him keep up with the lifestyle standards of his richer schoolboy contemporaries. He maintained his already developed taste for life in the First Class compartment.

I believe that this first taste of easy money also instilled in young John a gambling obsession that was eventually to cost him dear. It was to ruin not only his own life but also those of his future wife Veronica and the loving family of poor Sandra Rivett.

Lucan's extra-curricular gaming activities certainly improved his mathematics but further harmed the already low standard of his academic work. His mother and father were shocked to learn that John was not considered suitable university material and was abandoning any idea of further education. Their son was happy to avoid further study but now, at the age of 18, could not defer the then compulsory call-up for two years of National Service.

It was only natural despite the now distant military problems of the third Earl at Balaclava, that Lucan should follow the family tradition of joining the British Army. The young man's aristocratic background may not have got him into university, but it was certainly distinguished enough to ensure a commission. He went from Eton to Officers' Training School and graduated as a second lieutenant in the autumn of 1953. The newly graduated officer was posted almost immediately to West Germany, to serve with his father's old regiment, the 2nd Battalion Coldstream Guards.

The posting removed Lucan from his blossoming London social life to the considerably less attractive delights of Krefeld in West Germany. He learnt to speak a little German, but there was hardly any contact with the local population and nothing in the immediate surroundings of the army base to interest Lucan.

In the army the widest possible range of sporting activities were available, and Lucan became an expert member of the bobsleigh team. In the evenings he had no trouble in finding partners to indulge his passion for cards, and he supplemented his army wages and family allowances with consistent winnings. His illicit Eton training now stood him in good stead, and he became acknowledged as the regiment's best poker player. It was a rare evening when he did not leave the officers' mess with money in his pocket.

Back in London, casino gaming was still an illegal

activity. In Germany there were no such restrictions, and, when leave was available, Lucan would organize a small party of friends for a night out at the local casino. There he learnt the finer arts of blackjack, *chemin de fer*, baccarat and roulette. Lucan must have known in his heart that even the most skilful players can rarely beat the casino's built-in odds, but he would win or lose a week's salary without complaint. The casino trips were certainly less lucrative than his regular card schools but still a welcome diversion from the routine of army life.

In 1955 Lucan's army service came to an end, and he was discharged back into Civvy Street. Like many other young men completing their compulsory military service he had no job and no immediate prospects. He had attended England's greatest public school and yet managed to gain few qualifications that might make him attractive to potential employers. Without a job, how could he maintain the lifestyle he so desperately needed to have?

Once again his social position and family connections came to his rescue. Now that John's father had succeeded to the title of sixth Earl of Lucan, his eldest son was entitled to call himself Lord Bingham. Such a title was an attraction to certain employers.

Lucan had come out of the army and moved back into the family's home at Hanover House in the heart of the wealthy London district of St John's Wood. Now his mother Kait – 'Mummy' as he still called her then – galvanized the family network into urgent action. Kait began telephoning relatives, pulling every string to secure a worthwhile job for her son.

Mummy's pleas for assistance were answered by her sister-in-law, Lady Barbara Bingham, who was married to leading City stockbroker John Bevan. The couple had known Lucan since his earliest childhood, and Uncle John, then aged 61, had always had a soft spot for his charming young nephew. After a lengthy and distinguished career in the London financial markets, Uncle John had an enviable reputation within the Square Mile. He had no trouble in arranging a suitable post.

On his distinguished relative's personal recommendation the new Lord Bingham was appointed to a trainee management post with the merchant bank of William Brandt. It was a job at which Lucan was to prove particularly adept. Uncle John told me years later that he had been surprised at how quickly his protégé had demonstrated a sharp financial brain.

The trainee proved a quick learner. He was transferred from department to department within the bank, picking up an invaluable knowledge of money management and international banking procedures. He finally settled down to a permanent position in the bank's investment branch.

It may have been that the investment of other people's money temporarily satisfied Lord Bingham's own gambling urge. Knowing that his employers would frown on high-stakes gaming, he kept his private bets to a manageable and suitably discreet level. He played a little bridge for low stakes and even joined the bank's bridge team, bringing it some much needed success. Uncle John was delighted at his progress. 'I always knew that he was a gambler and had caught the bug at school,' he told me, 'but, at first, he really seemed to behave. I thought he was a credit to me . . . but it didn't stay like that.'

For the time being, however, regular employment appeared to suit Lucan well. With a steady income from the job and with money from the family he was able to move out of his parents' home and into a well-placed bachelor flat near Regent's Park. Compared with the great majority of the population he was a highly affluent young man, with money enough for winter sports, summer holidays and a busy social life in the booming London nightclubs of the 1950s. It was a playboy existence, and for many young girls, and more importantly their mothers, the playboy Lord Bingham was an attractive proposition.

He was undoubtedly handsome and charming. A bit of a 'cad,' all the fashion those days, but not enough of a cad to run off with one's daughter. He was sufficiently well educated and cultured to discuss music, the arts or politics, and he had a steady job in the profession of high finance.

It is unsurprising that Lucan was showered with invitations to coming-out parties. He joined the regular circuit of eligible young men who flitted from party to party, living inexpensively off the hospitality of eager upper-class mothers as they launched their debutante daughters on the London season.

There were always plenty of girls as evening escorts, or for weekends away in the country. For a while his friends and family thought that the eligible Lord Bingham had found a special someone, the daughter of a fellow Earl whose background and social standing matched up to his own. They dated and even went on holiday

16

together, but the relationship finally drifted apart.

Friends of Lucan believed that he may well have been still on the rebound when, in March 1963, he visited the Leighton Buzzard home of his close friend, the wallpaper millionaire, William Shand-Kydd. At the Shand-Kydds' country home at Horton Hall, he attended a cocktail party after taking part in a golf match. It was there he was introduced to a pretty, though shy, young lady. She was the sister of William's new wife, Christina. Her name was Veronica.

Other meetings followed during the summer of 1963, and, to the surprise of the friends on both sides, the relationship appeared to blossom. As the couple became closer, Lord Bingham took care to spell out the facts of his lifestyle to the impressionable young woman. He freely admitted to being an old-fashioned male chauvinist; a woman's place was in the home; a woman's role was fully to support her partner. Above all, he stressed to Veronica that she should never try to change him.

The good Lord was living the life of a man's man; a caviare and champagne high life, which he had always believed should come with his title. Woe betide the woman who stole this birthright from him.

CHAPTER 2

A LORD AND HIS LADY

For Veronica Duncan the summer of 1963 was a fairy-tale come true. When her sister Christina's marriage thrust her headlong into the rarified and wealthy world of the British aristocracy, it must have been bewildering, too, for the girl who was to become Lady Lucan later that year. She had been a student, a model and a secretary and had run her own small business – but nothing had prepared her to be swept off her feet by a Lord.

The two girls had been sharing a London flat together when Veronica's sister, Christina, met the well-to-do and well-connected William Shand-Kydd. She excitedly told Veronica all about Bill, including the fact that he was an exceedingly wealthy young man. Veronica would have needed to be superhuman not to experience a little pang of envy as she saw her sister walk down the aisle and into a life of riches, the like of which the two girls had never seen before.

Veronica was born in 1937, the daughter of an army officer, the late Major Charles Moorhouse Duncan and his wife Thelma. Tragedy struck in 1939, when Major Duncan, a distinguished army officer, was killed in a car crash. Veronica was just 2 years old, and although she was too young to remember her father in person, she has always been proud of his distinguished forces record, which culminated in the award of the Military Cross.

Veronica's grieving mother moved to South Africa and, soon afterwards, met and married her second husband, James Margrie. She and her sister were raised amid the white middle-class comfort of South Africa but returned to England when her stepfather took over the management of a large hotel near Guildford in Surrey.

Veronica and Christina attended the private St Swithun's Girls' School in Winchester. Veronica did not excel in her academic work, but showed a real talent for art and finally earned a place at an art college in Bournemouth. Here she lived a typical student existence, always short of money but helped out with an allowance from her mother and stepfather.

On leaving college she moved to a shared flat with her sister in London and worked as a model and later a secretary. There were boyfriends, mostly suitable young professional men, and an active social life with her flatmates. For a year she went out with Michael, a rich, young chartered accountant but, when that relationship ended, there was no other serious boyfriend in sight.

By the age of 25 Veronica was reasonably content with her life and had taken a job as the secretary to a small printing company. The firm was run by actor John Atkinson and naturally enough concentrated on posters and scripts for the theatre. It was interesting work, and Veronica did so well that she was made a director of the company.

When her flatmate sister Christina married Bill Shand-Kydd, Veronica stayed put in the flat, but socially she moved rapidly into a new and very different world. The Shand-Kydds knew the cream of smart London society. Veronica was carried along in her sister's wake to parties and nightclubs and weekends in the country. It was at a golf-club function near her sister's new country home that Veronica was to meet the handsome Lord Bingham.

Lucan had never been short of pretty girls to have on his arm, but something about Christina's petite and attractive young sister was to catch his attention. When, later that year, the Shand-Kydds invited their good friend Lord Bingham on holiday, it was he who suggested that the sister should be invited as well. During their stay in the South of France the couple surprised their friends by getting on so well together that a serious romance was obviously in the air.

Not long after their return to England Lord Bingham proposed to Veronica. By her later account it was an unromantic occasion, just a formal 'Will you marry me?' proposal, which was quickly accepted. But, the very next day, her new fiancé appeared with an impressive emerald engagement ring to seal their betrothal.

The marriage took place at Brompton's Holy Trinity Church on 20 November 1963. The guests, who included Princess Alice, were a cross-section of the society Who's Who of the day, and the couple honeymooned in Europe, naturally travelling first class and part of the way on the Orient Express.

At first Veronica was blissfully happy. She had, after all, married one of the most eligible bachelors in London, and her social life, her financial situation and her social standing had all changed beyond recognition. There were some sticky moments when she met with Lucan's aristocratic relatives, and a few of them made it clear that they considered her not quite of their class.

John's grandmother, widow of the fifth Earl, was a particular snob, complaining that Veronica had not been brought up with the right manners for polite company. It did not help that Lucan's parents had not been forewarned of his marriage plans. He just announced the fact to them one day, before they had even had a chance to meet with his wife-to-be.

Veronica also clashed early on with her prospective mother-in-law. They argued over politics, and the older woman, with a lifetime of Labour Party political experience already behind her, did not take kindly to Veronica expressing her Conservative Party views. However, despite such tribulations, there were substantial consolations for the new bride in being the wife of a lord who was heir to an earldom. She had thought, at the time, that one such consolation was money.

Yet, unbeknown to his wife and his parents, Lord Bingham's finances were already stretched by gambling debts. He was grateful when, immediately after the wedding, the sixth Earl increased his income by making a marriage settlement of which several other family members were the trustees.

Clearly the newly-weds faced the extra expense of running a larger home, and some provision had to be made for the expected future additions to the family. This substantial settlement from his father provided Lucan with the means of continuing his extravagant lifestyle over the next few years. He was able to finance his gambling losses and repay some of the people, such as his favourite Uncle John, from whom he had already borrowed money.

Some of his new-found funds were spent on leasing a family home at 46 Lower Belgrave Street and redecorating the house to Veronica's taste. In the course of my later inquiries I traced one of the interior decorators who had worked for the Lucan family at this time.

He told me that he had been repeatedly called in to redesign the interior rooms over a period of three years. He felt he had got to know the newly-wed couple well, and that there had never been any sign of friction between them over the space of 20 or more visits to their home.

The only sadness to mar the early married life of John and Veronica came barely two months after the wedding, with the death of John's father, the much respected sixth Earl of Lucan. Previously known simply as Lord Bingham, Lucan now inherited an impressive array of aristocratic titles. He became the seventh Earl of Lucan; Baron Lucan of Castlebar; Baron Bingham of Melcombe Bingham and Baronet of Nova Scotia. Veronica, of course, shared in his reflected glory and became the

Countess of Lucan.

Although only just back from honeymoon, the couple were shortly off on their travels again. In early spring the new seventh Earl took his new wife and the Shand-Kydds off on a sporting holiday to America. In the autumn there was the happiness of the birth of the couple's first child, a daughter, to be named Frances.

Born on 24 October 1964, the new baby was a strain on Veronica, but she wanted to do all that she could to look after the baby herself. Lady Lucan had not had an easy labour and suffered slightly from post-natal depression. Her husband was concerned, but proved both understanding and willing to help his wife pull through her depression. It was, therefore, not until a few months after the birth that Lord and Lady Lucan took on their first full-time nanny. Veronica was recommended by members of the family to seek help from the upmarket Beauchamp Bureau in fashionable Beauchamp Place. Early in the new year of 1965 the agency sent along nanny Lillian Jenkins to join the family.

Even with the new baby to look after, helped of course by the eminently suitable Nanny Jenkins, the aristocratic young couple seemed to have the world at their feet. Their financial situation, which had always been a closed book to Veronica, was eased by the money received after the death of Lucan's father. The seventh Earl was able to resume the playboy life that, for a while, had seemed threatened by money worries. Foreign holidays were plentiful, and when back home they joined in enthusiastically with the London social scene of glittering dinner parties and nights in clubland.

Even before the wedding, Veronica had known of

her husband's passion for gambling. Lucan had given her fair warning that he could not, and would not, change his lifestyle. He did, however, attempt, with little success, to involve Veronica in his gambling hobby, by buying her books that explained the rules and the strategy of his favourite card and casino games.

At the weekends there were frequent visits to the country homes of other, mostly more wealthy, friends. For a while Lucan also tried hard to interest his new wife in the hunting, shooting and fishing activities that he felt befitted a gentleman in his position. He paid for Veronica to have a series of golf lessons at a leading London golf clinic. She took to the game for a while but then stopped bothering with her tutoring sessions.

Lucan had a number of racehorses with the Newmarket trainer Arthur Freeman, some of which were frequently ridden by the professional jockey Stan Mellor. Mellor last rode a Lucan horse, named Le Merveilleux II, at Stratford racecourse on 6 April 1972. He remembers the Lord as a knowledgeable horseman. Lucan was, as always, a keen racegoer. Although he owned several horses either outright, or as part of a registered ownership syndicate, the hobby proved yet another drain on his finances.

In addition to substantial training fees there was also the expense of entry fees to races. Lucan's personal accounts with racing's owners' authority Weatherby & Sons show a consistent deficit. In 1968, for example, Lucan had a quarter share in the horse Komarov and interests in two other thoroughbreds, Prince Bleu and Sebasteen II, in addition to his main runner, the hurdler Le Merveilleux II. That year he paid entry fees for his horses at more than 20 different racecourses ranging from Ascot, Doncaster and Newbury through to the smaller tracks of Fontwell, Plumpton and Fakenham. His entry fees alone added up to more than £500, and yet the only return was a quarter share in the £60 second-place prize money for a runner at Bath in July.

Despite such expense Lucan was not averse to hiring a private plane to take a party of friends to the races, especially if his horses were running on the small racetracks, across the Channel in France, where a day's racing could be combined with a casino evening. Veronica, however, often ducked out of these trips. She was never keen on flying in the little light aircraft.

Lucan enjoyed shooting and owned a valuable pair of Boss shotguns, for which he had paid more than £3000. Ten years later, after his disappearance, the guns were to feature at the centre of several speculative newspaper stories, which claimed that he was armed with the matching weapons and could use them for suicide or to resist arrest. In fact Lucan was a responsible gunman, and, especially now that he had a young child around the house, he stored both shotguns for safety's sake at the London premises of the gunsmiths who made them.

To add even further to his playboy image Lord Lucan asked a car dealer friend to find him a second-hand Aston Martin drophead coupé, a car he had always desired. He drank a particular upmarket brand of Russian vodka and chain-smoked Peter Stuyvesant cigarettes with their, somewhat ironic, advertising slogan as, 'The International Passport to Smoking Pleasure'.

It was, however, in the field of power-boat racing that Lucan was to be seen at his most dashing. He had been converted to the sport at around the time of his father's death and, with his influx of capital, was able to pay for a new boat to be built. Once again Lucan would have only the best. He sought out Bruce Colin Campbell and asked him to build a boat capable of winning the forthcoming *Daily Express* Cowes to Torquay power-boat race.

Campbell, based at the boating centre of Hamble, near Southampton, built the vessel that Lucan named *White Migrant*. The Earl wanted the boat name to recall the happy days he had spent on the magnificent ocean-going yacht *Migrant*, which had been owned by his American childhood benefactress, Marcia Tucker.

Lucan ran his boat from marinas both at Hamble and along the coast at the Cresta Marina, Newhaven. For the Cowes–Torquay race he asked Campbell to be his co-driver. For a while the pair almost looked as if they might win the prestigious event but *White Migrant* sank before reaching the finishing-line. Lucan was devastated by the result but bought a new boat and continued his connection with the sport both in Britain and America over the following few years. He finally gave up racing, on financial grounds, around 1966.

Fox-hunting was another much loved activity, and a horse was purchased for Veronica. She found, however, that the animal was hard to manage and insisted that Lucan buy her another, more gentle horse. Later, after their relationship had deteriorated so seriously, Veronica was to suggest to friends that her husband had deliberately picked a skittish mount in the hopes it might harm her. Her fears were a foretaste of what was to come.

For the moment, however, the Earl and Countess

of Lucan made a most handsome young couple. The seventh Earl was glittering aristocracy personified, and it is not surprising that more than a few of Lucan's former girlfriends spoke bitchily behind Veronica's back about her lack of suitability for the role of Countess. Veronica herself has always put a great deal of their subsequent marriage problems down to pure old-fashioned envy by the girls who could not have him.

Throughout this period of the mid- to late 1960s, one of Lucan's closest friends was his Old Etonian chum, Charles Benson. Although they had lost touch in the years after Eton, the men shared a passion for gambling and gentlemanly sports that was to bring them together. Many years after Lucan's disappearance I read with interest an article by Benson, published in his own *Express* newspaper. He revealed that his friendship with Lucan had been closest between 1964 and 1974 when they lived in London within walking distance of each other and had many mutual interests. He described Lucan's life as one of golf, horse and greyhound racing, gambling and the cinema.

Benson said Lucky, as he became known, worshipped his children, and that he and Lucan had been together on the night of 21 September 1967 when the heir to the earldom, George Bingham, was born. The two men celebrated together at the Mirabelle restaurant and then gambled at the White Elephant Club until the early hours of the morning.

Lucky had lost many thousands of pounds that night, but he did not care a jot. Said Benson, 'He had a son, and he was as happy as Larry.' Unfortunately, Lord Lucan's happiness was destined not to last.

CHAPTER 3

UNLUCKY LUCKY

To an outward observer the newly ennobled seventh Earl of Lucan now had all that a young man could want. He was married to a devoted and attractive wife, had a private income and the love and respect of a wide circle of family and friends. The former Lord Bingham was reputed to have inherited one-quarter of a million pounds along with his title and clearly, for all to see, had the money to indulge an expensive range of sporting passions. On top of all that he was a 'man's man' whose loving partner did not want to change him. What clouds could possibly have marred his horizon?

The answer was gambling. What had started as a schoolboy prank and grown into an adult hobby had now developed into a full-scale and uncontrollable addiction. It was an addiction, I believe, that was fuelled by Lord Lucan's desperation for nothing but the best. Nothing less than a first-class ticket through life was acceptable – but he no longer had the money for his fare. Unbeknown to his trusting new wife, Lucan had been living beyond his means for some time, and, unlike his childhood days in America, there was now no Aunt Marcia to pick up the tab.

Soon after taking over the Sandra Rivett murder case, I had realized that the expensive Lucan lifestyle had never been all that it seemed. He did have access to substantial funds from the three separate trusts set up by his family, but I discovered that his outgoings were more than a match for his income. As Mr Micawber would say, 'Annual income twenty pounds, annual expenditure nineteen nineteen six, result happiness. Annual income twenty pounds, annual expenditure twenty pounds ought and six, result misery.'

It was a misery that, like most gamblers, he hid well from the rest of the world. As a police officer, my working life had many times brought me into contact with addicts. I have found that whether the addiction is drink, or drugs, or gambling, you can never trust the sufferers to tell you the truth. Alcoholics can 'take it or leave it', junkies have 'just one more fix' and gamblers 'just one last hand'. Be they peasants or peers of the realm, all gamblers have a natural tendency to lie about their winnings. One lucky evening is discussed at the greatest of lengths, while far more nights of cheerless losses are forgotten for ever.

Most know in their hearts that you cannot buck the odds, but the gamblers themselves begin to believe their own lies. It was into this trap of self-deception that Lord Lucan had already tumbled. Throughout his merchant-banking career, Lucan had continued to bet on his cards and his backgammon skills; on his golf; his horses; and his dogs. At some games, particularly bridge and backgammon, he was frequently a winner. At others, the losses were huge.

Even before his wedding, Lucan was already losing more than he could afford to pay off with one cheque. He had become a casino regular, one of the first members of the Clermont gaming club in Berkeley Square, London, and was soon in serious debt. One single gambling bill of more than £8000 had to be settled in a series of monthly payments. It was not surprising that it took some time to pay off. The sum represented around two-thirds of Lucan's entire annual income from the family trusts.

Lucan's more staid colleagues at William Brandt's merchant bank were far removed from the gaming set with whom he now mixed. Even so, rumours had begun to circulate at the firm about their aristocratic young manager's extra-curricular activities.

For obvious reasons, gambling – other than on the stock market – was not an activity that Brandt's encouraged among those responsible for the investment of clients' money. It was fortunate for Lucan that the rumours reached the ears of his own relatives before those of his bosses at the bank. It was Uncle John, the man who had first found him a job, who was to come to his rescue.

Stockbroker John Bevan had been concerned for some time about the welfare of his nephew. Then he heard that Lucan had lost a massive £10,000 in just one disastrous night in a London casino. When he tackled his errant young relative about the rumour, Uncle John was appalled to find that it was totally true. Lucan had lost at least that much money and had no means of paying it back. Even worse, he had agreed to settle the debt by instalments but could not even meet the payment that was due immediately. Years later John Bevan told me himself about the worry that Lucan had caused.

'I realized straight away that John was in serious trouble,' he said. 'He had virtually no money and was being pressed for an immediate payment of £1000. I knew that if the bank ever heard about the matter they would have no option but to let John go.

'I did not want to see John lose his job, and so I wrote out my own cheque for £1000 and told John to take it. He thanked me profusely and promised to pay the loan back – but I did not really expect to see my money again.'

Uncle John's lack of confidence in his titled relative proved to be unjustified. Lucan may have been by then a gambler, a liar and now a scrounger from his family, but you cannot deny the man a certain sense of style. Some two years later, after a fortunate night at the tables, Lucan sent back the borrowed £1000, along with a letter of thanks and a promise of interest still to be paid. It duly arrived, in the shape of a dozen bottles of uncle's favourite gin, delivered to his home a day or two later.

Despite these occasional wins, Lord Lucan's financial position remained at the heart of his problems. I believe that, rather than the much quoted love of his children, it is his lack of money, all of it lost through uncontrollable gambling, that provides the key to this case. For many years newspaper articles and books have mistakenly overestimated just how much money the seventh Earl of Lucan was worth. By comparison with other members of the wealthy aristocratic set in which he moved, Lord Lucan was a relative pauper – a fact that constantly troubled him.

It was commonly thought that he had inherited around £250,000 upon the death of his father on 21 January 1964. The truth is that Pat Lucan, who died from a stroke thought to have been induced by one of his frequent asthma attacks, had left nothing like that amount.

In his will the sixth Earl left his personal possessions to his widow Kaitilin, but the bulk of the estate was left in trust for his children with Kaitilin as the trustee. Probate documents, filed with the Family Division of the High Court in London, show that the estate was settled in two separate parts. The first grant of probate concerned £53,479 but did not include the disposition of settled land. A few months later a further grant was registered, valuing such land at £41,000 exactly.

Other documents, which I was shown many years later as part of Lucan's bankruptcy papers, revealed that the socialist sixth Earl also took few steps to mimimize death duties payable upon his estate. One document showed that more than £20,000 disappeared in taxes from Lord Lucan's inheritance.

A wealthy and titled relative of the Lucan family told me: 'The larger figure of £250,000 is completely untrue – I don't believe that Pat left much more than £50,000.'

Whatever the exact figure, the inheritance that he

did receive brought another welcome respite for Lucan's financial troubles. He was still spending money as though it were going out of style. There were regular foreign holidays in the days before cheap package travel was commonplace and frequent golf matches, often at Sunningdale or Wentworth. Lucan was a member of both of these exclusive and expensive clubs.

His growing obsession with gambling and his playboy lifestyle even began to alienate some members of his own family. Although devoted to her son, the Dowager Countess of Lucan was not averse to criticizing John's lifestyle. She called his gambling a 'most disreputable' way of earning a living.

There was a similar attitude from Lucan's brother, Hugh Bingham, who appeared to distance himself from his elder brother's activities. Hugh told me that he had been close to his brother as a child, but they had grown apart over the years. He never gambled himself, and, although he did not say so directly, he clearly disapproved of his brother's obsession. They lunched together every five or six weeks, but Hugh was not a member of any of Lucan's clubs and knew hardly any of his gambling friends.

One of the most established of the Lucan myths that have grown up since his disappearance concerns his decision to set up 'in business' as a professional gambler. Friends of the missing Earl portray his career change as a natural consequence of his skill and good fortune at the gaming tables. In fact my inquiries have shown the exact opposite to be true.

Partly because of the rumours about his gambling

life, Lucan's City career was not progressing as he had originally hoped. He boasted to his close friends that the bank was on the verge of making him a director. Everything was going well. Further promotions seemed certain. The reality was that the bank's management were worried about Lucan, and one of his closest office rivals was promoted over his head. In a fit of pique Lucan at first protested about his lack of advancement and then decided to quit.

Lucan was too proud to let his family know the true reason for leaving his job. Instead he boasted of a spectacular win at the tables. In yet another massive lie, the wayward Earl told all and sundry, 'Why should I work in a bank, when I can earn a year's money in one single night at the tables?'

The collapse of Lucan's banking career was confirmed to me by Uncle John, the man who knew more about Lucan's City activities than any other. John Bevan told me, 'John was deeply disappointed at not gaining promotion. He left when a colleague in his department was promoted, and John was certain that the job should have gone to him. Unfortunately, as far as I know, that was his last gainful employment. He never had another job from that day onwards.'

It was after taking up his new role as a professional gambler that Lucan met and married Veronica. He was to prove no luckier as a professional than he had been as an amateur 'mug punter'. He was undoubtedly a highly skilled backgammon player and at one time was rated among the top ten players in the world. He was champion of the West Coast of America and had won the St James's Club tournament. At bridge, too, he could more than hold his own. Officials at the Portman Club in London were convinced that Lucan won more than he lost over the years of his regular attendance. But in the casinos at night the losses continued on every other game he played.

As the situation worsened, Lucan still managed to keep up appearances. For a while he became a 'house player' funded by the casinos themselves and frequently playing with casino chips. His image as the immaculately dressed, high-roller, titled gambler was of value to the gaming establishments, which had already all but broken his own private bank.

New players being encouraged to try their hands at the tables were impressed by the image. To his closest friends he remained as the 'Old Fossil', but in the casino world he took on the nickname of 'Lucky' Lord Lucan. Only a few of his closest confidants realized that the nickname was ironic.

The commonly accepted story was that Lucan had earned his Lucky nickname after a spectacular evening at the Clermont Club casino, when he reputedly won more than £30,000. Some of his friends confirmed to me that the evening never happened. The Lucky tag was awarded him after a particularly long and consistent losing streak.

By this stage of his life Lord Lucan was living a lie. He maintained the myth that his professional gambling was earning him an erratic, but highly satisfactory, living. Outwardly, to his gambling friends and to his family, he remained a rich and successful aristocrat. The truth was known only to him and his several despairing bank managers. Lucky Lucan could no more beat the odds than anybody else. Consistent losses, coupled with his determination not to forgo his sporting activities and the outward trappings of his luxury life, were swallowing all of the family trust income and eating away at what was left of the Lucan fortune.

After leaving his steady employment in the City, Lucan felt increasing strain from his precarious financial existence. Bills that once had been settled by return of post began to be left until later. He had a total of four different bank accounts, and for the first time in his life he began to slip into the red with them all. The Lucan family noticed no difference. There were still clothing accounts at Savile Row tailors and the best Knightsbridge stores for Veronica. The household groceries still came on account from the Food Halls at Harrods. But the financial fabric was crumbling.

Lucan's new lifestyle began to alienate many former friends. The new gambling set who gathered around him gradually replaced old friends from his days in the army and his years in the City. Among those older friends was a City banker who had spent years at Eton with Lucan, had seen him occasionally in the army and had then become one of his closest friends for the following ten years. He had been an usher at the marriage of John and Veronica and had stayed friends with them both for the following few years. He recalled how Lucan gradually drifted away. He proved unambitious in anything but gambling, and during the late 1960s every social meeting had to involve a meal and a gaming session at the Clermont or other London clubs.

His friend told me, 'I have known John for many years. He is a very kind, understanding, generous and stable individual who I trust implicitly. He is much loved by a very large number of sensible people.' Despite this glowing character reference the friend recognized that the Lucan he knew was slowly changing out of all recognition.

Lucan's undoubted charm and his old-fashioned and courteous ways had always endeared him to many. Time and again, as I interviewed friends and relations shortly after the murder in 1974, I came across the same opinion. 'He is a loving, kind and gentle man,' I was told. 'He couldn't harm anybody.'

This gentle picture of the non-violent Lord Lucan was as false as the financial front he presented. In the years since the murder I have learnt of the other side of Lord Lucan – the less patient, the less even-tempered, the more violent man that he was becoming.

Even in the early 1970s there was the occasional dissenting voice to be heard among the chorus of Lucan supporters. Another City financier, who had known Lucan since he had started in the bank, had become an occasional golf partner. This colleague described how Lucan had, in the past, always been remarkably tolerant of the behaviour of Otto, his large Dobermann pinscher.

The dog frequently accompanied the Earl to the golf course. On one occasion it blundered clumsily across a room, knocking over tables and spilling the drinks. From Lucky Lucan there was a charming apology for the inconvenienced guests but hardly a word of reproach to his dog. And yet, shortly afterwards, when having a bad day at the golf course and losing a substantial bet, Lucan rounded on the animal and beat it so badly that one of the Sunningdale Golf Club caddies was moved to intervene.

Lucan had bought the Dobermann as a puppy from a Hertfordshire kennels in the autumn of 1964. Now it no longer fitted in with his temperament or lifestyle, and he took it back. He said he could keep it no longer. The fate of Lucan's dog appeared to me, on reflection, to be indicative of the stresses and strains on Lord Lucan himself. The beatings and the desertion, although unimportant in themselves, were forerunners of the far greater breakdown that was soon to engulf him.

CHAPTER 4

IRRETRIEVABLE BREAKDOWN

It was in the late 1960s that Veronica became more aware of the perceptible shift in her husband's attitudes and behaviour. He had always been a man of extreme right-wing views, indeed he had once insisted that she listen to recordings of the Nazi Nuremberg rallies while on holiday at the home of a German count. But now his attitudes hardened even further.

He was openly racist in his comments, calling one of his greyhounds Sambo's Hangover and frequently complaining that 'niggers, wogs and dagoes' were bringing the country to its knees. This toughening of Lucan's political stance coincided with his adoption of what Veronica was later to describe as a more 'aristocratic' air, a realization of his high place in society and a tendency, not shown before, to look down on 'lower' classes.

The irony is that his increasing snobbishness

coincided with a more and more desperate financial state. It may well be that the changes were his own way of coping with his failure to earn a decent living as a professional gambler. His even more extreme, right-wing and upper-class airs served as a façade, behind which he could more easily hide his impending poverty. Above all else he was determined to keep up appearances.

Even as Lucan's wealth decreased, his interest in his family history and his social position was growing in inverse proportion. Possibly he felt that his past family honour was all he had left. One episode from the time illustrated, for me, his desire to cling on to his family tradition. For generations the Lucans had enjoyed the right to appoint a vicar to the living of the parish of Laleham in Middlesex, where the family held substantial estates.

The incumbent at that time was The Revd Desmond Guinness who had been vicar for almost 20 years. Some time before, Lucan's father, the sixth Earl, had agreed to help pay for a new youth centre to be built in the parish. The vicar asked the son if he would honour his father's promises and was delighted when Lucan said that the money would be forthcoming. Indeed, despite financial pressures, Lucan made sure that the youth centre went ahead, and it was finally opened in 1966. However, he was considerably more resistant to the vicar's other request – that the Earl give up the now outdated rights over the politics of the parish.

Over lunch at one of Lucan's London clubs, the churchman was treated to a lengthy discourse on the history of the family. He learnt that Lucan was anxious to pass on his rights, as Patron of the Living in Laleham, to his own descendants. His only concession was an agreement to follow recent tradition by always rubber-stamping the choice of the local Church Council.

The new Earl also made it clear to the vicar that he was not likely to be seen as a regular member of the Laleham congregation. He described himself as a 'humanist' rather than a Christian, a legacy from his own parents who remained agnostic until their dying days.

As a child Lucan had laughed at his family motto, 'Christ Is My Hope', and as an adult he attended church only for the most important of family occasions. The Lucans have a family plot in the church graveyard at Laleham, and John and Veronica were there for the burial of his grandmother. Years later, however, when Lucan's own mother passed away, she insisted on an almost secret funeral ceremony in North London. There were barely a handful of mourners and no Christian service.

For Veronica Lucan, the glitter was beginning to fade from the glamour of being a countess. It was all very well having a high social position, a beautiful home and Knightsbridge accounts, but what she really wanted all along was a husband. She fundamentally disagreed with Lucan's perception of the role of a modern peer in twentieth-century Britain. Her husband still believed that he had a God-given right to a life of idleness and luxury. Veronica had realized long before that such days had now gone.

Driven to distraction by the stress of his money worries, John's increasingly desperate mood swings, and his now fanatical obsession with gambling, were taking their toll on the marriage. Veronica, kept in the dark about their financial situation, did not even know where to begin in trying to understand this new man, 'Lucky' Lucan, that John had become.

With the birth of their son in 1967 and the arrival of their second daughter, Camilla, in 1970, came further bouts of post-natal depression. Previously Lucan had helped Veronica through her illness. This time he proved unable to cope. He complained to his closest family and friends that Veronica was behaving oddly. He told his mother that he was hoping to get proper psychiatric help for Veronica, but that she was resisting his attempts to get treatment. His mother, who had always considered Veronica's behaviour as strange anyway, encouraged her son to take the matter seriously.

In fact, Veronica's illness was, by now, caused as much by her husband's careless and loveless attitude as by any post-natal depression. For more than five years she had loyally stood by her man through the tedium of his day-to-day life. His sporting interests, his friends, his relations, his 'job' as a professional gamesman had always come first.

For night after night, week after week, month after month, she had sat, mostly uncomplainingly, on the 'widows' bench' at the Clermont Club, while Lucky gambled away all their money. In company with the handful of other gamblers' wives she had listened uncomprehendingly at luncheons and dinners as the men compared their last hands or discussed the luck of the backgammon dice. Even Lucan's friends recognized that Lady Lucan's life was unfulfilled and unhappy. Nearly 20 years later, the Earl's close friend and Clermont companion, Michael Stoop, remembered well how Lady Lucan had spent most evenings in the club.

'She used to come with us every night, and it must have been a dreadful existence for her,' he told me. 'She would sit watching this boring game and had a very difficult life. I really rather liked her, she had a sort of quaint humour, which I thought was quite endearing. She would just sit there quietly and have a small drink and occasionally make some quite funny remarks.'

Another close friend, Charles Benson, also admitted to me many years after the event that he had some sympathy for Veronica Lucan's plight, although he had believed her behaviour to be unreasonable on many occasions.

'The problem really was that Lucky lived a certain life, and he wasn't going to deviate from that,' he said. 'His life involved going to clubs, and Veronica would join him for dinner nearly every night. It wasn't a terribly passionate or exciting marriage, but it worked in its way, and she was happy with her children and the title and her place in the world. But I suppose she must have been a bit disgruntled from time to time that she didn't see him enough or do enough.'

Veronica was an intelligent woman sentenced to a life as an upper-class bimbo. The occasional trinkets from Aspreys, his favourite thank-you when Lady Luck had smiled in his direction, did not make up for the mind-numbing dullness of the gambler's nightly routine. It was not surprising, then, that at last she began to complain – not so much for herself, as for her children. The elder daughter, Lady Frances, was growing up fast, young Lord George would soon be starting kindergarten, and nanny Jenkins was now in charge of the newest arrival, Lady Camilla. What was to be their future?

Veronica, coming not from the rich upper classes but from a family where school fees were a struggle to find, was sensing trouble. For the first time in their married life she started to ask questions about the money, and where it was coming from. Was Lucky really winning enough to secure her children's future?

For Lucan the questions from Veronica were a nightmare. He was already worried sick about the continuing losses. He was not so stupid that he did not realize the looming problem of public-school fees for his children; it was inconceivable that children from the distinguished Lucan line should not be privately educated. In addition, he recognized the eventual need to make financial provision for the still distant old-age care of his wife and himself.

He reacted to Veronica's questions in the only way he knew how, by refusing to respond or lying when an answer just had to be given. The arguments over money escalated from minor domestic skirmishes conducted behind closed doors, to full-blown rows and icy recriminations. The stress on Lord Lucan from the endless disputes over money made itself felt in other areas of the marriage. On a number of occasions Lord Lucan was violent, when previously he had appeared to be a gentle man.

The couple tried to keep their differences private, but inevitably gossip began to circulate in the clubs. All was not well. To his friends Johnny Lucan explained that the problem lay with his wife's continuing anxiety state: 'Not been well for a while, Old Boy . . . Under the doctor – psychiatrist actually . . . Not the sort of thing to talk about at the tables.'

It must have been around the late 1960s when Lucan first decided that his wife had to go. He did not believe in divorce, and anyway he wanted to keep control over his children, so some other way had to be found of getting her out of his life. Veronica seemed physically well and so was unlikely to die conveniently, which left very few options for regaining his bachelor status.

His chosen method was to try and prove that the Countess of Lucan was mad and in need of long-term psychiatric care. With calculated cruelty, he first tried to convince Veronica herself that she had to seek help.

On the pretext of taking her out for a drive, the Earl took his wife to a Hampstead psychiatric clinic and announced he was booking her in for treatment. For Veronica, the afternoon was a terrible shock. She had been pleasantly surprised that her husband was for once willing to spend the afternoon with her, away from his beloved gaming tables. Out of the blue she found herself having to argue her sanity.

After what Veronica later described as 'rather a to-do', she forced her husband to drive her back home to Belgravia. The row continued indoors, with Lucan repeatedly claiming that her anxieties over their finances were misplaced and simply a symptom of her illness. He even warned her that the surest sign of being neurotic was refusing to recognize that she was mentally ill.

Lady · Lucan was caught in a classic catch-22 argument. She did not need treatment – but refusing such treatment would be proof of her madness. Despite their differences and her fears over money, Veronica still loved her husband and wanted their life to get back to normal. In desperation she agreed to home visits from a psychiatrist and to a course of antidepressant drugs. It was the start of a slippery slope that Lucan was quick to exploit.

Among the tablets that Veronica was prescribed were tranquillizers containing fluphenazine, a long-lasting drug that needed to be taken just once a day and yet had significant side-effects. It is often used in cases of agitated depression, a state that justly described Veronica, although in her case both the agitation and the depression had an understandable cause. Along with other effects, such as drowsiness and a dry mouth, the drug frequently causes involuntary muscle contractions, twitching and foot tapping. The movements can resemble Parkinson's disease.

Lucan's friends, many of whom had already been warned by the Lord that Veronica was acting oddly, now saw for themselves how much she appeared to have deteriorated. On the widows' bench at the Clermont, Veronica mostly now sat quietly, paying little regard to what was around her and incessantly tapping her foot.

Events came to a head with an argument one night in 1972 between Veronica and another 'gambling widow' at the Clermont. In a row, over the woman making too much noise while Veronica was trying to watch the television, a glass of wine was thrown and harsh words exchanged. For Lucan the incident was deeply embarrassing. He did not expect his Countess to brawl in the club. For his gambling cronies and Veronica's enemies, the incident was the final straw. The woman was clearly quite mad!

Events in the Lucan marriage were now rushing headlong towards an inevitable conclusion. Veronica, still trying to make the marriage work, suggested a holiday abroad with the children. A few years before she had persuaded Lucky to take their first non-gambling holiday, with a tour of Venice and Rome. Perhaps he would try it again?

It was, by that stage, something of a forlorn hope to suggest that Lucan could go cold turkey on his gambling addiction. The family did go on holiday – but to the gambling mecca of Monte Carlo, where the Lucky Lord could lose even more of his now dwindling resources.

For Lady Lucan the holiday was close to being the final straw. After just one night of casino losses she packed her bags and headed back to London, leaving Lucan in charge of the two oldest children. In Britain her younger daughter Camilla was away with her nanny, so, rather than return to an empty house, Veronica went to visit her sister. She confided to Christina Shand-Kydd that her marriage now seemed on the rocks.

Some time later Veronica lunched with one of her husband's close relatives at a Chelsea restaurant. No longer able to cope with her solitary unhappiness, Veronica poured out her heart. She spoke of her husband's mental cruelty and hinted at sexual and physical abuses as well.

The story that Veronica told Lucan's relative was one that she later repeated to several close friends and to a number of women who worked for her over several years. She reported that Lucan had beaten her on a number of occasions – not out of anger but sadistically. The beatings had taken on an almost ritual air as he methodically caned his wife. The pain had been severe, but Lady Lucan had been so afraid of her husband that she was unable to stop the violence.

The story was confirmed a couple of years after the murder in an article by the writer and old Etonian James Fox, who revealed that one of the Lucan family nannies had spoken of Lucan beating up his wife, pushing her down the stairs and once trying to strangle her. He also reported that Lucan had caned Veronica, 'although more in sexual passion than in anger'.

Lady Lucan's story was a plea for help, but it fell on deaf ears. Lucan had already prepared for just such an eventuality, when he told his family that Veronica had been throwing herself, deliberately, against the furniture and threatening to accuse him of assault. The relative at first thought Veronica was joking and then decided she was mad. The much respected seventh Earl beating his wife – the idea was preposterous.

Matters came to a head, as is so often the case in family breakdowns, when the Lucans were confined together at Christmas in the country vicarage home in Guilsborough, Northamptonshire, of Lucan's sister, Lady Sarah, and her husband, The Revd Bill Gibbs. What should have been a happy holiday that December 1972 turned into a nightmare. The couple put on an act in front of the children but by Boxing Day could bear to be together no longer. Veronica and the children set off back to London. With nowhere else to turn, Lady Lucan at last consulted a solicitor about the state of her marriage.

She was by now concerned with far more than their financial situation. Her anxieties about the children's school fees had transformed into real fear of her husband's drinking, his gambling, his violence, his cruelty – a fear of Lord Lucan himself.

CHAPTER 5

SEPARATE LIVES

Two weeks later Lord Lucan moved out of the family residence at 46 Lower Belgrave Street. On 7 January 1973 he never came home from his club and instead moved into a tiny terraced house, just round the corner in Eaton Mews. The immediate cause of his departure was yet another row with one of Veronica's doctors. Lucan had tried to persuade the doctor that his wife should be certified as mentally ill. When the doctor dismissed his attempt as a nonsense, the Earl flew into a rage and stormed out of the house.

Within months Lucan found that the Eaton Mews house was too small for him. He arranged to rent it out to his friend Greville Howard, while he moved into a larger rented flat in nearby Elizabeth Street. Despite all of their disagreements, Veronica was deeply upset by their parting and never stopped asking him to return to her and the family, or expressing her love and affection for him. Some time after their separation she persuaded Lucan to join her for lunch at a London restaurant. They talked over their problems, and for a while Veronica thought that a reconciliation was in the air. At the end of the meal her husband kissed her on both cheeks and for a moment looked sad. But then he told her he must go.

For Lucan the break was clearly final. He had no wish ever to return to his wife. Equally, he had no intention of leaving her with the care and control of his three young children. All of his friends knew just how determined and competitive a man the seventh Earl could be. Now he brought the same single-minded determination to bear on his marital conflict. If Veronica had thought that his behaviour up until this point had been cruel and heartless – she had not seen anything yet.

The plan that Lucan had drawn up in his mind was simple, but it threatened everything that Veronica held dear. He approached the campaign to destroy her with an almost military precision. The first objective was to gain reliable intelligence about his enemy's movements and objectives. And so he set about spying.

At first Lucan tried his own hand at espionage. His dark-blue Mercedes car became a familiar sight in Lower Belgrave Street, as he sat watching his old house or following the children and nannies to school. On occasions Veronica or a nanny would spot him lurking in the road, and Lucan would drive quickly away, hiding his embarrassment behind the dark glasses that he habitually wore on his spying expeditions.

Even now, 20 years after the event, the mother of

one of Frances's schoolfriends remembers how she came across the Earl acting in a bizarre fashion. 'I had just picked up my daughter from Frances's home in Lower Belgrave Street when I noticed John Bingham parked nearby in his car,' she recalls. 'He was wearing dark glasses, and, when I tried to speak to him, he turned away, clearly not anxious to be approached. I suddenly realized how oddly he was acting and hurried off with my daughter.'

Such awkward incidents multiplied, and Lucan realized that a change of tactics was required. Money was desperately tight, but his need to prove that Veronica could not look after the children was greater. Lord Lucan sought professional help. In early 1974 he employed the services of London private investigators, Devlin & Co., to spy on Veronica and Lord Lucan's own children. The company, based in Baker Street, were asked to watch 46 Lower Belgrave Street and provide a full written report of all of its toings and froings.

As the detective in charge of the subsequent murder inquiry, I later asked the private investigators for the reports that they had written for Lucan. They assured me that they had never been asked to watch Sandra Rivett, and indeed their reports predated her arrival in the Lucan household. On the grounds that they had a confidential relationship with Lord Lucan, they refused to divulge further information.

It was early in 1994, while I was examining papers stored in connection with Lucan's bankruptcy hearing, that I finally saw the Devlin reports. In great detail the investigators described how they had watched the house for a number of days. For the most part the private detectives merely detailed the day-to-day comings and goings of life in Lower Belgrave Street. The agency used two different operatives, Mr Cranstoun and Mr Morris, to spy on Lady Lucan. Their record of 28 February 1974, for example, was typical of the mundane nature of the observations:

> At 10.55 am Harrods van made a delivery to the address.
> At 11.15 am a dry cleaner's van delivered and collected cleaning from the property.
> At 1 pm a Bedford van, reg. no. GLC 97C, returned Camilla to 46 Lower Belgrave Street.
> At 3.20 pm Lady Lucan left the address on foot and walked down the street.
> At 3.25 pm Lady Lucan returned to the address.
> At 3.40 pm a Liberal Party canvasser called at the address and spoke to Lady Lucan.

The second objective of Lucan's operation was for Veronica to be branded as insane. A madwoman would surely not be given custody of Frances, George and Camilla at any future custody hearing. Lord Lucan launched a systematic and thorough character assassination of his naïve and unsuspecting wife. With a word here and a story told 'in the strictest of confidence' there, the Earl began to throw mud. It was inevitable that some of it would stick to Veronica's reputation.

Since 1974 I have been regaled many times with Lucan-inspired myths about Veronica's behaviour. One woman, who admitted that she had never liked the 'airs and graces' Countess, told me of a tale that had been circulated among the clubland wives.

According to the legend, Veronica had drowned a

kitten or a puppy, supposedly a gift from her husband, and pushed its body through the letter-box of Lucky's new home in Elizabeth Street. Disregarding the difficulties of squeezing wet cats and dogs through letter-boxes, I knew that the story was pure fiction. The animal in question was indeed a cat, but it lived happily with Veronica for years after the murder. In fact when one of the Lucan daughters was told that her nanny was dead, she was understandably distraught. The young child was not so concerned for herself. Instead, she wanted to know who would now feed and look after her precious young kitten.

The woman who told me that story had been convinced it was true. It seemed that no tale was too far-fetched for the rumour machine that Lucan had set in motion. Other Clermont Club myths alleged that Veronica was failing as a parent; was insanely bad-tempered and impossible to talk to; even that she had attempted to drown her own children. She was reputedly paranoid about Lord Lucan's intentions; she believed that her husband was trying to kill her; she had accused him of buying her a dangerous horse in the hopes of getting rid of her in a riding accident; she claimed that he had wanted to turn his gun against her on a weekend shoot in the country.

The unjustified and untrue smears went on and on, and the plot was clearly working. But Lucan knew that people other than just his gambling cronies needed to be convinced of Veronica's insanity. He went so far as to enlist the unwitting help of the local vicar in his schemes against the mother of his children.

For years Lord Lucan had ridiculed his wife's

religious beliefs. Now that she was alone and free from her husband's sarcasm, Veronica sought comfort with the Church. She began attending adult confirmation classes at a Belgravia church. The vicar there was relatively new to the parish and had heard little about the Lucan family. He knew only that, like so many marriages these days, the couple were living apart. The reverend gentleman was somewhat surprised, therefore, to be visited one evening by Lord Lucan.

Outwardly charming and deeply concerned for the welfare of his wife and his children, the Earl cut an impressive figure. He explained that he was shortly to be leaving London on a business trip that was to take him out of the country for several weeks. The trusting vicar could not have been expected to know that the business trip was, in reality, a beach and gambling holiday at somebody else's expense in the sunshine of Acapulco.

Lord Lucan confided that he was worried about the family. He was sure that the vicar had heard that his wife was unwell? – No? Well, it wasn't something they talked about much. She was under the care of psychiatrists, having threatened some harm to the children . . . . Could he possibly keep an eye on his wife while the Earl was away?

The bemused vicar, who had until then found Veronica a pleasant and interesting young woman, was left deeply concerned at the weight of responsibility suddenly placed on his shoulders. Fortunately he was able to contact another churchman who knew Veronica and who assured him that the children would be safe in her hands. Still it was a worrying situation – and a little more mud had just stuck to Lady Lucan's reputation.

To a number of doctors, including the psychiatrists to whom Lady Lucan had voluntarily gone to please her husband, Lucan complained that his wife had gone mad. When the doctors explained that she was not mentally ill, only suffering from understandable depression and anxiety, Lord Lucan did not want to listen.

He found other professional people into whose ears he could whisper his poison. By now he had realized that his smear campaign was at its most effective when it concentrated on his alleged fears for the safety of the children. Soon almost everybody concerned with the education of Frances and George knew of 'Veronica's problem'. Lucan was an expert at playing the role of a worried and concerned father-figure. He fired off frequent notes to the children's teachers, keeping them up to date with his latest fears about Veronica.

Lucan told them that no nannies would work for the Countess. There had, it is true, been a succession of nannies passing through 46 Lower Belgrave Street, but it was not Veronica who drove them away. On the contrary, they usually found her to be a sympathetic and friendly employer. The nannies discovered that it was Lord Lucan whom they needed to avoid. It was hardly surprising that the staff found a job in which they could be spied on, or called to give evidence in custody cases, was not conducive to settled employment.

One woman cleaner had an amazing introduction to the lengths to which Lord Lucan was now prepared to go to uncover the dirt on Veronica. She had argued with the Countess on her very first day in the household, when she was accused of being slow at her job. Claiming that the house was too dirty to be cleaned in a hurry, the woman stormed out and went home.

The short-lived Lucan cleaner was astonished, one year later, to receive a telephone call at her own home from Lord Lucan himself. He was sorry to bother her – but why had she quit? On hearing of her reasons, the Earl was excited. He asked the cleaner to write down an account of her experiences as evidence against Veronica. Lord Lucan became angry and upset when the bemused woman refused to help. In the end she had to ask her husband to tell the Earl, in no uncertain terms, that they did not wish to get involved in his private matrimonial rows.

For one nanny, there was a very abrupt end to employment. In March 1973 nanny Stefanja Sawicka was employed by Lady Lucan to look after the children. She realized immediately that she was walking into a tense domestic situation. Deprived of adult conversation since the departure of her husband, Lady Lucan was quick to confide her troubles to the then 26-year-old girl.

She spoke to Stefanja of her fear of Lord Lucan and told how he had beaten her with a cane and on one occasion had pushed her down the stairs. Veronica confided that she was most concerned in the evenings and at weekends, when she was often alone in the house. The Countess dreaded that her husband would come back to harm her. On a number of occasions she told the young nanny, 'Don't be surprised if he kills me one day.' Her fears seemed to be confirmed by a series of odd telephone calls, made to the house at all hours of the day and night.

Stefanja found that the children were very well

looked after and loved by Lady Lucan. She enjoyed her first two weeks in the house with her new young charges. Then, on 23 March, she took the children for an outing to the park and walked into a nightmare.

The nanny was confronted by Lord Lucan and several other men, who said they had come for the children. The bemused woman was handed a document by a court official stating that the Lucan children had that day been made wards of court and authorizing their father to take them into his care. The bewildered children were driven away, and Stefanja hurried back, shocked and alone, to Lower Belgrave Street.

The kidnap of the children was Lady Lucan's worst fears come true. When her nanny told her what had happened she went completely to pieces. It was perhaps an understandable reaction from a mother who feared she might never see her three children again.

As Stefanja tried to comfort her, the distraught Lady Lucan began screaming hysterically and running up and down the stairs. In desperation, the nanny called her family doctor to the house to calm the Countess down. The children's schools were informed of what had happened, and Lady Lucan insisted that the police be called. In the face of the court order there was nothing that the sympathetic officers could do to return the children to their mother.

Veronica was to remain alone in her home in Lower Belgrave Street for nearly three months, while the children lived with their father at his nearby flat in Elizabeth Street. Lucan had gained control of the children through a one-sided, ex-parte application to the High Court.

Veronica had been given no chance to defend herself against charges that she was unfit to look after her family. Now she was determined to win back the children as soon as possible.

The Countess's solicitors applied for a new court hearing, at which both parents could be represented. Within two weeks a hearing had been arranged before a judge in chambers. Veronica went along with high hopes of regaining her children but was to be disappointed. The judge decided that because of the allegations made by both parents the case was likely to be lengthy. He said that he wanted to hear all of the facts before making a final decision, and a date was set, three months ahead, for the custody hearing.

Devastated by the court decision, Veronica set about preparing her case for the forthcoming hearing. Her first step was to disprove her husband's wilder allegations about her sanity. Although Lady Lucan's doctors had already told her estranged husband that she was not mentally ill, Veronica now needed the proof.

A few weeks later she voluntarily booked herself in, for observation, to the Priory Clinic in Roehampton. She stayed for four days so that a full report could be prepared on her mental state. The doctors found no indications that she was mentally ill, and the psychiatrist's report was later instrumental in destroying Lord Lucan's case for care and control of the children.

The custody case opened before Mr Justice Rees, in chambers, on 11 June 1973. This time Veronica was not only prepared to defend herself but also to go on the attack. Lord Lucan had expected the hearing to look into his allegations that Veronica was mentally unstable.

Instead, he was shocked to find his own violence towards Veronica was also on the agenda. The once meek Countess was prepared to fight like a tigress for her children. And, this time, she was determined to win.

After a two-week hearing and a succession of witnesses, Lucan gave up the fight. On the advice of his lawyers, he conceded the case. The children remained wards of court, but care and control was restored to their mother. The decision was a disaster for Lord Lucan, even though he was granted access rights to his children every other weekend. He left the hearing a shattered man.

The seventh Earl of Lucan was never to recover from the body-blow of losing the custody hearing. He had lost his greatest battle with Veronica; he had lost his children; he had lost his pride; he had lost a very great deal of money.

The Earl's immediate reaction was one of anger. He determined to hit back at his wife in every possible way. With a twisted logic, Lucan considered that Veronica had broken the rules by divulging intimate details of their personal life. Now the gloves were off. He went back to all his old tricks – and threw in some new ones for good measure. The first priority was gathering yet more evidence for use in another custody hearing. The Earl once again started watching Veronica, the children and their nannies.

Lady Lucan was desperately lonely – and alone. Compared with the lifestyle to which she was accustomed, she was suffering severe financial hardship. As so often happens in bitter marital disputes, both sides of the battle had totally different perceptions of the truth.

Lord Lucan was by now telling all and sundry that his wife was 'spending money like water'. During an interview with his Coutts bank manager he explained away his own gambling losses by alleging that Veronica was overspending by £10,000 a year. He told friends that she was wasting his money out of spite.

Veronica, on the other hand, felt she had far too little cash coming in to maintain the household and feed and clothe her children. Since the separation she had been receiving £40 a week, paid by standing order from her husband's Coutts bank account. During the subsequent inquest Lady Lucan stated that she had been receiving only £40 a month from Lord Lucan – but this was an error on her part. The Earl's bank statements clearly showed that he was paying her that amount weekly by standing order.

The family had always ordered their food on a Harrods account, but now Lucan accused Veronica of overspending. He stepped up the pressure against her by cancelling the arrangement with Harrods. With no income of her own Veronica sold some of her jewellery and for a while took a part-time job in a local hospital – ironically the hospital in which she herself was soon to be a patient.

Lucan bought a small Sony pocket tape recorder and recording equipment for his own phone in order to keep a record of his conversations with Veronica. To paint as black a picture of his wife as possible he would engage her in conversation, and cleverly insult, threaten and goad her into losing her temper. Only then would he switch on the recorder to capture her verbal retaliation.

On these carefully doctored tapes Lucan could be

heard to be sweet reason itself, while his wife would appear beside herself and mad with rage. The Earl took to carrying the tape machine around in his pocket and playing the Veronica tapes to as many of his friends as would listen. With a few exceptions, mostly women acquaintances who were willing to think any evil of Veronica, most of his friends had no wish to be dragged into the sordid details of Lucky's domestic arguments and became embarrassed at listening in on Veronica's supposed tantrums.

Lucan began making telephone calls to his wife's home at all hours of the day and night. At times he would simply threaten Veronica, at others she would find only a chilling silence on the line. If one of the nannies answered, then the phone would either be hung up, or he would pretend to have obtained a wrong number and ask for a non-existent subscriber.

Veronica had lost touch with most of her own acquaintances over the years of the marriage, and many of the couple's joint friends had been scared away by the Earl's distortion of her character. She was not, however, completely alone. As a condition of the court custody ruling Veronica was required to have a live-in nanny to help look after the children. The appointment of all these nannies was subject to the approval of the Official Solicitor, responsible for the welfare of Frances, George and Camilla. Over the latter half of 1973 and into 1974 there had been a number of nannies employed at 46 Lower BelgraveStreet.

One girl who proved highly satisfactory was Christabel Martin, who was to work several times at the house as a temporary stand-in nanny and who got to know

Veronica more as a friend than an employer. Christabel had started working for Lady Lucan in December 1973 when she received a frantic call one day from the agency for which she was working, issuing her with orders to go immediately to the Lucans' Belgravia home. Once there she found that Veronica was in a panic because her regular nanny was not at home, and her estranged husband was returning the children that day after an access visit.

Under the terms of the court order, Lady Lucan was required to have a nanny on duty at all times. She knew that her husband would make an instant complaint to the Official Solicitor if no nanny was waiting to greet the children. Having solved that problem for Veronica, the new girl, Christabel, became the regular stand-in and also a close confidante. She was shocked at some of the things that the Countess of Lucan was to tell her.

Many of Veronica's friends had abandoned her, and one close relative had even told her that the best thing she could do was to commit suicide. Over the months of their friendship, Veronica told Christabel of beatings from her husband and of being forced to accept psychiatric treatment against her will. Perhaps most worrying of all were the constant telephone calls, many of which were from a man asking for fictitious people or simply an empty line. One of Christabel's friends who also spent time at Veronica's home subsequently told her that in just one hour she listened in on 22 heavy-breathing telephone calls.

Veronica had been very scared and said she was worried because her husband still had a key and on occasions had let himself in, uninvited, into the house.

Christabel was instructed that she was never to give Lord Lucan information because Lucan would twist anything she said to try to gain custody of the children. During a later spell of duty, Christabel noticed a man watching the house. He would stand on the opposite side of the road, always with a small mongrel dog, but would only stroll up and down with the animal when he noticed that somebody was paying him attention.

Christabel was aware of other more subtle ways in which Lucan was determined to make his wife's life difficult. On some occasions he refused, or was unable, to pay regular household bills. The milkman stopped delivering after his bill was left unpaid for months. The unfortunate Express Dairies milkman wrote an apologetic letter to Lord Lucan on 10 December 1973. He reported:

> Your wife Lady Lucan asked me to send her account to you, but the amount of £57.62 has not been forthcoming. As we have sent several accounts, we have been forced to stop supplying. However Lady Lucan assures me on the telephone that you will pay this account directly you receive this bill.

This time Lord Lucan did settle the overdue bill, but it was little more than a reprieve for the hard-pressed milkman. By September 1974 he was writing once again, pleading that the milk bill was now five months overdue for payment. He was, however, a little luckier than most of Lord Lucan's creditors. The milk-company records show that on 5 November 1974, just two days before the murder, Lucan settled his overdue £43.80 account. It was one of the last bills he was ever to pay in person.

More seriously, Lucan delayed payment to the nanny agency upon which Veronica depended. Knowing that under the terms of the court order Veronica was required to have a nanny, Lucan was supposed to foot the bill. By April 1974 he had built up such a bad financial reputation with the staff agency that they issued a writ to try to recover unpaid fees. Christabel believed that Lucan was trying to make it harder and harder for Veronica to keep a nanny and satisfy the court restrictions.

It was clear to me at the time of Sandra Rivett's murder that Lady Lucan had found a true friend and strong supporter in Christabel. The young woman was full of admiration for the Countess, who she felt had great internal strengths enabling her to withstand the pressure of her husband's attacks. Christabel told me, in no uncertain terms, that she believed Lord Lucan had been callously attempting to drive his wife over the edge of a nervous breakdown.

The story of Christabel Martin had its own tragic postscript, one of the most astonishing and unhappy coincidences that I was to come across in my entire police career. More than ten years later, long after Christabel had married and left her job as a nanny behind, she also met her own death in a bizarre criminal case.

Christabel's husband, Nicholas Boyce, killed his wife by striking her with a karate blow during a violent argument at their home in East London. The facts of the case were astonishing. While the couple's two young children slept soundly upstairs, Nicholas Boyce cut up and dismembered the body because he feared that nobody would believe her death was not premeditated. He was terrified that his children would be left with no parents at all.

Boyce, who was sentenced to six years' imprisonment for manslaughter at the end of his 1985 trial, had gone to extraordinary lengths to hide poor Christabel's remains. Having sawn up the body, he roasted parts of her corpse in the oven in an attempt to disguise the human parts as the remains of a cooked Sunday joint. Then he distributed the dead woman's limbs and torso in separate builder's skips and rubbish dumps all over London. Boyce, a science graduate, was unable, however, to dispose of her head in the same way. This he encased in concrete and dropped over the side of Hungerford Bridge, while taking his 3-year-old son for a walk.

The tragic story, astonishing because of the long odds against two nannies employed by the Lucan family meeting a violent criminal death, also has one other bearing on the case of the missing Earl. It has been suggested that after the murder Lord Lucan could have killed himself and planned for his body to stay hidden for ever.

In the Boyce case, despite the extraordinary lengths to which the guilty man went in order to dispose of the remains, the police were still able to find physical evidence. Divers were able to recover Christabel's entombed skull from its resting-place on the bed of the River Thames after Boyce had finally confessed to the crime. What clearer demonstration could there be of the difficulties Lucan would have faced in committing suicide and ensuring that his body would never be found?

Christabel had only been employed as a temporary

measure, and Lady Lucan was soon back on the phone to the employment agency for a permanent replacement.

Nanny Elizabeth Murphy, another in the long line of qualified staff to serve the fragmented Lucan household, appeared to be a godsend to the Earl. She had a drink problem, which Lucan quickly recognized. Unbeknown to the nanny or to his wife, Lucan made extensive inquiries to check up on Mrs Murphy's background. Through his international network of friends he even obtained damaging evidence that the nanny had been sacked by her former employers in Spain.

Lucan went to extraordinary lengths to build up his own secret dossier on the unfortunate nanny. Past employers were traced and reluctantly persuaded to give written statements, which suggested her references were forged. He discovered that the nanny had been fired for drunkenness, for walking naked around the house and for encouraging children to drink.

The level to which Lord Lucan now sank in his battle against Veronica was demonstrated by his subsequent behaviour towards the unfortunate Mrs Murphy. Outwardly he befriended her, playing on her weakness by buying her drink and thereby seeking new gossip about the Countess and her treatment of the children. The trusting Mrs Murphy never suspected a thing as she sipped Lord Lucan's whisky; little knowing that, behind her back, Lucan would first ruthlessly use her and then set out to destroy her reputation.

Mrs Murphy was not a well woman, and Lord Lucan provided a sympathetic ear for her troubles. What she never knew was that throughout their conversations the

Earl was secretly tape-recording every word she uttered
with his pocket Sony. Lucan gleefully reported back on
the success of his plot in a letter to one of his friends.
The typewritten letter on Lucan's own Coronet-headed
notepaper was dated 20 February 1974. It mentioned an
earlier recording made in the street and continued:

> There is no shouting and despite the noise of the traffic
> nearly all of the conversation is distinguishable. However
> I am certain it is the wrong moment to disclose this as
> Mrs Murphy will surely be indiscreet in front of Messrs
> Sony before long.

Lucan instructed his private detective agency,
Devlin & Co., to watch every move that Mrs Murphy
made. He wanted evidence that she was failing to care
for his children. The agency had put Morris and Cranstoun on the case in early 1974, and Lucan was delighted
at the report he received. Headed PRIVATE & CONFIDEN-
TIAL and dated 28 February, it began:

> Dear Lord Lucan,
> re: Lady Lucan
> In accordance with your instructions, we confirm
> that observation was maintained upon the address of
> Lady Lucan during the period Saturday 23rd February
> 1974 – Tuesday 26th February 1974.
> At 8 am on Saturday the 23rd February 1974, our
> Mr Cranstoun commenced observation upon 46 Lower
> Belgrave Street, London SW1, when he located the
> brown DAF motor car, Reg. No. LPK 389K, parked
> outside the address.

The investigators' report detailed every movement
in or out of the house that morning, including the

postman, the paper-boy and even the delivery of four pints of milk by Express Dairies. It continued:

> At 11.45 am a woman hereafter referred to as fitting the description of Mrs Murphy left the address with the three children, Frances, George and Camilla. Mrs Murphy was wearing a dark blue coat with a fur collar, Frances was wearing a black jacket and blue tartan trousers, George was wearing a grey jumper and grey trousers, and Camilla was wearing a fawn jumper and blue trousers.
>
> Mrs Murphy and the children were followed to a newsagent's shop, McQuillan at 31 Ebury Street, London SW1, and a few moments later they left those premises and were followed to The Irish Club, 82 Lyall Street, London SW1, where they arrived at 12.10 pm.
>
> Thereafter Mr Cranstoun observed Mrs Murphy and the three children sitting at the bar drinking from glasses.
>
> Mr Cranstoun telephoned our Mr Devlin from the club when we reported the foregoing to you as the premises are situated close to your own property.

This evidence that the wayward Mrs Murphy had taken all three of the children to the local Irish club, where she was in the habit of having a lunch-time drink, was invaluable to Lucan. It was the opportunity for which he had been waiting – a chance to cause more problems for his estranged and hostile wife. Eager for more ammunition to use in the custody battles, Lord Lucan wrote urgently to the investigators:

Dear Mr Devlin,
    Thank you for your most useful report. I would like if possible the same arrangement for next Saturday and Sunday.
    Remember that my wife is extremely suspicious (the psychiatrists agree on a form of paranoia) so that if she

was to go out with the three children and your man
followed them he would have to be very careful.

If the whole party got in the car (assuming Mrs
Murphy was with them or had gone away) it might be
an opportunity to install the telephone device. . . .

Yours sincerely,

The investigation agency never did agree to plant a
telephone bug, despite Lord Lucan's insistence, and the
surveillance operation was called off soon afterwards
when Lucan received bills totalling several hundreds of
pounds for their services.

Watching Mrs Murphy was paying no further
dividends. She was rapidly becoming seriously ill. The
middle-aged nanny visited her doctor and was referred
to a hospital for further tests. None of these mattered
to Lucan, and with disregard for both her medical condition and their supposed friendship he set about destroying
Mrs Murphy just to score points off Veronica.

He spoke first to the Official Solicitor, to whom
he voiced his suspicions about Mrs Murphy's references
and his fears that the children might come to moral
harm. It was plain, the Earl said, that Veronica was
unable to choose suitable staff. Lucan detailed the results
of discussions with the Marquesa de la Puente in Spain,
who had employed Mrs Murphy in 1967. Although Mrs
Murphy had produced a satisfactory reference on headed
notepaper, the Marquesa now revealed that the nanny
had been fired for 'excessive drinking, heavy smoking
and encouraging the children to drink'.

Similarly Lucan revealed his findings from 1972
when the nanny worked for a solicitor in Cyprus. 'She
drank to excess, had hallucinations and was sacked,' he

said. Coupled with Lucan's new information about the Irish Club visit, there was only one inevitable conclusion. Still mystified as to the real reasons of how her past had come back to haunt her, Nanny Murphy was sacked.

Perhaps the greatest hypocrisy was still to come from the seventh Earl of Lucan. Shortly after losing her job, Mrs Murphy's mystery illness was finally diagnosed as cancer. She was rushed into hospital for an operation but told she had little time to live. In hospital she received a visit from her concerned friend Lord Lucan. He was sorry to hear that Veronica had fired her.

A relative gave Mrs Murphy a home for the last weeks of her life. From there she wrote to Lord Lucan, the man whom she thought had been so kind throughout all her troubles. Her handwritten note made it clear that she knew the terminal nature of her illness. The dying woman spoke of her new home in Camberley and her rapid escape from hospital, 'even if of a temporary nature'. The letter continued:

> Although I left hospital full of bravado, on arrival here, it took all the Irish spirit to keep upright.
> This is a beautiful spot and I go daily to feed a vast swarm of ducks and their hungry babies – it is refreshing to walk through the woods, so clean after Eaton Square.
> May I say 'thank you sincerely' for visiting me in hospital, and your gift of lovely grapes, it was most considerate of you. I did not see Lady Lucan, perhaps she was tied up with household affairs. I will take advantage of that good drink you so kindly offered before entering hospital again, will probably need it to get up courage. Will ring on my return to The Irish Club.
> Yours sincerely,
> Elizabeth Murphy

Soon afterwards Mrs Murphy went to her grave, never knowing that the unhappiness of her later days had been directly caused by the Lord she had thanked so profusely.

For Lucan Mrs Murphy's departure proved to be a set-back. All his carefully prepared evidence had harmed Veronica not one jot. Nanny Murphy had gone; the succession of temporary girls had gone; and in their place was a new and eminently suitable young woman. She was a delightful girl whom Lady Lucan took to immediately. As the new nanny's mother was later to describe her, she had the ability to cheer up everybody she met. The date was 26 August 1974, and the new girl's name was Sandra Rivett.

CHAPTER 6

THE POINT OF NO RETURN

S andra Rivett's appointment to look after Frances,
George and Camilla marked a major turning-point
in Lord Lucan's attitude and led directly to the
tragic events of 7 November 1974. By then Lucan's
position was truly desperate. He had pinned all of his
hopes on portraying Veronica as mad, proving that she
was so eccentric that no properly qualified staff would
stay with her to look after the children.

Now he had to face the fact that Sandra was not
only good for the children, she was good for Lady Lucan
as well. Through his carefully nurtured intelligence network, Lord Lucan heard that Sandra and Veronica had
quickly become fast friends. They called each other by
their first names, and Sandra regarded Lady Lucan as
more of a companion than an employer. The number
of distressed telephone calls from Veronica to her few

remaining friends had dropped markedly since Sandra had come to live in Lower Belgrave Street. It was precisely the moral support that Lord Lucan did not want his estranged wife to enjoy.

I believe that it was at this point that the seventh Earl of Lucan realized that his tactics had failed. New, and far more drastic, measures were called for. For not only had his hopes of regaining the children been dashed, but he was also in the deepest financial mire. Only he knew just how bad his financial situation had become. For years he had been skating on the edge of a financial precipice; the massive costs related to that summer's High Court custody case had finally tipped him over the edge.

Many of his friends and gambling acquaintances told me that from the summer of 1974 onwards the big stakes games played by Lucan were a thing of the past. Where once he had played backgammon for £50 a point, his stakes were now a tenth of that level. There were similarly drastic changes in his behaviour and attitude. His moods became more morose, and he drank far more heavily, to the point where close friends became worried for his health. He started to chain-smoke his favoured Peter Stuyvesant cigarettes.

The one man who probably knew Lucky better than anyone, Charles Benson, still has regrets that he was unable to help Lucan more in his times of troubles after he had lost the custody case. Charles told me: 'He certainly drank more – and maybe we should have noticed that his whole demeanour was changing.

'I was playing in a big backgammon tournament about a week before this all blew up, and he started slumping over our board and making silly comments and actually touching some of the pieces, which is absolutely not done.

'If it had been almost anybody else involved in that tournament he would have been slung out. It was undignified and very sad, and that, in a sort of small way, gives you an indication of the deterioration of his state of mind.'

Once again, though, Lucan's pride and his desire to project the public image of a successful gambler ensured that few people knew how much he had lost through his vendetta against Veronica. He was warned by his financial adviser that Carey Street beckoned. The thought terrified Lucky, but the gambling was an obsession he still could not stop.

He laid plans to end his money worries, once and for all, by making a clean-break settlement with Veronica. He hoped to offer her money to part with the children. His American godmother, so good to him throughout his life, was his last hope of borrowing substantial sums. Lucan flew to the United States to see her and beg for a loan of £100,000, more than he could ever have repaid.

The now elderly Marcia Tucker was unable to meet his request, so the Earl wrote to her son, The Revd Luther Tucker, then living in Munich, to explain that he had recently spent a few days with Marcia in New York. He outlined his plans to 'buy the children' off his Countess wife. He explained:

Dear Luther,
　　Although I have made my proposals in the bluntest possible way as being a straight purchase of the children

74

by your mother on my behalf, the offer would have to be dressed up in order to give Veronica the maximum amount of face saving.

It may seem incredible to you that Veronica might entertain such a monstrous proposal or that it should be necessary to go to such extreme lengths when a solution should be obtainable in the Courts.

I regret having to involve you and your family in my domestic problems, but I did everything I possibly could in court and although we did not have judgement given against us (we conceded after 2 weeks ruinous court action) we ran into a brick wall in the shape of the current psychiatrist.

Yours ever,
John

Lord Lucan's Munich letter sparked off further correspondence between The Revd Tucker and Lucan's solicitors, but the money that Lucan required was never forthcoming. In desperation Lucan fell back on the traditional last resort of hard-up aristocratic rakes from throughout the centuries. He made plans to sell the family silver. What nobody really knew then, possibly not even Lucky himself, was that even this desperate move would be totally inadequate to save him.

The Earl began borrowing money from anybody who would lend it. Some, such as the wealthy millionaire businessman Sir James Goldsmith, were happy to help out an old friend in trouble. When Lucky approached Sir James he willingly guaranteed him a £5000 overdraft with the Midland Bank. It was the gesture of a true friend, and one that was to cost Sir James several thousands of pounds when the bank called on his guarantee to be honoured after Lucan had fled. His loan was not repaid for many years, until Lucan's bankruptcy accounts were finally settled.

Others were not so willing to help. One businessman whose only real contact with the Earl was as an occasional golfing partner was surprised to receive a telephone call one night. 'I knew straightaway that he was going to be after money,' he told me later. 'I told him I couldn't lend him any, but he said that wasn't what he was after. He had already arranged a loan with a finance company, and they wanted a guarantor.'

It was on 11 September 1974 that Lucan called into the Mayfair offices of the Edgware Trust, a company that specialized in lending money to the rich and famous in the most discreet of circumstances. The firm's director, Charles Genese, later told the Rivett inquest that their company was well known in the sort of circles that Lord Lucan frequented and that the Earl had been recommended to them by a close friend.

The moneylenders requested details of the seventh Earl's income and were told that he received some £12,000 each year from family trusts. He frankly admitted that his expenditure was some way in excess of that figure. Lucan said that he was planning to sell family silver in order to pay back the loan and that the money would be required for no more than six months. Mr Genese said that it was not company policy to ask an aristrocrat like Lord Lucan to fill in any application form, but that a surety would be required.

It was then that Lucan began calling around his friends to find somebody willing to provide the guarantee that he needed. An old Etonian colleague finally agreed to help, and the loan transaction was finalized on 20

September. A banker's draft for £3000 – still £2000 less than Lucan had wanted – was handed over. The agreement called for the capital sum to be repaid after six months and for Lucan to provide a series of post-dated cheques to cover the six monthly instalments of £120 interest.

Lord Lucan found himself trapped in an ever ascending spiral of debt. In the past he had frequently borrowed small sums of £500 or £1000 from friends, just to tide him over a bad evening or two at the tables, but his friends were beginning to tire of the repeated requests for larger and larger amounts.

Many separate individuals were now providing Lucan with loans, none of them realizing the true extent of his borrowings from others. One acquaintance, the chairman of one of Britain's biggest companies, was surprised to be asked for £5000 by the Earl at a Mayfair dinner party.

His dining companion for the evening, a woman who had known Lucan for years, had been even more surprised at the amount of attention that the handsome Lord had showered on her during the course of the evening. Lucan had appeared to hang on her every word; had laughed at all of her jokes; had flirted and flattered. It was only later that she realized to her annoyance that he had clearly been buttering her up so that her partner would provide the money for which Lucan was apparently so desperate.

Lucan's mother, the Dowager Countess, was an even easier target. She was the very first person to whom the impoverished Earl had turned immediately after the custody case. Kaitilin, by no means a rich woman, had nevertheless advanced him a total of £4000, which she believed would be used by her son to help pay off his outstanding legal fees. In fact Lucan used that money, like all of the rest, to maintain the façade of success. At the time he disappeared he still had not settled the legal bills that his mother had believed she was paying.

Another £4000 came that autumn from a stock-broker friend who agreed to an interest-free loan. And Lucan was quick to call in every penny that was owed to him, from loans that he had made to others in his more affluent times. One woman friend, who had borrowed £1000 to help start a business some years before, now found her offers of repayment accepted at once.

Despite all of the money that he was able to scrounge, beg and borrow, Lucan was still unable to maintain his lifestyle because of the continuing drain of his out-of-control gambling. He had accounts with four different British banks – and all were overdrawn. At Coutts, bankers to Her Majesty The Queen, the debt was £2841; at Lloyds £4379; at the National Westminster £1290; and at the Midland £5667. It was only in 1994, when I saw his bankruptcy papers for the first time, that I fully realized the phenomenal amounts of money that Lucan's gambling had cost him in the year or two before the murder.

Statements from his Coutts bank account give a good day-to-day picture of his expenditure in the Clermont and other clubs. On 16 November 1973, for example, he cashed three separate cheques for £2000 each and one for £3000 at the Clermont Club casino. The cheques, totalling £9000, were all made out to 'Cash'. On

21 November a further four cheques 'to cash' totalled £12,000 in a single day. On the very next day, 22 November, seven more cheques for cash added up to an astonishing £22,000.

In just 24 hours Lord Lucan gambled and lost a sum that in 1973 would have purchased two three-bedroomed, semi-detached homes in Greater London. The cheques cashed in a single day represented virtually twice his entire annual income from the family trusts. Less than a week earlier his Coutts bank balance had been over £10,000. Now that account was vastly overdrawn.

Other accounts, too, were suffering in much the same way as Lucan switched cash around from bank to bank, trying to give each bank manager the impression that all was well, and there was plenty of money being paid in every day. It was a financial merry-go-round that could not continue.

Even the most tolerant bank managers were beginning to worry. At Lloyds Bank Cox's and King's Branch in Pall Mall, London, Lucan enjoyed the privilege of an account with the special Guards and Cavalry section of the bank. The section manager, Mr J.E. Chapple, treated all his special customers with due respect. By the autumn of 1973, however, his tolerance was beginning to wear a little thin, as can be seen in the reproduction of the letter dated 26 September (see p. 81).

By October of that year the overdraft, far from diminishing as Mr Chapple had hoped, had grown to £3772. His letters took on a more urgent tone, as can be seen in that of 23 October (p. 82). In December a note of desperation was creeping into the unfortunate manager's communications with the errant Lord (see p. 83).

Temporary Address During Rebuilding 59, Strand, London, WC2N 9LJ

with Messrs. Coutts & Co.

4,11, Strand, London, WY2N OQS

THE RT HON RICHARD J EARL OF LUCAN

DATE	DESCRIPTION	DEBITS	CREDITS	BALANCE CREDIT −+ DEBIT −DR
14 NOV 73	BROUGHT FORWARD			10,917.56
14 NOV 73	CASH	2,000.00		8,917.56
14 NOV 73	CASH	2,000.00		6,917.56
14 NOV 73	CASH	3,000.00		3,917.56
14 NOV 73	CASH	2,000.00		1,917.56
19 NOV 73	RECD		12,500.00	13,917.56
19 NOV 73	RECD		1,000.00	14,917.56
19 NOV 73	E J HAYDEN	25.20		15,492.36
21 NOV 73	RECD CASH	2,000.00	3,000.00	16,492.36
21 NOV 73	RECD SPECIAL PRESENTATION	5.00		16,487.36
21 NOV 73	CASH	3,000.00		12,487.36
21 NOV 73	CASH	2,000.00		9,487.36
21 NOV 73	CASH	2,000.00		5,497.36
21 NOV 73	CHEQUE NO 55104?	590.00		5,297.36
21 NOV 73	CASH	2,000.00		3,297.36
22 NOV 73	RECD		2,000.00	5,297.36
22 NOV 73	SPECIAL PRESENTATION		3,275.00	8,572.36
22 NOV 73	ECD SPECIAL PRESENTATION		4,000.00	12,572.36
22 NOV 73	CASH	2.50		12,569.86
22 NOV 73	CASH	3,000.00		9,569.86
22 NOV 73	CASH	2,000.00		7,569.86
22 NOV 73	CASH	3,000.00		1,569.86
22 NOV 73	CASH	3,000.00		1,130.19 DR
23 NOV 73	RECD CARRIED FORWARD		2,000.00	549.86
23 NOV 73	BROUGHT FORWARD			549.86
23 NOV 73	RECD		3,000.00	3,569.86
23 NOV 73	CASH	3,000.00		549.86
26 NOV 73	RECD CASH	9,000.00		1,130.19 DR
29 NOV 73	RECD		9,000.00	569.86
3 DEC 73	CARRIED FORWARD			569.86

Lord Lucan's November 1973 statement of his account with Coutts Bank.

THE POINT OF NO RETURN

Lloyds Bank Limited

COX'S AND KING'S BRANCH

P.O. BOX 220 · 6 PALL MALL, LONDON, SW1Y 5NH
Telegraphic Address: Coxia LondonSW1 · Telephone: 01-930 7001

In replying kindly quote
this reference both on the
letter and envelope

GUARDS/CAVALRY/JEC/JE   26th September, 1973

The Rt. Hon. The Earl of Lucan,
5 Eaton Row,
London, SW1 0JA.

Dear Lord Lucan,

    I was very pleased when you paid in £6,000 the other day to restore the position on your Current Account.

    You can imagine my disappointment when cheques totalling no less than £3,500 were presented to me for payment yesterday in the absence of funds, particularly as these cheques were all in favour of Cash or Clubs and have, I surmise, all gone in one particular direction.

    After careful consideration I have met these drawings to result in a renewed overdraft of no less than £2,978 and I do hope that you will be able to provide funds forthwith to restore this position and to ensure that in future the account works on a credit basis.

Yours sincerely,

J.E. CHAPPLE,
Section Manager,
Guards & Cavalry.

Letter to Lord Lucan, dated 26 September 1973, from J. E. Chapple of Lloyds Bank.

Lloyds Bank Limited

COX'S AND KING'S BRANCH

P.O. BOX 220 · 6 PALL MALL, LONDON, SW1Y 5NH
Telegraphic Address: Coxia LondonSW1 · Telephone: 01-930 7001

In replying kindly quote
this reference both on the
letter and envelope   Gds/Cav/WAC/LC   23rd October 1973

The Rt.Hon The Earl of Lucan,
5 Eaton Road,
London,
SW1 0JA

Dear Lord Lucan,

    I am extremely disappointed that I cannot trace a reply
from you to my letter of the 10th October regarding the borrowing
on your account. In the circumstances therefore, I would be most
grateful if you would let me know as a matter of urgency what
arrangements are in hand to adjust the present borrowing.

    For your records I enclose a "print-out" showing the
present position and look forward to an early reply.

Yours sincerely,

J.E. Chapple
Section Manager
Guards and Cavalry.

Letter to Lord Lucan, dated 23 October 1973, from J. E.
Chapple of Lloyds Bank.

The much disappointed Mr J.E. Chapple may well
have been even more disappointed, and certainly more
worried, had he been aware of the true picture of Lord
Lucan's finances. There were, for example, letters from
his counterpart at the Midland Bank, where millionaire
Sir James Goldsmith had guaranteed a £5000 overdraft for

Lloyds Bank Limited

COX'S AND KING'S BRANCH

P.O. BOX 220 · 6 PALL MALL, LONDON, SW1Y 5NH
Telegraphic Address: Coxia LondonSW1 · Telephone: 01-930 7001

In replying kindly quote
this reference both on the
letter and envelope

GUARDS/CAVALRY/JEC/JE   4th December, 1973

The Rt. Hon. The Earl of Lucan,
5 Eaton Row,
London, SW1 0JA.

Dear Lord Lucan,

     You will know from my recent letters how disappointed I
am that you have not been in touch before this to let me know
what arrangements are being made to adjust your overdraft here
which stands at £4,238.94 as I write. I must confess that I
find it difficult to understand why you have not corresponded
with me.

     Surely you appreciate that the present position is far
from satisfactory and certainly I do not wish to be placed in
an embarrassing position because of your lack of co-operation,
and I am sure that you share the same feeling. Obviously though
I cannot undertake to continue to meet substantial drawings in
the absence of acceptable arrangements.

     Can you please be in touch with me as a matter of urgency
and meanwhile I must ask you to restrict your drawings to the
absolute minimum as I would prefer that the present debt shows no
appreciable increase.

               Yours sincerely,

                   J.E. CHAPPLE,
                   Section Manager,
                   Guards & Cavalry.

Letter to Lord Lucan, dated 4 December 1973, from J. E.
Chapple of Lloyds Bank.

Lucan. In September, Mr M.G. Taylor, Assistant Manager of the Midland's Newgate Street Branch, was a little more gentle in pointing out to Lord Lucan that his £6291.64 overdraft had exceeded even this guaranteed amount.

'I have thought it desirable to acquaint you of this position, and may I ask you to give the matter your kind attention and arrange for your borrowing to be reduced,' he wrote.

Lord Lucan's problems were less surprising to yet another one of his bankers, the up-market Coutts & Co., with whom Lucan had held an account for more than ten years. In October 1973 Lucan went to their offices in the Strand in London, explained some of his problems and begged for their help. He told the manager that he had recently lost £25,000 gambling and asked for a £20,000 overdraft. They refused that, even though he claimed that he was due to go to America to ask for financial help from an old friend and that the overdraft could be repaid by this means.

The Earl's desperation then led him into blatant lies to the bank. Towards the end of November he told his Coutts manager that his American friend had agreed to help to the extent of £100,000, but that due to complications of gift tax he might not get the money for several months. In truth his request for funds had by then been turned down flat by Marcia Tucker, Lucan's American fairy godmother. Lucan's big lie was enough to keep the bank off his back for several months, after which he resorted to other tactics. He told Coutts he had sent silverware to Christie's for auction and that this would undoubtedly raise between £20,000 and £30,000.

(When the sale did finally take place, after Lucan's disappearance, it was to raise only £15,000.)

Lucan pleaded that he needed a £4000 overdraft to take his children away on a planned holiday to Portugal. He stressed that the money would not be used for gambling, and, having seen the auction catalogue, Coutts agreed to further overdraft facilities. The bank could not have known that the proceeds of the same silver sale had already been promised to just about every one of Lucan's many creditors.

Even then the Earl frequently exceeded the agreed limit, and many of his gambling cheques were presented with insufficient funds being available. In some cases Lucan was able to pay in money to meet the cheque demands, and in others the cheques were returned to drawer marked 'Orders Not To Pay'.

Perhaps the greatest sign of the near bankrupt gambling addict's desperation came in his plan to milk the family trusts of money in the guise of helping his children. On 13 September 1974 his Coutts overdraft had risen to more than £5000, and he approached the Coutts Trustee Office. The managers of the family trusts were asked to release investment funds to Lucan. He said the money would be used to help pay the children's school fees.

Faced with this unusual request, the bank said it would require the approval of the Official Solicitor, because the children were wards of court. Their decision was a fatal blow to Lucan's plans. He could not risk this kind of approach to the Official Solicitor. It would wreck any chance of gaining custody of the children by exposing his desperate financial state – and the gambling addiction that had led him to such a plight. He immediately withdrew his request to the Trustee Office and said he would find other sources for the money.

By now Lucan was gambling out of desperation, rather than with any real hope of being able to keep his head above water. To give some idea of the amounts involved, I calculate that his personal loans, gambling debts and the overdrafts that he had run up amounted to more than £50,000 in just the months of September and October 1974.

Most of Lucan's contacts were, by this time, under the impression that his high-stakes gambling was a thing of the past. In fact, in these last desperate days, the opposite was true. He needed the money so badly that he fell into the trap of chasing his losses and throwing good money after bad.

Some two years before, the luxurious Clermont Club, which had been his Mayfair second home for more than a decade, was sold by John Aspinall to the Playboy organisation. Along with the new ownership came changes in the gambling games that were on offer for the upper-class punters. Some of the older, established members were horrified to find that fruit machines had been installed at the club. These held no attraction whatsoever for Lord Lucan, but another innovation was to lead him even further astray.

The new management installed an American-style craps table, and Lucky Lucan was soon hooked on this most dangerous of gambling games. For decades the game of craps has been the downfall of many a gambler. Played with two dice and a complex system of odds, craps is more heavily slanted in favour of the casino, and against the gambler, than almost any other game.

To an outsider the craps table can seem impossible to understand. Play moves at a furious pace, barely giving the participants time to slap down their money before the dice are thrown, and a fortune is won or, more often, is lost. Few serious, professional gamblers, exactly the description that Lord Lucan liked to have applied to himself, would have anything to do with this game of pure chance. For Lucan, however, the point of sensible thinking was passed, and this new American pastime had one great attraction. Because of the speed of the play it is possible to win, or lose, a great deal of money very quickly. Staff at the Clermont revealed to me just how great an addict Lucan had, by now, become.

Immediately before the killing of Sandra Rivett, he ran up a debt of £10,000, almost all of it lost on the green baize dice table. The casino was forced to call a halt to Lord Lucan's virtually unlimited credit and only allowed him to carry on playing after he assured the credit manager that he would shortly be selling the family silver to repay the debt. The much promised silver once again saved the day, and in the meantime he made an arrangement to pay back some £200 a month towards the substantial capital sum he still owed.

Over the months since the disastrous High Court hearing, Lucan had been a changed and unhappy man. His friends repeatedly told me that he was drinking more; to the point where some of them began to fear that the alcohol might be taking an unshakeable grip. One woman explained how Lucky had always been able to handle his drink, usually vodka, or wine with his evening meal, but that since June he had begun to show the effects of too many drinks by the end of an evening.

'You would never really know if he was drunk,' she said, 'but certainly I noticed more and more that his eyes would be glazed over, and he would become more reckless at the gaming tables.' Lucan confessed to her and others that he was having difficulty in getting to sleep in the early hours of the morning – after spending the night at the casino. He had started habitually using sleeping tablets to ensure a little rest.

Another woman acquaintance reported how Lucan had become someone to be avoided. He talked of little other than his fight for the children and the way in which his wife was spending his money. 'He was like a firework that had never been lit,' said the friend, 'depressed, often morose and introspective and, quite frankly, rather boring to be with towards the end.'

Significantly, however, there came a point in this sorry saga of depression when Lucan once again regained his former sparkle. I believe that it was at this moment – around the start of October 1974 – that Lucky Lucan finally decided to murder his wife.

He, at long last, seemed to accept that he was never going to win the custody battle with Veronica. He appeared more relaxed, more charming, more like his old self. He told a number of people that the arrangement of seeing his children every other weekend now appeared to be working out well. He even stopped the incessant criticism of Veronica and shut up about his fears for the safety of Frances, George and Camilla.

In late October and early November 1974 Lucan was almost back to being his old self. For three days at the end of October he was visited by his old friend, John Wilbraham, who stayed with him at the Elizabeth Street flat. John, who had been Lucky's best man at his wedding to Veronica, was pleasantly surprised to find that, although Lucky was still worried about money, his apparent obsession with regaining the children seemed to have faded.

Another witness also spoke in that final week of Lucan's apparent high spirits. His mother Kaitilin had one of her regular dinner dates with her son in the week before the killing and thoroughly enjoyed his company. The Dowager Countess was almost as obsessed with her daughter-in-law's behaviour as was her son, but on this night he had wanted to talk of other things.

Over dinner they discussed politics, always a lively debate between mother and son as they sat on diametrically opposed sides of the fence. Kaitilin was pleased when John agreed to borrow a book from her that outlined her socialist side of the argument.

Books also featured in another of Lucan's activities that week. Since early the previous year, he had been a regular customer at G. Heywood Hill Ltd, a bookshop in Curzon Street, Mayfair, calling, on average, once a fortnight to pick up new works. Lucan read a great deal, but, most interestingly for my crime inquiry, his tastes in recent months had been for crime murder mysteries. On the very day before the murder he had asked the bookseller for two more books by the author Michael Gilbert, one of England's most prolific crime-writers who specializes in tales of mysterious murder. I never did find out which of Gilbert's books Lucan had read, but the suspicion lingered that he may have been using the crime thrillers as research material for ideas on how to murder his wife.

Crime stories were not the only ones Lucan was reading. On his same visit to the Curzon Street shop he paid cash for a book about Greek millionaires, which he had earlier reserved and which I was later to find still unread in his flat on the night of his disappearance.

Lucan's helpful uncle John was also to receive a visit from his nephew that week. On the previous weekend in Guilsborough, Lucan had left his spectacles behind at his sister's home. Uncle John's daughter, Jennifer Lowther, had offered to take them back to London and deliver them to her father's house.

Accordingly, on Wednesday, 6 November, just the night before the killing, Lucan turned up at Uncle John's apartment to 'pinch a drink' and collect the glasses. The two had not met for about a year, and there was plenty to talk about. Lucan was cheerful, talkative and the best of company. The Earl spoke of his children being well and remarked on how much he and the children had enjoyed a recent holiday at Palm Beach. The children wanted to go back again to the house that had been loaned to them by Marcia Tucker.

Earlier, on the Sunday night, Lucan returned his children for the very last time to the care of their mother in London, then joined a friend for dinner at the Ladbroke Club. His friend told me, 'Lucky was in wonderful spirits that evening. He didn't drink much and hardly mentioned Veronica. It was good to see him back in his old form.'

It may well be that Lucan, by now coldly calculating how he could, quite literally, get away with murder, was laying the ground for the violence that was shortly to follow. He knew that he would be the prime suspect should anything happen to Veronica. It would have appeared much better for him in any subsequent police inquiry if he appeared to have come to terms with the loss of his children and to have finally given up the running battle with his estranged wife. This sea change in Lucan's behaviour coincided with two other significant events, which lead me to believe that he had by then decided upon the broad details of his murder plot.

The first was an unusual approach to his old friend Michael Stoop. In late October Lucan met Stoop at the Portland Club and asked if he could borrow his car. Stoop, one of the best backgammon players in London and a regular golfing companion of the seventh Earl, was happy to accommodate his friend. He was surprised, when, though, Lucan rejected his offer of a Mercedes and instead asked for the use of his old banger, a Ford Corsair. He agreed without question and thought that the somewhat odd request may have been because Lucan wanted to continue spying on his wife in Lower Belgrave Street from a car that she would not instantly recognize.

I, however, have always believed that there was a clear motive in the decision to borrow the Corsair. Lucan did not want to use his own car to carry the body away from the scene of the murder for two reasons. Initially he was worried that witnesses might notice and later report on his Mercedes car parked outside Lower Belgrave Street on the night of the killing, and subsequently that the police would forensically examine the vehicle after Lady Lucan's disappearance.

The second and even more clear-cut indication that

Lord Lucan was by now thinking of murder came from yet another gambling friend, the banker Greville Howard, who had known Lucky since the earliest days of the Clermont Club. For a while Howard and his wife had also been friends with Lady Lucan. He would sometimes accompany the Countess to Annabel's Club, when the many hours of watching Lucky gamble had reduced her to tears of boredom. Eventually, however, Veronica's rather odd behaviour had alienated her from their friendship, and Howard had begun to believe Lucan's repeated assertions that his wife was mentally ill.

After the murder Howard revealed details about a meeting with Lucan earlier that year, at which the Earl talked about his relationship with Veronica and how he could solve some of his financial troubles. The full details of Howard's evidence have never been fully revealed because he was unable, through illness, to appear at the subsequent inquest into the death of Sandra Rivett.

A later newspaper article, however, printed the text of the conversation that had not been put to the inquest jury. Howard had reportedly been astonished when Lucan started talking of killing his wife as a means of solving his financial problems and saving himself from going bankrupt. He had even suggested that there were others among his gambling friends who would do well to follow his suggestion and murder their own wives to solve their money worries.

According to the newspaper reports, Howard had told Lucan that it would be better for his children to see him at a bankruptcy hearing than in the dock at a murder trial. Lucan replied that the body could be dumped in the Solent and never be found. Completely confident of his own abilities to outwit the law, Lucan boasted: 'I would never be caught.'

Perhaps the most damning evidence that Lucan was now planning a cold-blooded murder came from his own children. On what turned out to be their last weekend together, Lucan took his son and two daughters to the Guilsborough vicarage home of his sister Sarah. It was a regular routine on weekends when Lucan had access to his children.

His small Elizabeth Street flat offered few opportunities for play, so Frances, George and Camilla preferred to get away for the weekend. Popular Saturday and Sunday haunts included the Wiltshire country estate of Lucan's close friend, the Earl of Suffolk and Berkshire, the Shand-Kydd home at Horton Hall, and the Gibbs family's Northamptonshire vicarage.

To the adults in the party, Lucan appeared charming and relaxed. On the Sunday morning of 3 November, he spent some time quietly chatting to his three young children. The Earl asked about schoolwork; and friends; and the games they had been playing. All part of a normal father's parental concerns. I am convinced, however, that behind this façade Lucan was now in the final stages of coldly calculating his chances of getting away with the murder of their mother.

The conversation was far from being the concerned and caring, fatherly chat that it outwardly appeared. For Lucan even used his own children as part of his extraordinary spying operation. The Earl steered conversation with his youngest daughter, Camilla, around to her new nanny. Yes, nanny Sandra was nice and looked after them well. Yes, nanny did have a boyfriend. And, yes, they often went out for the evening together, on nanny's night off.

For Lucan the young girl's giggles about Sandra Rivett's romance provided the opportunity he had been seeking. A chance to catch Veronica alone in her Belgravia home. But little Camilla was too young to remember which night of the week her nanny was off duty. Her daddy could not rely on her words alone. He turned instead to Frances, his eldest child and now a sensible 10-year-old. She, too, confirmed that Sandra Rivett always went out on her nights off. That, she revealed, was on Thursdays, always a Thursday. What child could possibly have imagined that talking with daddy would be helping to plan her own mother's murder?

For Lucan, the children's innocent chatter put the final jigsaw pieces in place. He could now afford to relax. With a little luck the children would soon be his alone. Veronica would bother him no more. No longer the expense of two homes; nor the costs of an extravagant wife. Following in the footsteps of so many deluded men and women, Lucan now believed he had planned the perfect crime. It all seemed so easy. Surely, nothing could go wrong.

CHAPTER 7

THE ABSENT HOST

In Lucan's gambling heyday of the late 1960s, London casinos were the most closely regulated gaming operations in the world. Just a decade before, any form of private, organized casino gambling had been strictly illegal, but most common games, such as roulette, *chemin de fer* and blackjack, were finally legalized by the 1960 Gaming Act.

For people of Lucan's class, illegal gaming had been available for many years. This took the form of private games, which floated from house to house around the wealthy homes of Mayfair and Belgravia. These parties, sporadically raided by an unenthusiastic police force, were part social gatherings and part gambling dens. Uncontrolled by any authority and with organizers motivated only by greed, the odds were often heavily weighted against the 'punter'. Running an illegal casino was an easy way to make a fortune for those willing to risk a criminal record by taking part in the operation.

The 1960 Act, which decriminalized the situation, was a traditional British compromise between those pushing for total freedom and the 'nanny knows best' establishment. British citizens were to be allowed to gamble – but only with a mass of rules and regulations controlling how, where and when they could fritter away their money.

Foreign gamblers on their first visits to London are frequently still astonished to find that the casinos are obliged, by law, not to permit them to lose their money too foolishly. On blackjack tables, the gaming regulations insist that notices are displayed, advising the punter on the best method of betting and banning some of the more silly wagers by which the casino could relieve them, more quickly, of their money. They also find that alcohol is banned at the tables to prevent them throwing cash away while drunk – although there is nothing to prevent them from drinking at the casino bar before going back to their game.

One further area in which the rules have always been strictly interpreted is in the hours during which a gambler may gamble. In Las Vegas they serve breakfast at the roulette wheel, but for some inexplicable reason the British law was determined to turn our gamblers into night-owls. Casinos open after 2 pm and close their doors by 4 am.

Lord Lucan was therefore obliged to adopt an almost nocturnal lifestyle if he wished to follow his chosen career as a professional gambler. On occasions, particularly if he were losing serious money, he would chase his losses until the last legal moment of gaming. For many months before the 1974 murder, having fallen into the habit of taking tablets to help his insomnia after a late night at the tables, he frequently did not rise from his bed until lunchtime.

Unusually, on the morning on 7 November Lucan appears to have been an early bird. My investigations after the crime revealed that he had telephoned his solicitor early that morning and, at about 10.30 am, had received a telephone call from his current girlfriend, Charlotte Andrina Colquhoun.

Charlotte, known to Lucky by her shortened middle name of Andy, had known the Earl for about nine months, since being introduced by a mutual friend over lunch at the Clermont Club. She described her relationship with Lucan as friendly but not intimate. Her description tallied with my own investigations into Lucan's personal life. I never heard a single suggestion that the Earl was a womanizer or had intimate girlfriends either before, or after, the separation from his wife.

Andy was just 21 when she met the then 39-year-old seventh Earl, but they became firm friends, with frequent lunches at the Clermont, or dinner and dancing dates at Annabel's. She told reporters later, 'I found him very quiet and interesting and very relaxing.'

'He was very interested in photography at a good amateur level, and I advised him where to get his printing done. We discussed all sorts of things such as the price of gold, stocks and shares. He used to confide in me about his wife, although I have never met her. But we never discussed marriage – after all he isn't yet divorced.'

After the murder, I spoke at length to Miss

Colquhoun. She was a pleasant girl who did her best to help but had little to tell me of Lucan's real character. I formed the impression that their friendship was no more than a social convenience for Lucan. He wanted an occasional dinner partner when required, and I thought it unlikely that he would have turned to this young girl for help in his flight from justice.

Andy, the step-daughter of timber millionaire Peter Meyer, later spoke again to the newspapers. This time she publicly pleaded with Lucan: 'Come forward – I'm sure it will be for the best.'

She also spoke about her last date with Lucan, at Annabel's on the Wednesday evening before the murder. 'He seemed very happy, just his usual self, and there was nothing to suggest that he was worried or depressed,' she said.

On that Wednesday evening it had been agreed that Andy would telephone Lucan the next day. During the morning call, however, he had seemed vague about his arrangements that evening. Finally he suggested that she join a small party, with whom he was dining, at the Clermont Club. Andy agreed and at about 3 pm on the day of the killing she visited the Clermont Club, hoping to see Lucan to confirm the arrangements. She was disappointed to find him not there.

With some persistence, she again telephoned his home but could get no reply. Because she had planned to spend the weekend with friends, Andy particularly wanted to see Lucky before leaving town. So at 4.30 pm she left her office and made one last attempt to find him. She drove home past the Clermont and Ladbroke clubs and the end of Elizabeth Street but failed to spot

Lucan's Mercedes car parked outside any of these places. Because of Lucky's failure to confirm their arrangements, Andy did not go to the Clermont Club for dinner that evening. She was never to see him again.

Other close friends who were let down by Lucan on that fateful day included artist Dominic Elwes and banker Daniel Meinertzhagen. They had arranged to have lunch with their friend at their regular haunt of the Clermont Club. When he did not turn up at 1 pm as arranged, they both began to be worried. For all of his faults, Lucky did not usually fail to keep his appointments. After waiting a decent interval, the two men decided to go into luncheon without him. They were sure he would turn up at the club that evening, as usual.

The next confirmed news of Lord Lucan's whereabouts on 7 November came from a more unlikely source. At about 4 pm, wearing a smart blue suit, Lucan called at a chemist shop at 9 Lower Belgrave Street – just a few hundred yards from his estranged wife's home. He had an unusual, though not unprecedented, request. He asked the shop pharmacist to identify a capsule that he produced from his pocket.

The chemist had no difficulty at all in putting a name to the tiny pink and green capsule in Lord Lucan's hand. It was Limbutral 5, a drug available on prescription for the treatment of various nervous complaints. The chemist later told me that over the previous couple of years Lucan had been in several times asking about various drugs used by neurotic people. Although he never explained his requests to the pharmacist, Lucan gave the clear impression that he was keeping a check on which drugs were being prescribed for his wife.

At about 4.45 pm Michael Hicks-Beech, a literary agent who had been a friend for many years, received a telephone call from Lucan, inviting him to call at his home at Elizabeth Street. The Earl wanted some advice on an article he was writing. Hicks-Beech agreed to help and arrived at the flat some time between 6.30 pm and 7 pm. Lucan explained he was writing an article on gambling for the student son of another friend. He had agreed to write around 2000 to 3000 words for an Oxford University magazine on the strict condition that it was published anonymously.

Hicks-Beech examined and corrected the article, and they had a few drinks. He was later to recall that Lucky had a couple of sherries or vodkas, while he drank two large scotch and sodas. They discussed books and the current political situation in the Middle East and laughed together over the gambling article. Lucky Lucan had been asked to share his knowledge on the art of hustling mug punters, a game for which he had a proven aptitude, and at one stage Lucan had telephoned the young man for whom he was writing, to assure him that the article would be ready a day or two later. Years later I found the full text of Lucan's gambling article. For legal reasons it cannot be published.

Michael Hicks-Beech was certain about one important factor in the Lucan saga. He revealed that when Lucan drove him home at 8 pm that evening, a time later confirmed by the literary agent's wife, he had definitely not been driving the Mercedes. Instead, Hicks-Beech recalled the car as being an old, dark and scruffy Ford, almost certainly the Ford Corsair that had been borrowed from Stoop. He also confirmed that Lucky had been wearing grey flannel trousers and a jersey, possibly a polo-necked jumper.

One puzzling aspect of the Hicks-Beech visit revolved around a second telephone call that Lucan made in his presence. Hicks-Beech heard Lucky telephone at about 7.30 pm to reserve a table for dinner at the Clermont Club. My inquiries revealed that Lucan did make a call with just such a dinner reservation – but the call was received by the assistant restaurant manager at the Clermont at 8.30 pm, some 30 minutes after Lucan had driven Hicks-Beech back to his own home in Oakley Gardens, Chelsea.

The restaurant manager, who did not come on duty that evening until 7.30 pm, was certain about the timing of the Lucan call, and the mystery of the dinner reservation has never been satisfactorily resolved. Did Lucky Lucan simply call the restaurant twice, to make certain of his reservation? It seems an uncharacteristic and unnecessary act. Or was he trying to establish an alibi for later that night in as many people's minds as possible?

Certainly he does seem to have invited a good number of his friends to share his Clermont dining-table that night. Earlier in the afternoon, at about 5.15 pm, Lucky had received a call from Greville Howard, who asked him to come to join a small party of friends at the theatre that night, as he had spare tickets for a performance at the Mermaid. Lucky sounded cheerful but declined his invitation. 'That is very kind of you, but I don't think I will,' he said. Instead, Lucan suggested that Howard join him for dinner at the Clermont Club.

Also invited to dinner was secretary Sarah Smith-

Ryland, a friend of Howard who had met Lucan a year before at the Clermont. She was in the party who had gone out with Howard to the theatre that evening along with merchant banker James Tuke and his wife Caroline.

The entire group of invited guests were to turn up as arranged at the Clermont to be met by yet another mystery. When they got there at around 11 pm, knowing nothing of the horrors that had occurred in Lower Belgrave Street, they discovered that their host was nowhere to be found. Greville Howard tried telephoning Lucky at his London home, but when he could get no answer the foursome decided to go ahead with their dinner.

It was then they discovered that Lucan had booked a table for four – perfect for them, but one place short if their host was to join them. The group insisted on another chair being brought to the table for Lucan. The drama that had been played out two hours earlier at 46 Lower Belgrave Street had much delayed their absent host. His chair would stay empty for the rest of the night.

CHAPTER 8

MURDER MOST FOUL

I n the first-floor bedroom a mother and daughter
sprawled lazily across the woollen blanket covering
the king-sized double bed. Upstairs in the nursery
the two youngest children were already abed, tucked up
by their loving nanny Sandra, while 10-year-old Lady
Frances stole a few grown-up moments alone with her
mummy. The little girl, already in her pyjamas, was
bathed but sitting up way past her bedtime.

Copying her mother, Frances doubled up a single,
white pillow against the headboard. It made it more
comfortable and easier to see the colour television at the
end of the bed. Mummy, still dressed in her best brown
jumper and green pinafore dress, had already pinched
the other three pillows for herself.

The bedroom, with its large-flower patterned wallpaper, was softly lit by the two large lamps, competing

for space on the crowded bedside table with Lady Lucan's packets of Embassy cigarettes, lighter, an overfull ashtray, family pictures and a chrome water jug. On the bed, alongside Lady Frances, lay a copy of that night's *Evening Standard* newspaper, turned to the page of television times.

Unheard by children or adults up above, a key silently opened the front door's Yale lock. The door to the deserted street opened quietly, unhindered by the security chain dangling by the door jamb. The women of the house had forgotten once again to put the chain on. A figure slipped into the house, tiptoed soundlessly to the basement steps and descended into the darkness.

On Lady Lucan's side of the bed a clock showed a few minutes before nine when nanny Sandra Rivett popped her head round the open bedroom door. 'Would you like a cup of tea?' she asked with a smile. An already sleepy Lady Frances barely looked up as Veronica replied, 'Yes, I'd love one.'

On the first-floor landing Sandra paused, listening, for a moment. Not a sound to be heard from the nursery above. Both Lord George and Lady Camilla were safely asleep for the night. Reassured, the petite and pretty young woman trod carefully downstairs, balancing in either hand the used cups and saucers she had collected from the room up above. At the top of the steps leading down to the basement breakfast room and kitchen, Sandra once again stopped for a moment. She tried without success to switch on the downstairs light. The light bulb must have blown, always a problem to change when the ceilings were so high and both she and Veronica so small.

Sandra was happy in her new job, settled in comfortably to this friendly, family home. The creaks of the stairs and the dark of the waiting kitchen held no fears for her. Once again she set off down the last flight of stairs.

In the darkness below, crouching at the side of the staircase, Sandra's killer was waiting. His mouth dry, his heart pounding, he struggled to control his breathing, fearful of betraying any sign of his menacing presence. In his right hand the murderer grasped the short but heavy length of bandaged lead piping he would use in his crime. The weight felt familiar. He had practised wielding the weapon before, swinging different lengths of pipe to find the best size for his bludgeon. He could afford no mistakes.

Sandra reached the bottom of the basement steps on her way to the kitchen and, her eyes not yet accustomed to the dark, stepped gingerly on to the wooden parquet flooring. She flinched in terror and started to turn when she heard a sound behind her. There was never the time to cry out.

The bludgeon crashes down with sickening force, and all becomes dark; and, in a frenzy, the murderer leaps forward towards the helpless young woman; cups and saucers go crashing to the herring-bone wooden floor; a teaspoon tinkles across the room before coming to rest in the kitchen doorway. He grasps her roughly by the elbow, bruising her skin and stopping her from collapsing completely to the floor; he swings back his arm and strikes down yet again; and there is no sound now from the unconcious woman, yet the violence goes on unabated and blows rain down unremittingly on Sandra's unprotected face and body; the pipe splits open the dying woman's scalp, across her forehead, by her ears, at the side of her face, while his other fist punches out to split open her lip, and, as Sandra doubles up on the floor, the bludgeon smashes into her shoulders, her arms, her fingers; blood sprays across the walls; across the ceiling; across the piano, six feet away; it splashes over the empty glass rosebowl and the two volumes of a child's encyclopaedia, resting on the piano top; across the family photographs and portraits gazing down in silence on the scene of unparalled, bloody horror.

When, finally, the frenzy subsided, the killer was left panting, exhausted, his arms by his side; at his feet lay the crumpled, still warm body; a thin gold chain still circled round her neck; blood already soaking her flower-patterned smock, her dress and her tights. Sandra's sensible black working shoes had fallen from her feet, coming to rest in a jumble against the wooden blanket chest at the foot of the stairs; a pool of blood already forming around her deathly still body. She died quickly and without a sound.

In the immediate aftermath of the attack the killer acted with cold and calculated precision to clear up the scene of the crime. Firstly, still working in the dark, he scooped up the now dead body and doubled it up and into the waiting canvas mailsack. A sash cord had been threaded through metal eyelets at the top of the sack, and he drew the cord loosely together to close the bag.

He folded the top over, but Sandra's arm flopped out, bent at the elbow and dangling at the side of the sack, a gold ring set with a single small diamond on her second finger, her tiny, square-faced watch still ticking on her wrist.

It is likely that the murderer, at this stage, still

did not realize whom he had killed. He expected the nanny to be out; Veronica was the only woman who would walk down those stairs; the women were of identical height and similar build; he was working in the dark; his sole contact with the body through the leather-gloved hands that had beaten and punched and lifted it into the unwelcoming canvas shroud.

His subsequent actions also support the theory that he believed he had murdered the Countess. Expecting there to be no other adult in the house, he left the body downstairs in the sack while walking calmly up one flight of stairs to the ground floor. He went into the adjacent small cloakroom, intending to wash off the blood. But the cold tap did not work, and he was left, literally red-handed, as he heard a noise outside the washroom door.

In the different world of the quiet and cosy upstairs bedroom, Veronica was becoming impatient for her tea. The BBC news had been on for fifteen minutes with no sign of Sandra returning. Lady Frances remained, half-asleep, on the bed. It was late for the little girl, and school beckoned in the morning.

The Countess of Lucan left her young daughter on the bed and walked down one flight of stairs to the top of the basement steps. At her side was a glazed and wooden partition; to her front the door leading out to the street; to her rear the cloakroom door and a corridor in which the children had left their bicycles half-propped up against the wall. Veronica leant down into the basement stairs, surprised to see no light in the downstairs kitchen; 'Sandra . . . Sandra,' she called; and she heard a sound from behind the cloakroom door.

For the murderer the sound of the Countess's voice was the greatest shock of his life. What must he have thought at that moment? The woman he had battered to death was outside of the door. Was he going insane? Had he not killed her, after all? Had she got out of the bag and come back to haunt him? With his senses reeling and still grasping the bloodstained piping, he flung open the door.

> Veronica has no time to grasp what is happening before a stunning blow to her head knocks her down to her knees; the bludgeon falls again and again; the force of the blows distorting the metal and once again spraying blood over the walls, the partition, the ceiling lampshade, her attacker. Now she is fighting for her life; screaming and screaming, until a voice in the darkness hisses, 'Shut Up' and, with horror, she recognizes the voice of her husband, Lord Lucan; he is trying to kill her; grabbing at her arms; thrusting his fingers deep into her mouth, scratching her throat; and now she bites hard, as hard as hard can be; to force his hand away, to let her breathe, to save her own life. She feels herself spun round, face down to the carpet, with his hands round her neck, tightening, throttling; she fears she is going to die; and she twists, and she wriggles, and she gets between his legs; and she reaches up and grabs hold of his testicles; and squeezes and wrenches with a desperate strength; and his grip weakens around her throat, and the air rushes into her lungs; and she gasps and pants as Lord Lucan gives up the fight, and Veronica struggles up into a sitting position between his legs. She has survived; her scalp cut to the bone, bloody and battered and beaten; but alive.
>
> Then she asks, 'Where's Sandra?'

In semi-darkness, sitting exhausted on the stairs, Lady

Lucan demanded to know what had become of her nanny. At first Lord Lucan was evasive – she had gone out, he claimed. The words sounded weak even as they were uttered, and she asked once again. Suddenly he blurted out the true horror of what he had done. Standing on the staircase Lord Lucan confessed to his wife that he had killed the nanny.

His chilling confession terrified Lady Lucan. She and her children were alone in the house with a cold-blooded killer. Her fear spurred her into action. Now she knew he could try to finish off the job at any time. She resolved to play along with her husband as the only way to survive.

The Countess suggested that she could help him to escape from the consequences of what he had done. If he were to stay at the house and look after her for a few days, her bruises would go down, and nobody would be any the wiser about what had happened. She suggested that they go upstairs, but first she pleaded for a drink of water. Despite the massive injuries to her face and scalp, Lady Lucan was most troubled by the pain in her throat. The inside of her mouth and throat had been gouged and lacerated by Lord Lucan's fingers, and her throat felt on fire.

She received little sympathy from Lord Lucan. He allowed her to get up and walk into the ground-floor washroom, where only the water-heater tap was working. When Veronica complained that the water would be too hot to drink he grew more impatient. She bent over the wash-basin, cupping her hands to catch enough hot water for a sip to drink.

'Hurry up,' he told her, 'look at yourself.'

If Veronica had looked at herself, she would have seen an awful sight. Her face was a mask of blood, still flowing profusely from several splits in the skin of her scalp. Her hair was tangled and matted with blood, and dark bruising was already developing around her cheeks and her eyes.

The couple were a frightening sight for young Lady Frances when they made their way back up to Veronica's bedroom. Lady Lucan had gone first up the stairs, still terrified that her husband would hit her again but in too much pain to move too fast. Trying to prevent her daughter from seeing the full extent of her injuries Veronica ran into the adjoining bathroom.

Lady Frances, who had earlier heard a faint scream from downstairs but thought that the cat had scratched mummy, was quickly sent off to bed by her father. She was surprised to see her daddy who had not lived at the house for so long, but she said not a word and went straight up to bed. She lay there wondering what was happening.

In the bedroom one floor below, Lord Lucan was starting to think once again. When Veronica went to lie on the bed, he stopped her and insisted that she first put a towel down so the pillows would not be stained with her blood. He had earlier asked if she had any Tuinol, a prescribed drug that he knew made her sleepy, or barbiturates. Veronica confirmed that she had some tablets in the bedroom but complained again that she felt very ill and had to lie down.

As she lay on her own side of the bed, Lord Lucan said she must clean up her face and went into the bathroom to get a wet cloth. Veronica heard the taps running and realized that for a few vital moments her husband would be unable to hear her. She slipped off the bed and, despite excruciating pain in her back and her neck, fled down the stairs and out of the house.

Moments later Lord Lucan emerged from the bathroom to find the bedroom empty. The wrong victim was dead, and now the right one had fled. He lurched out into the corridor in search of his wife. Up above, the frightened face of his daughter Lady Frances peered down the stairs. Lord Lucan ignored her and turned down the staircase.

Fleeing from the house into a wet and deserted Lower Belgrave Street, the Countess of Lucan heard the last words she was ever to hear from her husband. 'Veronica . . . Veronica,' he called; but Lady Lucan did not look back. Instead she fled down the street to the safety of the one building where she knew she could get help. The handful of drinkers in the Plumbers Arms public house were astonished when the door burst open, and a blood-stained Lady Lucan fell in.

Lady Frances had, meanwhile, watched her father disappear down the stairs. She did not know what to do. Her nanny Sandra was nowhere to be found, mummy had been hurt and had disappeared, and now daddy had gone off without a word. The little girl retreated to the only place she felt safe, her bedroom.

Lord Lucan's movements were not hard to deduce in the few moments after he ran out of the front door of No. 46. He appears to have walked towards the Plumbers Arms but then turned off to the right and into Chester Square. At around 10.30 pm Madelaine Florman, the mother of one of Lady Frances's schoolfriends, heard a knocking at the door of her Chester Square home. As she and her children were alone in the house, she decided not to answer such a late-night caller. Soon afterwards she received a telephone call from a man who spoke incoherently and whom she later identified as Lord Lucan.

She did not hear the distinctive 'pips', which in 1974 indicated that a call was being made from a public telephone box, and so assumed that the call had been made from a private address. Having been roused from her sleep Mrs Florman was unable to make any sense of Lord Lucan's rambling telephone call and put the receiver down.

She later discovered bloodstains on her doorstep, and although police were not informed until some three days later, forensic examination of these marks revealed the blood was a mixture of groups A and B. These blood groups were a mixture of the blood of both Sandra Rivett and Lady Lucan, and to my mind confirmed that Lucan had been the unknown caller on the night of the murder.

Between 10.30 pm and 10.45 pm Lord Lucan's mother also received a telephone call from her son asking her to collect his three children from 46 Lower Belgrave Street. Once again no pips were noticed by his mother, indicating the call was not made from a public telephone box.

The puzzle of from where Lord Lucan made these two calls remains one of the many unsolved mysteries of the case. He would hardly have stayed put in the house after Lady Lucan had run off for help, and anyway the call to Mrs Florman came after he had knocked on her door. He does not appear to have returned to his own flat, because he could then have changed clothes and picked up more of the personal belongings that we found left in his bedroom. In addition, nobody has ever admitted letting him into their home to use the telephone.

From wherever the calls were made, the one thing we do know is that Lord Lucan did not tarry long. He must have got straight into his borrowed Ford Corsair car and driven hell for leather out of London. Just an hour or so later he turned up 42 miles away, on the doorstep of friends the Maxwell-Scotts. It was to be the last time that anybody has ever admitted to seeing the long-lost Earl of Lucan.

While Lucan was speeding through South London, on his way to the Maxwell-Scotts' home in the Sussex village of Uckfield, his badly injured wife was being taken by ambulance to the nearby St George's Hospital after rudimentary first aid from the shocked bar staff at the Plumbers Arms. At St George's she was rushed into a cubicle in the casualty department, and her wounds were cleaned. The doctors and nurses remember her being in a lot of pain and yet repeatedly voicing her concern for her children. At times she became almost hysterical with the worry of what her husband might have done to Frances, George and Camilla.

More bizarrely, the Countess also objected most vociferously to the nurses' attempts to cut off her heavily bloodstained brown jumper. 'It's my very best jumper,' she protested, before being persuaded that treating her wounds was more important than her concern for her clothes.

Even before Lady Lucan had been taken to hospital, the police had forced their way into her home in Lower

Belgrave Street and found the ground floor and first floor deserted. In the nursery upstairs, the still awake Lady Frances and the other sleeping children were found safe and well. In the basement below, the subsequent discovery of the very dead body of their nanny Sandra Rivett was to set in train a police investigation that continues to this day.

CHAPTER 9

LETTERS
FROM A LORD

DAY ONE

Protecting the scene of a crime is the essential first step for any detective during the initial stages of a criminal investigation. It is all too easy for vital evidence to be destroyed, and it is necessary to restrict, as far as possible, the number of people with access to the scene.

As soon as I arrived at 46 Lower Belgrave Street, in the early hours of that Friday, 8 November 1974, I realized that too many people were already inside the house. I ordered everybody out and posted a young police constable on the door to prevent any unauthorized entry back into the premises. Then, I and Detective Chief-Inspector Dave Gerring had a quick conference on the doorstep so that he could bring me up to date with the action he had taken already.

I was informed that the first two officers on the

scene had examined the front and rear of 46 Lower Belgrave Street and had found no sign of any forcible entry to the premises. They had found it necessary to kick open the front door to get into the building. I learnt that the divisional surgeon had already been to the house and had officially pronounced life extinct in the body of Sandra Rivett. To disturb the scene as little as possible he had examined the body without removing it from its canvas shroud. As a matter of routine fingerprint officers and photographers had also been called to number 46 to examine and take photographs of all the relevant rooms.

Dave told me that all three of the young Lucan children had already been taken away by their grandmother, the Dowager Countess of Lucan, and were staying with her at her apartment home in St John's Wood. I also discovered that Lucan's mother had received a telephone call from her son at about 10.45 pm on the Thursday night, asking her to collect the children. Lucan had spoken of a 'terrible catastrophe' at number 46 and told his mother that the nanny had been badly hurt. The Earl had asked her to contact his friend and brother-in-law, Bill Shand-Kydd.

My first move was to inspect the house from top to bottom. Lady Lucan's first-floor bedroom appeared normal with the exception of a bloodstained towel that lay draped across the pillows on the far side of the bed. On the ground floor there was a hallway with a short flight of steps. Immediately next to this was a wood and glass partition and a doorway giving access to the staircase that led down towards the basement breakfast room and kitchen. This entire ground-floor area was heavily bloodstained. Lying on the floor just a few feet away was what appeared to be a bloodstained cosh.

As I went down the stairs to the basement area, I could see the pictures on the walls were awry, the walls themselves were bloodstained, and even one of the metal banister rails had been distorted and dislodged. I picked my way carefully down, trying to avoid the bloodstains. Two cups and saucers with a bamboo-leaf pattern had been dropped on the floor at the foot of the stairs. They were lying in a pool of blood, and one of the saucers had broken.

To my right was a piano and, nearby on the floor, a large canvas bag, from which a human arm was protruding. All around this bag was a dark and still spreading pool of blood. A colleague pointed out to me that the light fitting, designed to illuminate the bottom of the stairs, did not have a bulb in the holder. However, there was a light bulb lying on one of the dining-room chairs nearby.

The door that led to a small, rear garden had been found closed but was unlocked. I went outside and found the garden surrounded by a six-foot-high wall, which was itself topped by a three-foot-high trellis. To complete the barrier the trellis was covered in rambling roses. I looked closely at the walls, which were covered in moss, but there was clearly no trace of anybody having attempted to scale them in an endeavour to escape the premises. In the rear garden there were also some bloodstained leaves, which were covered up to protect them for later, detailed forensic-science examination.

Back inside the house, I found that the door leading to the front area of the basement had been locked. I examined this area but found nothing to assist my inquiries. There was a safe in the basement, which appeared to be locked, although I could not examine it closely at that stage because fingerprint experts had not yet had the chance to go over it in detail.

I remained at the murder scene until the fingerprint experts and photographers arrived so that I could personally direct the operation and tell the photographers exactly what pictures I needed to be taken. I also had the sad task of ensuring that the coroner's officer had been told about the death, so that arrangements could be made to have the body of the nanny, Sandra Rivett, taken away to the mortuary.

Leaving the scene of the killing, I went around the corner to 5 Eaton Row, which our inquiries had already established was owned by Lord Lucan's family trust. We searched the premises, together with the garage, and went on to 72a Elizabeth Street, the rented apartment where Lord Lucan was living at that time.

The scene at his flat was bizarre – a little like walking into a cabin of the *Marie Celeste*. To all intents and purposes it appeared as though the owner had just popped out and left all his clothes and belongings ready for his return. A suit and shirt, still on their hangers, were neatly laid out, waiting, on the bed. Also in the bedroom were what appeared to be the entire contents of Lord Lucan's pockets: his cheque-book, credit cards, driving licence, about £80 in notes and a small sum in small change.

The immediate thought went through my mind that Lord Lucan had emptied his pockets in order to avoid any danger of dropping identifying items at the scene.

It seems likely that when he entered his wife's house he was carrying only the keys to his Corsair car and the front-door key for 46 Lower Belgrave Street.

It had proved necessary to force entry into each of the houses and leave police officers behind me to guard each of the buildings. My next port of call was the nearby St George's Hospital, since converted into London's most expensive and luxurious hotel, but at that time one of the capital's busiest hospitals. There, I found that Lady Lucan had already been heavily sedated but was able to give me a short version of what had happened that evening.

Her head was still covered in blood, which had matted her hair and had run down across her face. Incongruously, I noticed that she was wearing a beautiful sapphire necklace and matching ring. She had clearly been very badly injured, but I was reassured by the casualty officer doctor on duty, Dr Neil Scott, who told me that he believed Lady Lucan would eventually make a full recovery.

It was clear that Lady Lucan had been the victim of a severe and sustained attack, one that she had been fortunate to survive. I had to consider the possibility that her assailant might return and try to finish his deadly assault, and so I detailed a police officer to stay at the hospital and guard her from further harm.

By now it was well into the early hours of the morning, but I still had one other morbid task to perform. Returning to Lower Belgrave Street, I supervised the removal of Sandra Rivett's body to the mortuary. It was essential that all possible evidence of the attack be preserved, and so the dead girl had, of necessity, to be left in the mailsack. With all the dignity they could maintain, the undertakers eased this unwieldy form on to a stretcher, manœuvred it up the stairs, out of the front door and into their waiting van.

I knew that the results of the post-mortem examination would be vital to my inquiry and so was pleased to learn that it was to be carried out by Professor Keith Simpson, one of the country's most experienced pathologists.

Back at Gerald Road police station, the necessary staff had already been called from their homes, and a murder office had been set up. My first task was to appoint an office manager and the all-important exhibits officer. Arrangements were made for teams of detectives to make house-to-house inquiries along Lower Belgrave Street and its immediate vicinity.

I also set up a search of all the rubbish skips in the district, every basement area and garden of nearby houses and any open spaces. It was necessary to search for any weapon used in the murder, although I was satisfied, even at that stage, that the weapon used on both Sandra Rivett and Lady Lucan had been abandoned at the scene of the crime.

Police officers involved in the search were particularly asked to look for any abandoned bloodstained clothing or gloves. One oddity that was turned up at this early stage was a wig, found abandoned in a rubbish skip. We had this examined, but it was found to have never been worn and proved to have no connection whatsoever with the case.

It was by now 8 am and both myself and Dave Gerring had been busy all night. Taking a short break, we visited a nearby old-fashioned barber-shop in Horseferry Road, and for the first time in my life I had the barber give me a shave with a cut-throat razor and was freshened up with hot towels. I can heartily recommend this to anyone who has worked through the night and still faces a heavy day's work. I always kept a spare set of clothing at my office for just such emergencies, and, having changed, I returned to work in the investigation room at Gerald Road.

That morning I reviewed the statements that had already been taken, making sure that all possible witnesses had been traced and that further statements were being taken from the staff and customers who had been in the Plumbers Arms public house when Veronica Lucan burst through the door.

Later that day I had the unpleasant task of going to the mortuary where I identified the body, which was still in the canvas bag, to pathologist Keith Simpson. We had asked for a police photographer to be present, and he took a number of photographs of the body as it was removed from the canvas bag and laid on the mortuary slab. The exhibits officer was also present to take possession of the clothes and the mailsack. These items were labelled, entered into the Exhibits Book of the case and taken away for storage. In addition, he photographed each of the various wounds that had been brutally inflicted on the body of Sandra Rivett.

Immediately afterwards Professor Simpson began the post-mortem. He told me that he was certain that death had taken place before Sandra's body had been placed in the bag and confirmed that it had been due to the blows on the head with a blunt instrument.

We had brought with us from the scene of the killing the short length of heavy lead piping, which was still wrapped in a layer of surgical tape. This had already been examined for fingerprints and placed into a plastic bag. Professor Simpson examined the piping carefully and said that, in his opinion, the weapon could certainly have been responsible for Sandra's many injuries.

Back at Gerald Road it soon became apparent that the case was of great interest to the press and TV media. The police station was besieged by reporters who repeatedly requested to interview me and tried to tackle any members of the murder squad as they entered or left the building. A statement giving the brief details of the case had been released on my authority to the Metropolitan Police Bureau, based at Scotland Yard, who handle all media inquiries relating to London police operations.

Throughout the day the house-to-house inquiries that I had initiated and the search for any other possible weapon or clues such as bloodstained clothing continued without success. The homes of both Lord and Lady Lucan were searched, and an array of address books, diaries, telephone numbers and letters were examined and taken to the investigation headquarters.

Cases of brutal murder affect all police officers, however long their experience in the job. It is impossible ever to come fully to terms with the grief that such incidents can cause for the innocent families of the victims. Often one way of coping with the stresses involved, however, is to use humour. I was not surprised, therefore, when I discovered that my detective staff were already running a sweepstake to guess how long it would be before Lord Lucan resurfaced.

As far as I can remember nobody had bet on the open-ended option that he would disappear for the next 20 years, and, at first, I was convinced that he would walk into the station some time that day to face the music. I believed that he was probably consulting a lawyer and would turn up with a legal representative to answer my questions. How wrong time has proved me to be.

I thought it unlikely that the answer to this particular murder mystery would lie in the background of the victim, Sandra Rivett. It was necessary, however, to investigate fully that background to make certain that there was nobody lurking in her past who would have had good reason to attack the Lucan family nanny. One of my team had already traced the dead woman's estranged husband, Roger Rivett, who had officially identified her body.

Sandra's parents, Albert and Eunice Hensby, a pleasant but totally bewildered, ordinary family couple, had been visited and told about what had happened but were clearly far too upset to take on the task of identifying their dead daughter. Roger Rivett, separated from Sandra, but not yet divorced, gave me a detailed account of his marriage. It had clearly been as amicable a separation as these situations can allow, but it would have been foolish of me not to have considered the young man as a potential suspect. It was no surprise, however, when he was able to explain to me exactly where he had been on the night of the killing. His alibi was checked out with the witnesses concerned, and he was, as expected, eliminated completely from our inquiries.

Sandra had been living apart from her husband for many months by the time of her death and, as a normal and attractive young lady, had not been short of male admirers. I found nothing unusual in the fact that so bright and personable a woman should have had a series of men friends, some serious and others of a more casual nature.

We traced all of her recent boyfriends, and each agreed to be interviewed and provide details of what they were doing on the night of 7 November. In every case they were immediately able to provide checkable alibis, although the process did cause some embarrassment to one married man who had become friendly with Sandra unbeknown to his wife and family.

The dead woman's current boyfriend, Australian pub manager John Hankins, had contacted us very shortly after the killing. He had heard about the incident from people who had been in the Plumbers Arms when Veronica ran in for help. His job, acting as a public-house locum, took him to numerous pubs in West London, and he had first met Sandra while working a few weeks before at the Plumbers Arms.

The couple had become close very quickly, and John was clearly deeply distressed to learn of her death. He told me he had seen her on the night before the killing and had telephoned her that very evening to arrange their next date. Once again, he had a totally convincing and truthful alibi for the time of the crime, having been working at the nearby Kings Arms public house.

Sandra's grieving parents lived in a caravan home near Basingstoke in Hampshire. They were interviewed at length but were unable to give me much information of real use in the inquiry. However, Sandra's mother did stress that in recent conversations her daughter had told her how happy she was to be working with Lady Lucan who was treating her more as a friend than as an employee. It also became clear that Sandra had a great affection for the Lucan children under her care.

As day one of the inquiry drew to a close, and my initial belief that Lord Lucan would appear to make a statement appeared less and less likely to happen, I decided to circulate his description to police forces throughout the country. The report described Lord Lucan as being wanted for interview, and this fact was also released to the national newspapers and television stations.

The resulting publicity led to a flood of telephone calls into the incident room, with reports of having seen the missing Earl from the complete length and breadth of the country. Many of the calls proved impossible to check out in detail, having been sightings simply of a man resembling Lucan in buses, cars, trains and railway stations all over Great Britain. Others were more substantial and carried greater detail. These were passed on to local police forces for further inquiries to be made.

During this entire busy time it was necessary, before the age of computers, to keep the extensive paperwork system fully up to date. The results of inquiries coming into the murder office had to be read by the office manager and entered into the records, indexes and cards. When further inquiries needed to be made, such details went into the action book for allocation to one of the many detectives now engaged on the case. To keep an overview of the whole inquiry it was vital for me to read all of the statements that had been taken – always a time-consuming if necessary task.

One of the statements that passed over my desk that Friday was from Lord Lucan's mother, the Dowager Countess of Lucan, Kaitilin Elizabeth Anne. She revealed that her son had telephoned her at about 10.45 pm on the previous evening with the news that an 'awful catastrophe' had occurred at 46 Lower Belgrave Street. The Dowager Countess said that in her son's telephone call he had claimed to have been driving past the house when he saw a fight going on in the basement between a man and Veronica. He had rushed into the house to find his wife shouting and screaming.

Lucan told her that his wife Veronica and the children's nanny had been hurt and asked her to collect the children. The Dowager Countess had hurried to the house, arriving shortly after 11 pm, where she had been seen by the first CID officer to arrive at the scene. He had told her about the murder of the nanny and that her daughter-in-law had been taken to hospital with serious injuries.

Lord Lucan's mother had taken the children back to her own flat at St John's Wood after informing police officers at the scene that her son was separated from his wife and normally lived in a flat at 72a Elizabeth Street, Belgravia. A police constable had accompanied her and the children back to her home and had been with her after the children had been put to bed when, at about 12.30 am on the Friday morning, her son had telephoned again. He had declined to speak to the police officer present at the time but had told his mother he would be in touch later that day.

By late on the Friday night the hunt had been intensified, and detailed scientific examinations were continuing at the scene. One of the country's foremost experts on blood, Dr Margaret Pereira, had agreed to examine the house. It was clear that Lucan was not going to turn up voluntarily, and I was already experiencing what I perceived to be a lack of co-operation from some of his friends and acquaintances.

By now the news of the killing and of Lord Lucan's disappearance was widespread, and yet very few people had come forward with offers of help. We were having to contact everybody who we wanted to talk to by telephone for an appointment to be made and full statements to be taken. It was not a promising beginning.

DAY TWO

Having managed to get home late on the Friday night to snatch a few hours' sleep, I was back at Gerald Road early on the Saturday morning to finish reading the mass of statements that had been taken by my detective team the day before and to plough through the many messages that had come into the incident room. On the previous day we had contacted William Shand-Kydd, Lucan's brother-in-law, who was clearly a close friend of the missing man. I was surprised to hear from him early on the Saturday, when he telephoned to say that he had startling news.

Earlier that morning he had been called by another Lucan friend, Ian Maxwell-Scott, who revealed that the Earl had turned up at his Uckfield, Sussex home just a couple of hours after the murder had been committed in London. While at Uckfield Lord Lucan had written two letters to Bill Shand-Kydd, and these had been posted to his London address. Although staying in the country at the time, Bill Shand-Kydd had immediately telephoned his London home, and, upon being told that the letters had arrived, he had straightaway driven back to London.

He had opened both the letters from Lucan and immediately brought them, and the envelopes, to the murder office at Gerald Road police station. I met him there and was handed this vital evidence personally by Mr Shand-Kydd.

In contrast to some of the people with whom I was now dealing, I found Bill Shand-Kydd to be a most helpful and forthright man. He pointed out to me that he had already noticed that there were bloodstains on the envelopes that he had opened. In addition he told me that he had contacted as many of Lucan's friends as he could think of during the previous 24 hours, but that none of them knew any more than he about his brother-in-law's whereabouts.

What was most surprising, and not a little annoying, was that it had taken so very long for news of this vital sighting of the wanted man to be passed on to me at the murder headquarters. It seemed inconceivable, given the immense amount of publicity in newspapers, television and on radio, that the case had received, that anybody could have failed to realize just how important a visit from Lucan would be. How could anybody who had been visited by Lucan after the murder have failed to contact the police?

One of my senior officers at once telephoned the home of Ian and Susan Maxwell-Scott to try to find out

The 1963 engagement picture of
Lord Bingham and his fiancée,
Veronica Duncan
(Universal Pictorial Press)

Above Veronica Lucan with eldest daughter Lady Frances and her only son Lord George Bingham *(Express Newspapers)*

Right Lord Lucan's mother, the Dowager Countess of Lucan, never ceased protesting her son's innocence of all charges. It was to his mother that Lucan first called for help in the first minutes after the murder

Opposite In the happiest days of her marriage, a radiant Lady Lucan poses proudly with her first-born daughter, Frances, in 1965

Above The young Lord Bingham in his army days, preparing for the bobsleigh run at St Moritz

Right Shooting practice for the ex-guardsman Earl of Lucan *(Express Newspapers)*

Above Lord Lucan was regarded as one of the foremost bridge players in Britain and regularly competed for high stakes at the Portland Club in London
(Express Newspapers)

Left Bill Shand Kydd with his wife Christina, the sister of Veronica, the Countess of Lucan. The couple has looked after the Lucan children for years

Above Zoo-keeper and gambling club owner, John Aspinall, moments after being punched on the jaw by an angry relative at the London memorial service to the late Dominic Elwes

Below Lucan's gambling friend, the late Ian Maxwell-Scott, hotly pursued by a press reporter after Lucky Lucan's disappearance

Above Lord Lucan's old Etonian schoolfriend, who stayed his closest companion in life, Charles Benson, the *Daily Express*'s racing tipster 'The Scout' *(Hulton Deutsch)*

Above Greville Howard, to whom Lord Lucan confessed he was planning the murder of his wife

Opposite Mrs Susan Maxwell-Scott to whose home in Uckfield, Sussex, Lord Lucan fled on the night of the murder. 'Loyalty to friends is the highest morality'

Above Playboy
artist Dominic
Elwes and friends
at a London Ballet
premiere of
Sleeping Beauty
(Hulton Deutsch)

Right Multi-
millionaire
financier and now
Euro-politician,
Sir James
Goldsmith, who
guaranteed a
£5,000 overdraft
for his friend,
Lucky Lord Lucan
*(Universal
Pictorial Press)*

Top The basement window of 46 Lower Belgrave Street, through which Lucan claims to have seen a mystery assailant attacking his wife

Above The unfortunate nanny, Mrs Sandra Rivett, battered to death in the basement of the Lucan family home

Above The author, ex-Detective Chief Superintendent Roy Ranson outside the Lucan family house in Lower Belgrave Street

Left The doorway of Mrs Madelaine Florman's house in Chester Square, Belgravia, where drops of blood from the murdered Nanny were found on the doorstep

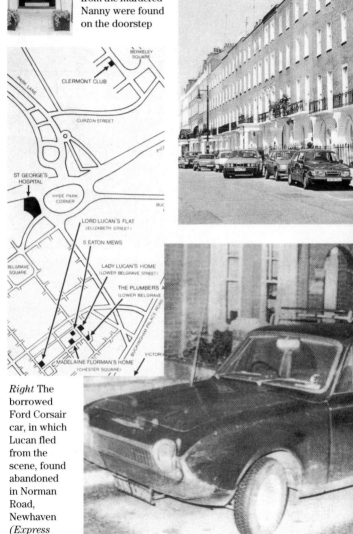

Right The borrowed Ford Corsair car, in which Lucan fled from the scene, found abandoned in Norman Road, Newhaven *(Express Newspapers)*

Above middle Lower Belgrave Street, along which a beaten and bloodstained Lady Lucan fled from her husband to seek refuge in the Plumbers Arms public house

Above The author outside 72A Elizabeth Street, Belgravia, the apartment where Lucan lived at the time of his disappearance.

Left The tiny home at 5 Eaton Mews where Lucan first moved after the break-up of his marriage and where Lady Lucan now lives alone

Above The Lucan family silver collection on show to be auctioned after the Earl's disappearance in 1974. Lucan had pledged the proceeds of this sale many times over to a number of his unsuspecting creditors
(Express Newspapers)

Right The Countess of Lucan, escorted by her detective bodyguard slipping into Court for the inquest on Sandra Rivett, the headscarf-covered scars still present from the attack by her husband

Right The Countess of Lucan at her London home a year after the murder. She still treasures the portrait of her husband from the earlier, happier days of her marriage
(Express Newspapers)

Right The author, Roy Ranson, looking for Lucan on safari in the Tuli Block in Botswana

Below The Polana Hotel in Maputo (formerly Lourenco Marques) in Mozambique. Lucan allegedly found temporary refuge here with British doctor, Brian Hill

Right The Debswana House office and shopping complex in Gaborone, Botswana, where Lucan was allegedly seen alive, well over a decade after his flight from Britain

Left Former
safari guide,
Janice Mullen,
who had a close
encounter with
the missing
Earl in
Gaborone,
Botswana :
'I turned
around ... and
there he was.'

The missing Earl as he is now likely
to look around his sixtieth birthday
in December 1994. The image was
created by computer-blending the
features of the Earl's mother and
father at a similar age

what had happened, while I despatched other members of the murder-squad team hotfoot to Uckfield. They were instructed to find out as much as possible about Lucan's movements and pass the information back to me immediately.

While I waited for the results of these latest inquiries, I turned my attention to the two separate letters, both postmarked from Uckfield and both addressed to Bill Shand-Kydd's London home. The first and more interesting letter was dated 7 November 1974. Complete with lack of punctuation, it read:

7th Nov. 1974

Dear Bill,
The most ghastly circumstances arose tonight which I briefly described to my mother. When I interrupted the fight at Lower Belgrave St. and the man left Veronica accused me of having hired him. I took her upstairs and sent Frances up to bed and tried to clean her up. She lay doggo for a bit and when I was in the bathroom left the house. The circumstantial evidence against me is strong in that V will say it was all my doing. I will also lie doggo for a bit but I am only concerned for the children If you can manage it I want them to live with you – Coutts (Trustees) St Martins Lane (Mr Wall) will handle school fees. V. has demonstrated her hatred for me in the past and would do anything to see me accused For George and Frances to go through life knowing their father had stood in the dock for attempted murder would be too much. When they are old enough to understand, explain to them the dream of paranoia, and look after them.

Yours ever
John

The letter had been handwritten, apparently in a hurry. The writing was sprawling and, in parts, was hard to decipher. In particular some words of the last sentence were little more than a squiggle. It was only after examination by handwriting experts that the phrase 'dream of paranoia' was deciphered. Putting that letter carefully aside, I unfolded the second and much shorter message from the missing Lord Lucan. It was brief and to the point.

FINANCIAL MATTERS

There is a sale coming up at Christies Nov 27th which will satisfy bank overdrafts. Please agree reserves with Tom Craig.
Proceeds to go to:
Lloyds: 6 Pall Mall,
Coutts, 59, Strand,
Nat West, Bloomsbury branch,
who also hold an Eq. and Law Life Policy.
The other creditors can get lost for the time being.
    Lucky

I thanked Bill Shand-Kydd for bringing the letters to me so promptly, and both letters and envelopes were placed in plastic bags for labelling and for the appropriate entries to be made in the various files. Immediately afterwards the exhibits officer took them personally to New Scotland Yard, where I had requested an examination by fingerprint experts and the forensic-science laboratories.

On the night of the killing the officers who had searched Lucan's flat in Elizabeth Street had found his Mercedes motor car parked outside the building. The engine had been cold, and evidence coming in from our questioning revealed that Lucan had been seen driving what was described as an old banger of a motor car. I had ordered urgent inquiries to find the index number of that car, and the team had finally found a witness to provide the missing number.

When this was traced, the owner turned out to be yet another friend of Lord Lucan's, Michael Stoop. He freely admitted having lent his old, blue, D registration Ford Corsair to Lord Lucan a few weeks earlier. Details of the car and its number plate, KYN 135D, were now sent to all British police forces, along with a more detailed description of Lord Lucan, which we had drawn up over the past 24 hours.

The basic facts of the case appeared to be crystal clear. From Lady Lucan's version of events, one would have to believe that Lord Lucan had a great number of tricky questions to answer. And yet he had given his own account in the telephone call to his mother and subsequently had repeated a similar story in his letters to Bill Shand-Kydd. We could not afford to ignore any possibility in order to establish the truth.

The three Lucan children had been collected earlier that day from the Dowager Countess's St John's Wood flat by their aunt, Lady Sarah Gibbs, and taken back with her to Guilsborough Vicarage. For the next few weeks they lived there, in the quiet Northamptonshire village, with their only distraction being the ever waiting posse of newsmen standing outside the vicarage gate.

I learnt later that, unlike many of the characters involved in this case, Lady Sarah had earned the gratitude of the entire press corps through her attitude to the reporters and photographers outside. Although she protected the children fiercely, she was unfailingly polite to those who approached her for comments.

It was Aunt Sarah who had to break the tragic news of what had happened to the children. Frances, then aged 10, was the only one old enough to understand that mummy was badly hurt and that their nanny was dead. Lady Sarah told one of my officers later that the young child had been deeply shocked at the news and had questioned who would look after the Lucan family kittens and the children themselves, now that nanny Sandra had gone.

DAY THREE

On the Sunday morning I found that Lady Lucan's latest and far more complete statement was waiting upon my desk. It had taken one of my officers a painstaking two days to produce, because the Countess had only been able to talk to us when her treatment, and the routine of hospital life, allowed.

The Countess had confirmed all of her earlier version of events and had remembered some more detail. Despite the severity of her injuries, which might well have been fatal, Lady Lucan was proving to be a credible and reliable witness. In all my contacts with her, over many months to come, she never varied from the essential facts of her account of that night – to my mind a clear indication that she had told the plain, unvarnished truth. More and more of the evidence was now pointing directly at Lord Lucan, not least the fact that he had conspicuously failed to contact the police as he had promised his mother in the first-night telephone call.

Another version of events that had now been more fully investigated was that of Susan Maxwell-Scott, who had been interviewed at length by some of my officers at her Uckfield home. She and her husband had been friends for many years with both Lord and Lady Lucan, who had often visited the Maxwell-Scotts' beautiful Uckfield house together with their children and their dog. Mrs Maxwell-Scott always insisted that it was her husband and not her who had been the closest friend of Lord Lucan. The two men shared a passion for gambling. Over the years, however, she has turned out to be one of the missing Lord's staunchest defenders. Years later she was to mount a spirited defence of her concept of loyalty and friendship, after I had been quoted as criticizing his friends in a *Daily Star* article. In a letter to the paper she wrote:

> I fully and truthfully answered all questions. I also gave permission to search the house and the grounds. Later still, I allowed police forensic science experts to examine my chairs for blood stains – they did not find any! I cannot imagine in what way I could have helped Ranson more!
>
> Friends have loyalty to each other – else they are mere acquaintances NOT friends. Loyalty among friends is, in my opinion, the highest morality in life. Without it friendship could not exist – only acquaintanceship.

I understand that Susan Maxwell-Scott trained as a barrister but had never practised. Certainly I found her to be a highly intelligent woman, a fact that made it harder still to understand her failure to report the matter to the police in the aftermath of Lucan's late-night visit to her home. The explanation given was that they did not see newspapers or radio and television news broadcasts about the Lucan case during the day after his nocturnal visit, and were therefore unaware of its consequence.

The latest version of the Maxwell-Scott saga added very little to the facts that we had already established. Susan and her children had been alone in the house on the night of 7 November when, at about 11.30 pm, there was a ring on the doorbell. It turned out to be Lucan, who apologized for disturbing her at such a late hour and asked to see Ian. Susan explained that her husband was spending the night in London but invited Lucan into the house.

In the course of a two-hour visit Lucan told her roughly the same version of events as he had given his mother. He had been passing the house and had seen a stranger attacking his wife in the basement kitchen of number 46. When he ran into the house, he had slipped in a pool of blood, and the man had fled.

After telling his tale Lucan asked if he could telephone his mother to check up on what had happened to the children he had abandoned in the Lower Belgrave Street house. He had also made an unsuccessful attempt to contact his brother-in-law, Bill Shand-Kydd. When he could not get through once again on the telephone, he asked her for writing paper and wrote two letters, both addressed to Bill Shand-Kydd at his London home.

Susan offered to post them for him in the morning, and he eventually agreed, having at first suggested that he did not want to get her involved by having an Uckfield postmark appear on the letters. She then made coffee and also gave Lord Lucan two drinks of whisky. He had left her at about 1.15 in the morning, disappearing down her drive in a dark saloon car.

Dave Gerring and I did not understand why neither Susan, nor Ian Maxwell-Scott, who had returned home the next day, had contacted the murder squad about this late-night visit. Since Friday morning the case had been headline news in the newspapers, on the radio and on the television news bulletins. Why, then, had we not been informed that the man being sought by police throughout Great Britain had sat drinking whisky in the Maxwell-Scott drawing-room?

We were still debating the issue when shortly before 3 pm that afternoon we received a telephone call that appeared to throw yet more light on Lord Lucan's movements and to strengthen the Sussex connection. It was from an excited Detective Sergeant David De Lima, of the Sussex Police Force. He told us that he had found a blue Ford Corsair motor car in Norman Road, just a quarter of a mile from the docks in the coastal town of Newhaven. Sgt. De Lima told us that the registration number of the vehicle was KYN 135D, a slight discrepancy from that listed in the nationwide police bulletin asking officers to search for the Lucan car.

We quickly discovered there had been an error in the transmission of the message, which had incorrectly listed the number as KIN 135D. Over the telephone I thanked the officer for his help and requested that the vehicle be kept under observation until I drove down from the murder-squad office to Newhaven.

The discovery of the car was clearly a much needed major breakthrough in the case. It took but a glance at the map to see that Newhaven was only about 16 miles from the Lord's last-known sighting at Uckfield. It was, in fact, the nearest coastal port to the Maxwell-Scotts' home.

I arrived at Newhaven about two hours later, and a cursory inspection found the Corsair to be locked. By then a full detective team with scientific back-up was on the scene, and the car was photographed before a key was found to open the doors and boot.

The interior of the boot was a jumble of vital evidence. The centrepiece was a length of lead piping, covered in surgical tape, which appeared to me to be similar in almost every respect to the murder weapon I had seen just three nights before lying in the ground-floor hallway where Lady Lucan had been attacked. The only apparent difference was that it was some three or four inches longer. Also lying in the boot was a full bottle of vodka, the spirit that we had by then established was Lord Lucan's favoured drink.

It was hard at that stage closely to examine the interior of the car. The seats appeared to be heavily blood-stained, and I did not wish to take any chance of damaging this vital evidence. After more photographs had been taken of the interior and the contents of the boot, I asked for a low-loader to transfer the entire vehicle to the forensic laboratory for detailed examination.

Even before the results of such scientific studies I knew that the car represented the last physical link in the chain connecting Lord Lucan and the events in Belgravia. With high hopes that the case was finally breaking, I travelled back up to London and called in to check on any final developments before a welcome return home to my bed in the early hours of the morning.

DAY FOUR
My absence from the incident room had resulted in yet a further build-up of new statements, messages and entries in the action book, which it was vital for me to read in order to stay on top of the overall picture. The next morning, while I ploughed through this paperwork, Sussex police made door-to-door inquiries in Norman Road, the quiet residential street of terraced houses where the Corsair had been abandoned.

The car's proximity to the small Newhaven docks clearly required further investigation, and another team of policemen questioned witnesses throughout the port and the car ferry terminal. They were armed with our description of Lord Lucan who I felt would have stuck out like a sore thumb on a cold and wet November day in Newhaven. As far as we knew, he had been wearing simply a light blue rollneck sweater and brown sleeveless pullover over a pair of dark grey trousers. He appeared to have no coat with him at all. Among the inquiries I requested from the Sussex police was for visits to any charity shops in the district that might have sold second-hand clothing.

My conviction that a breakthrough was imminent was further strengthened at about 5 pm on that Monday afternoon, when a telephone call came into the murder-squad office from Michael Stoop informing me that he, too, had received a letter from Lord Lucan. Our missing suspect was turning into a prolific correspondent. In fact, the letter to Stoop proved to be another dead end.

The Stoop letter had been sent, unstamped, to his club, the St James's. However, by the time it was handed to the police, the envelope had been thrown away in one of the club's waste-paper bins, and, despite the most extensive inquiries, it was never to be found. I traced the club porter who had paid the 7p postage due when the letter was received at the club, but neither he nor Stoop had any recollection of the postmark and therefore the town from where the letter had originated.

Once again we were frustrated by an unfortunate event – in this case Stoop's lack of interest in such a vital communication from a dear and trusted friend, which had led him carelessly to discard the only evidence of Lucan's present whereabouts. Still, we had the letter itself. Once again it was terse, but this time shed just a little more light on the motivations that could have driven Lord Lucan to run away from our inquiries. The letter read as follows:

My Dear Michael,
I have had a traumatic night of unbelievable coincidence. However I won't bore you with anything or involve you except to say that when you come across my children, which I hope you will, please tell them that you knew me and that all I cared about was them. The fact that a crooked solicitor and a rotten psychiatrist destroyed me between them will be of no importance to the children. I gave Bill Shand-Kydd an account of what actually happened but judging by my last effort in court no-one, yet alone a 67 year old judge – would believe – and I no longer care except that my children should be protected.
    Yours ever,
    John

By this stage we were asking every witness to give us details of any boats or holiday homes that they owned, any properties to which Lucan could have gained access and be hiding out. Michael Stoop was one of those who had a country cottage, and this was fully checked out by local officers on the off chance that Lucan could have been hiding there without his knowledge. There was, however, yet again no trace.

We were now in possession of three separate letters written by Lucan within 12 hours of the murder. I realized that the letter to Michael Stoop had been written partly in the past tense, which could be taken as an indication that Lucan was contemplating suicide. He had, after all, suffered as he said in one of his letters 'a traumatic night of unbelievable coincidence'. Considering that I by now believed he had tried to murder his wife and succeeded only in killing the wrong woman, I thought the phrase was something of an understatement.

Clearly one option was that either through shock, or guilt, or just plain fear he would have taken his own life rather than face capture and the ignominy of a trial at London's central criminal court, the Old Bailey. If suicide were an option, then it seemed highly possible that he had killed himself somewhere on the Downs or in the sea around Newhaven.

I decided that to discount all possibilities it would be necessary to search as much of the Downs around Newhaven as was possible, along with the coastline stretching as far as the notorious suicide spot off Beachy Head. The local coastguards and fishermen had already told me that any person who drowned in the sea around Newhaven would be liable to be washed ashore near the cliffs of Beachy Head. I originally contemplated searching the entire area within a five-mile radius of Newhaven itself. It was only when I discussed the matter with the local police, and saw just how much land that would involve, that I realized it was an impractical request.

The local experts told me that a search of that magnitude would require up to 1000 men for as long as a month, and there would still be no guarantee that any corpse would be found. I went up on to the Downs with local police officers and was shown patches of impenetrable gorse, some of them stretching for 200 yards or more. I realized that, if Lucan had been determined for his body never to be found, it would have been possible for him to worm his way into the bushes via the numerous animal runs, kill himself and lie there undetected for years.

Still determined on a search I contacted the army who offered me the services of 100 men – but for only three days at the most. I realized then that the search I had wanted to carry out was an impossibility.

Throughout my inquiries in Newhaven I received magnificent co-operation from the men on the ground, but the same could not be said for some of the senior officers of the Sussex force. I had unwittingly crossed over the delicate boundaries of co-operation that exist between different police forces, and on my return to London I was contacted by an irate officer who asked me how I even dared to consider a search on his patch without his permission. Astonished at his pettiness in view of the seriousness of the crime I was investigating, I told him that his permission would have been sought if the operation had ever proved a realistic possibility.

As a postscript to my abortive attempts to search

the Newhaven Downs I was contacted in May 1975 by a Home Office scientist who had been conducting experiments in finding bodies that had been buried or hidden away. He worked for a government research department that had been having some success in this work, which involved burying the carcasses of pigs in a specific area and then having infra-red photographs taken over the various sites. From these photographs the burial sites had successfully shown up.

The scientist offered to search an area of six square miles of the Downs above Newhaven to assist me in my hunt for Lucan. I readily accepted his offer, and we agreed on the area to be examined. A few weeks later he informed me that the necessary photographs had been taken, and there were about 20 sites worthy of further physical exam-ination. We made the appropriate arrangements, and a few days later we met. My teams, together with the scientists, spent a tiring day going to all the relevant sites, which were covered in numerous patches of gorse, measuring from 20 yards to 200 yards in circumference.

To check some of the suspect ground we had to fight our way into the centre of this dense gorse. There we found only household items, such as abandoned re-frigerators, or piles of discarded rubbish consisting of petrol cans, strips of plastic or carrier bags; and even old picnic sites showed up where the ashes of fire remained. In one case a telegraph pole, where seagulls or other birds had perched and left a circle of white droppings, had appeared on the infra-red photographs. By the end of the day we had checked more than 20 suspect sights, none of which had provided the slightest clue to the whereabouts of the missing Earl.

CHAPTER 10

A WARRANT FOR MURDER

I t was in front of the Chief Magistrate at London's Bow Street Magistrates' Court on the morning of Tuesday, 12 November, that I requested and was granted warrants for the arrest of Lord Lucan. The documents permitted his arrest to answer charges of attempting to murder his wife and of murdering his children's nanny, Sandra Rivett. Descriptions of the wanted man had already been circulated via the internal police bulletins of the *Police Gazette* to all forces in Great Britain, and now, armed with a warrant, through Interpol I was able to send his details to all member police forces, covering most of the western world.

This Tuesday morning following the murder had once again begun with the promise of new information. The Sussex police had found two witnesses in Norman Road, where the Corsair car had been abandoned. One of these was certain that the car had not been parked in the road when he looked out of his window at five o'clock on the morning of Friday, 8 November. The other witness, living just a few doors away, had confirmed that the car was parked in the street by eight o'clock that morning.

If these accounts were true, and both seemed to be reliable witnesses, it followed that Lucan had taken many hours to drive the 16 miles from Uckfield to Newhaven. Where had he been in the meantime?

Back at the murder-squad offices one other fact had emerged from the slow but steady tracing and interviewing of Lucan's friends and acquaintances. John Aspinall, at one time the owner of the Clermont Club, had met with five other close friends of the wanted man at a lunch on the day after the killing.

This meeting, later to be dubbed by the press as the 'meeting of the six just men' had taken place at Aspinall's home in Lyall Street, Belgravia. Those present in addition to Aspinall were Daniel Meinertzhagen, Charles Benson, Stephen Raphael, Bill Shand-Kydd and Dominic Elwes. Over the years there has been a great deal of press speculation and ill-informed opinion in books, concerning 'the Just Men' and their influence on the search for Lord Lucan.

In fact it appeared, from the earliest days of the inquiry, that none of the so-called 'Lucan set' really had any information about the murder itself, or the Earl's subsequent whereabouts. Members of the group, such as Dan Meinertzhagen and stockbroker Stephen Raphael, have always insisted that the Just Men meeting was nothing more than a gathering of good friends who were worried about Lucan and were anxious to share any news. Many of the group were concerned that he might well have killed himself, and the whole lunch-time meeting was very far from forming the escape committee that the tabloid press have suggested.

Among those present was the *Daily Express* racing tipster, Charles Benson, who had already contacted us to offer his help in contacting Lucan's friends. In the subsequent weeks, as rumours circulated about the unhelpful attitude of many of the powerful and wealthy men with whom I was now dealing, one MP, Marcus Lipton, took it upon himself to criticize Lucan's friends *en masse* for their attitude. It was Charles Benson who was to take him to task. On 22 November 1974 he wrote a letter to *The Times* refuting the allegations that people were being 'a bit snooty' with the police.

Years later Benson told me that the Just Men lunch had been a spontaneous response to the tragic events. He explained: 'It was a perfectly normal reaction to a horrifying situation, in which none of us knew very much about what had happened.

'We were originally going to have lunch at the Mirabelle restaurant, and then John Aspinall quite rightly and sensibly decided that it would be better, so that we weren't stared at and misunderstood, to have it in his own house.'

Charles Benson insisted that the lunch has been misrepresented by many people over the years – not least by the suggestion that vast quantities of smoked salmon had been consumed along with bottles of expensive wine. 'In fact it was a rather sombre occasion,' he said. 'There was a little hock – but not much – some cold meat and some cheese.

'Some people were of the opinion that he should be helped if he appeared, and Dominic Elwes said we must get him on a banana boat to South America. But he was not taken seriously. Most of the others felt we should just wait and see, and I felt it was pointless wasting time on hypothesis.

'Another misconception is that we asked Dominic Elwes to go and see Lady Lucan in hospital as some sort of group representative. Dominic did go to see her, but it was entirely off his own bat. He went to be sympathetic, and he was pretty shattered by seeing Veronica lying back and battered and not in very good shape.

'When she saw him, she hauled herself up on her elbows, and she said to him: "Who's the mad one now?" and that had a profound effect on him, and he came back very shaken.'

A number of people at the Just Men lunch had, in fact, been courteous, charming and helpful in my inquiries. Bill Shand-Kydd, in particular, had provided the Lucan letters that had been sent to him as soon as they were in his possession, and I had no complaints at all about his attitude.

One man who was most definitely not at the Aspinall lunch was international entrepreneur Sir James Goldsmith, who took great exception to a subsequent and inaccurate report in the satirical magazine *Private Eye*, which suggested that he had been one of the dining companions. The truth of the matter was that Sir James, a good friend of Lucky Lucan for very many years, had been on business in Ireland on the night of 7–8 November and nowhere near the Just Men meeting. When

Sir James came to Gerald Road police station to make a statement about his friendship with the missing Earl, I found him a courteous and helpful witness.

The same, however, sadly, could not be said about others on the fringes of the Lucan set. After extensive experience in questioning criminals and witnesses of all persuasions and from all walks of life, I was still not prepared for the unhelpful attitude that I found in some quarters as I investigated the tragic death of an innocent girl.

Even hardened criminals tend to 'play by the rules' and if you were to ask an East End villain to come down to the police station for questioning, he would generally be there within hours. In the Lucan case there were many times when a similar request was met with obstruction and delay. 'I'm afraid I'm off skiing for three weeks, old chap', I was told on occasions; 'I'll be happy to pop in with my solicitor when I'm back from the trip.'

As the investigation continued the Lucan children had been staying with a succession of family members while their mother slowly recovered in hospital. Partly to get away from the constant attentions of reporters, they had been taken from the Gibbs family vicarage in Northamptonshire to the country home of the Shand-Kydds.

Lady Lucan was now medically fit to be discharged from hospital, but there was still some doubt as to whether the children would immediately return to live with her. The matter was resolved by yet another High Court hearing on the day that Lady Lucan was released from hospital.

Accompanied by police officers, she attended a

specially convened morning hearing in chambers at the London High Court. In a thirty-minute hearing, conducted behind closed doors and followed by a two-hour discussion between lawyers representing various members of the Lucan family, the children were given back into the care of their mother.

However, 7-year-old Lord Bingham, Lady Frances, aged 10, and 4-year-old Lady Camilla were still officially wards of court. Because of the intense press speculation surrounding their future the Official Solicitor, Norman Turner, took the most unusual step of inviting reporters into the court after the matter had been decided to issue a formal statement. The press release, which had been authorized by the judge, simply said that the children would now live with Lady Lucan but added: 'The parties are united in the hope that the children may now be allowed to resume their lives, undisturbed, and they will now be spared any further publicity.'

Lady Lucan wore a black pillbox hat for the court hearing, before Mr Justice Rees who had been responsible for all of the previous decisions about the Lucan family future. In the months to come, leading up to the inquest in the summer of 1975, Lady Lucan was never to be seen without such a hat. She wore it to cover the massive and still livid scars resulting from the ferocious attack that she had been so lucky to survive.

The Official Solicitor's plea for the children to be left in peace fell on deaf ears in the offices of Britain's national newspapers in Fleet Street. To safeguard the Countess and the children from the constant attentions of photographers, it was decided that she should take up the offer of staying with a friend at a farm in the

West Country. Accordingly she set off for Plymouth by train, accompanied by a police escort. The posse of journalists who followed the group thankfully lost sight of their quarry after she alighted from the train in Exeter, and she was taken on by police car to her hideaway home near Plymouth.

It was in the peaceful surroundings of this West Country farm that a sympathetic woman detective, Sally Bower, began talking to the Lucan's eldest child, Lady Frances. She encouraged her to tell what had happened on the night of the killing. The young girl was able to give a coherent account, but I was unable to estimate just how much reliance I could place on the words of a 10-year-old girl who had been through such a shocking experience.

In broad terms the statement, which was later to be read out in full at the Sandra Rivett inquest (see pp. 178–81), supported the Countess of Lucan's version of events in their home that night. It was impossible not to be moved by the young girl's simple words, as she described the last moments when she saw her father disappear down the stairs in the aftermath of the murder.

As Lady Lucan and the children began the formidable task of rebuilding their lives, work was continuing with all possible speed on the main murder inquiry. Awaiting my attention in the incident room were a series of forensic science reports into various aspects of the case. Both the lead piping, which we believed to be the murder weapon, and the similar length of metal recovered from the boot of the Corsair had been examined for fingerprints, but nothing useful was revealed in the experts' report.

Dr Margaret Pereira, as one of the country's foremost experts on the study and classification of blood groupings, had also now had the opportunity to look at the bloodstained piping. She discovered that the lead bludgeon, totally and tightly wrapped in an adhesive tape, bore traces of a mixture of the blood of both Lady Lucan and Sandra Rivett. Hairs found on the tape covering were identified as those of Lady Lucan, but none was found that could be linked to Sandra. Dr Pereira had also examined the lead pipe found in the Corsair boot, which, although similarly wrapped in tape, was totally clear of any blood or hair.

Both sections of piping were studied by Home Office scientific officers who stated that they believed, but could not prove beyond doubt, that they were cut from the same original length of piping. They also said that the two pieces were most unlikely to have been adjacent sections of that pipe. Similarly the adhesive tape wrapped around both weapons was examined and found to be similar, although the experts could not link them conclusively.

In a bid to leave no stone unturned in solving the mystery of the two pipes, I asked for them to be sent to the laboratories of the Atomic Energy Authority at Aldermaston. There they were subjected to the most detailed and modern scientific examination techniques available, but no further useful evidence was uncovered.

Over the years since the death of Sandra Rivett, there have been various attempts to confuse or discredit the important forensic evidence relating to the many bloodstains that were found at the scene. From the outset, however, there has been no doubt in my mind that Dr

Pereira's initial findings were correct and incontrovertible.

From examination of the extensive blood splashes in the house her report clearly showed that Sandra had been attacked in the basement area, while Lady Lucan was attacked at the head of the stairs, which led from the ground floor to the basement. The two women had quite separate blood groups. Sandra Rivett was group B, while Lady Lucan was group A.

Looking further into Dr Pereira's comprehensive report, I found that both of the envelopes that had been sent to Bill Shand-Kydd bore bloodstains that were considered to be a mixture of blood from both women. Some pages of the letters were also stained, but it had not been possible to identify clearly the blood group involved.

The last letter, sent to Michael Stoop, had been written on a piece of blotting paper, which bore no bloodstains at all. However, examination of a Lion brand writing pad, which had been found in the boot of the car, proved that the blotting paper had been torn from this pad.

Further forensic science reports dealt with the examination of the Ford Corsair, which had been taken direct to a laboratory from the road where it was found parked in Newhaven. Once again there was extensive blood-smearing on various parts of the vehicle. I read that blood had been found on the front offside door, on both front seats, on the map box between them, on the steering wheel and the dashboard.

On the floor of the driver's side of the vehicle the experts had recovered some strands of bloodstained hair, similar to that of Lady Lucan. The bloodstains gave a scientific reaction to the AB blood group, which the report concluded could well be a mixture of blood from both of the women victims.

Sitting alone late at night in the murder incident room at Gerald Road, I pondered the conclusions to be drawn from this first week of the murder inquiry. A vast number of Lucan's friends, colleagues and acquaintances had been traced and interviewed at length by detectives from the murder team. There had been hundreds of sightings of the missing Earl, which had all proved inconclusive. The forensic-science reports had painted a clear picture of the likely course of events and had broadly confirmed the account of both the Countess of Lucan and her eldest daughter.

In my own mind the case appeared straightforward. But, as always in every serious crime inquiry, a series of unanswered questions and downright mysteries had already begun to rear their heads. From where had Lucan made his telephone calls, immediately after the murder, to both Madelaine Florman's house in Chester Square and the first call to his mother's home?

It would appear not from a public telephone box, as neither woman remembered hearing the distinctive pips from the coin-boxes of the period. And not, I suspected, from his nearby flat in Elizabeth Street. If he had returned to that home he would surely have left traces of blood behind. Would he not also have changed his clothes, or picked up some of the essential possessions we found in the flat?

How was he managing to stay on the run without all of those day-to-day possessions that we had found in his home? As far as we could ascertain he had emptied the contents of his pockets before leaving for Lower Belgrave Street and had left behind his passport, his driving licence, his cheque-book and ready cash.

Perhaps most puzzling of all was the time-lag between Lucan leaving the home of the Maxwell-Scotts in Uckfield and abandoning his car in Newhaven. He had somehow taken at least 3½ hours to drive the 16 miles from Grants Hill House to Norman Road.

Had he really driven that route himself? Or had he contacted a friend to spirit him away in another direction while the car was left by a seaside port to lead me on a wild-goose chase? If that were the case, then I knew that he might even now be in another part of Britain or the world, as I was left concentrating my inquiries on the Newhaven area and the ferries that run between England and France. It was a worrying thought.

CHAPTER 11

THE INQUEST OPENS

For varying reasons the inquest into the death of Sandra Rivett posed problems for almost everybody involved in the case. The hearing, though necessary by law, was a distraction for me and my police team, still actively involved in investigating this most serious of crimes and in searching for the missing Earl. Some witnesses were anxious about giving evidence that might incriminate him further, or expose weaknesses in their own statements to the police.

For Lady Lucan, and not least for the family of Sandra Rivett, the inquest threatened to be a public ordeal, made worse by the frantic attentions of scores of television, radio and newspaper reporters. It was even a problem for the numerous lawyers, who had been hired to represent various interested parties, and who worried that evidence presented at the inquest could prejudice future criminal trials and compensation claims.

The court official who had to try and reconcile each and every one of these conflicting interests was perhaps the most worried man of all – the Coroner for Inner West London, Dr Gavin Thurston. In the mid-1970s the post of coroner still carried an impressive amount of power and personal discretion as to how an inquest should be conducted. Dr Thurston's task in this case was most definitely not, however, a role to be envied.

As the inquest opened, I still hoped that Lord Lucan would soon be found to help shed light on the tragic occurrences at 46 Lower Belgrave Street. Accordingly, I told Dr Thurston that an adjournment would be desirable in order that further police inquiries could be made. It was, anyway, unusual for any other than the most simple of inquests to be opened and concluded on the very first day, and so Dr Thurston was happy to agree to my request.

The opening of the inquest on Wednesday, 13 November 1974 was notable only for the extraordinary amount of press interest for a hearing that everybody, including the reporters, knew would be concluded within just a few minutes. In the event, we all crowded into the tiny and distinctly old-fashioned courtroom in a red-brick building in Horseferry Road, Westminster, to open the formal inquiry into the tragic death of Sandra Rivett.

Only two witnesses were called on that first day. One was Roger Rivett, who took the stand and gave his occupation as a security guard from Coulsdon in Surrey. In the formal language of the courtroom he confirmed to Dr Thurston that he had earlier attended the mortuary and had there identified the dead body of his wife, Mrs Sandra Eleanor Rivett, née Hensby.

Next came Home Office pathologist Professor Keith Simpson who gave the briefest of details of the cause of death. In open court he said only that he had performed a post-mortem examination, which revealed that death had been due to blows on the head with a blunt instrument. With the reporters still scribbling furiously in their notebooks, Dr Thurston then adjourned the hearing indefinitely. The entire proceedings were over within five minutes.

Two further adjournments followed over the next few months. The first was on 11 December of that same year; the second, three months later, on 10 March. Both of these hearings were no more than formal remands, but by now the Coroner and the police team were agreed that there was little point in delaying the matter further. Accordingly, the full inquest hearing was finally set for 16 June 1975.

Throughout this period I had stayed closely in touch with Dr Thurston, who admitted to me that, despite his vast experience, he was worried about this most unusual of cases. In the months between the opening and the final hearing, Dr Thurston took soundings, not only from official sources and the highest judges in the land but also from many friends and colleagues in both the legal and medical professions. The Coroner was fortunate in having the ideal background for obtaining the best possible advice.

Dr Thurston had spent almost ten years as Westminster's Coroner and was widely respected by all who had dealings before his court. A frequent contributor to both legal and medical journals, his background and experience spanned the two professional disciplines that are of the greatest use to any coroner.

He had qualified as a doctor at Guy's Hospital in London some 40 years earlier and had served with the Royal Army Medical Corps in the Second World War. During that time he became interested in the work of coroners and subsequently started legal studies to add to his medical qualifications. He was eventually called to the bar in 1952. There then followed many years, and thousands of cases, which had prepared Dr Thurston well for the trials and tribulations he was to face from a raft of lawyers and laymen at the Sandra Rivett inquest.

The crucial problem facing the Coroner was that he had been forced by the circumstances to hold a full inquest in advance of any possible trial for the murder of Sandra Rivett; or for the near fatal assault on Lady Lucan. To complicate the matter further, there were strict legal rules about what evidence Lady Lucan would ever be allowed to give in any future trial.

At the time of the Rivett murder, a wife was considered in law to be neither 'compellable nor competent' to give evidence against her husband in the great majority of criminal cases. If she had witnessed him commit a crime, even the most serious of offences such as murder, or robbery, her evidence could never be heard by a jury. She could neither be made to give evidence against her will, nor speak against her husband even if she wanted so to do. The sole exception to this rule arose in the case of an assault or some fraud offences committed against herself; in which circumstances her evidence could be admitted to a criminal trial.

The rules had clear implications for any future trial of Lord Lucan. His wife Veronica could tell a jury of how her husband had attacked her; but was forbidden to reveal anything about the death of Sandra Rivett. In particular, she would be unable to discuss her husband's virtual confession, which she had heard just minutes after the killing.

Clear legal precedents had also been set, which meant that Lady Lucan's evidence about the attempted murder of herself would have to be heard before a totally different jury, in a totally separate trial, in order to avoid fatally prejudicing the murder trial.

Just a few years earlier, the Appeal Court had freed a man named William Deacon from a life sentence for murder. Deacon had been convicted of murdering his own brother-in-law who was shot dead in a family row. Deacon's wife had also been shot in the incident and had given evidence in the trial only about the assault on herself. Quashing the conviction, the Appeal Court ruled that the two charges should have been heard before different juries in separate trials.

Dr Thurston knew that these strict legal rules did not apply to the evidence that he could call before his own selected jury in the Coroner's Court. In the inquest it was quite possible for Lady Lucan legally to speak out against her husband, not only about the injuries that she sustained on the night of 7 November 1974 but also in relation to the murder of her children's nanny.

Such evidence would help the jury come to an honest conclusion but, if Dr Thurston allowed Lady Lucan to speak freely, she would give details that should not be revealed to any future murder trial jury.

To add to the legal minefield in which Dr Thurston now found himself, there were the further complications of 'hearsay' evidence; the facts learnt not firsthand but from another person's account of events. Such hearsay is strictly banned in criminal trials and yet could freely be bandied about in a coroner's court.

With the benefit of hindsight, others have criticized Dr Thurston's handling of the inquiry. Some accused him of being too repressive of the evidence; others of allowing too much to be heard. On balance, I believe he got it as right as these most bizarre of circumstances would allow.

I had supplied the Coroner's office with copies of all of the hundreds of statements, lists of exhibits, photographs and plans that had been gathered by my team of detectives and uniformed officers in the course of the inquiry. Just reading his way through the mass of documentary evidence was a major task for Dr Thurston, but eventually he gave me a list of 33 witnesses whom he felt could contribute to a full and fair hearing.

The Coroner well knew that his conduct of the hearing would be scrutinized by the participants and by legal experts throughout the country. Even he, however, could not have predicted the final verdict and the subsequent changes to the law that were to flow from this case.

I remember the atmosphere of the opening day as extremely expectant and tense. Interest in the case had been fuelled by a vast number of news and feature items about the murder in almost every one of that day's national newspapers. In the continuing absence of the main suspect, each of the newspapers had concluded that the inquest would be an acceptable substitute for the trial of Lord Lucan.

The court benches were packed to overflowing with police officers, witnesses, lawyers and reporters as the jury were sworn in. Comprising six men and three women picked from the Westminster voters' register, the jury was subsequently to elect a 62-year-old local resident, William Thomas, as their foreman.

For the most part, inquests tend to be rather informal hearings, conducted in the saddest of circumstances and designed to uncover the truth of a person's passing, rather than to try and apportion blame. Any illusions that the Sandra Rivett inquest would follow this comfortable and sympathetic pattern were soon shattered as a succession of lawyers rose to introduce themselves to the Coroner and the jury.

Lady Lucan was represented by Mr Bruce Coles; the family of Sandra Rivett by Mr David Webster; the Commissioner of the Metropolitan Police by Mr Brian Watling. The Dowager Countess of Lucan had also engaged a lawyer, Mr Michael Eastham, who, it soon became clear, was there to represent not only the Lucan family but also Lord Lucan himself.

Dr Gavin Thurston ensured that the jury had no links with the Lucan family and then addressed the hushed and expectant court.

'I will explain why you are here,' he told the jury. 'The circumstances are very unusual – the death of Sandra Rivett, who was the nanny to the family of Lord and Lady Lucan.

'I have already taken evidence of identification and

cause of death and matters appertaining to the death, which took place on 7 November. She was aged 29 years, a married woman living apart from her husband. The cause of her death, given by Professor Keith Simpson, was blunt injuries to the head.

'There is a warrant for the arrest of Lord Lucan for the murder of Sandra Rivett and the attempted murder of his wife. The coroner's situation, when there is a death, is that he inquires into the cause of death which appears to be violent or unnatural.

'Firstly, if a person is found killed, and somebody is charged, the coroner comes out of the picture entirely. If there is a murder, followed by a suicide, or a person is battered to death, if, after some months nobody is traced, the jury is directed in a way in which they reach a verdict, of murder by person or persons unknown.

'The Coroner's Court has the power to commit a person for trial to the Crown Court. Proceedings are started by indictment at the Crown Court. We are here, in a position where you have the person who has been killed and to hear evidence of who is responsible, and what should be done about the situation. Lord Lucan has disappeared. Your function is to decide who the deceased person was, how, when and where she died, and then the persons, if any, to be charged with murder or manslaughter.

'There are difficulties, and the one which caused me considerable anxiety and thought is the difficulty of the wife giving evidence adverse to her husband. With certain exceptions, a wife cannot be called to give evidence adverse to her husband, but the exceptions are frauds claiming sickness benefits and the one exception is where a man has assaulted his wife, and this is the exception.

'This arises in calling Lady Lucan as a witness and the assault on herself and the death of Mrs Rivett. This is the difficulty we have to untangle. We are going to hear 33 witnesses, and I think this hearing will last about three days. This case has received an enormous amount of publicity – it is my duty to say, as you already know, you must only come to your conclusions on evidence you have heard in this court.'

Then followed a succession of witnesses giving the formal evidence necessary to confirm the identity of the dead woman and to introduce scientific and photographic evidence into the case. For the packed press benches this opening section of the proceedings was something of an anticlimax. But their interest soon revived when the Countess of Lucan rose and walked towards the witness box.

CHAPTER 12

'WHEN DID YOU LAST SEE YOUR HUSBAND?'

There was a hubbub of excitement as Lady Lucan was sworn in to give her evidence to Dr Thurston. She took the oath and confirmed that her full name was Veronica Mary Bingham, of 46 Lower Belgrave Street, London, SW1. Dr Thurston, clearly anxious to keep a tight rein on proceedings, told Lady Lucan that he intended to ask her three separate sets of questions. Firstly about her marriage and family; secondly about Sandra Rivett; and thirdly the events as far as she could remember them on the night of 7 November 1974.

In response to the first set of questions, Lady Lucan stated that she had married Richard John Bingham in 1963, when he was heir to the earldom. Soon afterwards he succeeded to the earldom and became the seventh Earl of Lucan. She said that they had three children, but that the marriage had deteriorated greatly in recent years.

Throughout her evidence, Lady Lucan was guided towards her answers by the Coroner who framed almost every question in such a way as to encourage a simple, 'Yes' or 'No' response from the witness. In this manner she confirmed that her husband was a professional gambler and had always stayed out a great deal in the evening. He had left her early in January 1973, when he had gone to live at his nearby mews house at 5 Eaton Row.

Lady Lucan told Dr Thurston that they had not lived together since that date and that the children had stayed with her until 23 March, when they went to live with her husband at 72a Elizabeth Street – just a few hundred yards from her home. After a High Court action, however, the Countess regained custody of the children, and they had gone back to live with her on 1 July.

She confirmed that her husband had been highly affectionate towards the children and that they filled a very great part of his life. 'They were very important to him,' she said.

The Earl had been allowed access to the three children every other weekend and had usually collected them at around 5.30 pm on alternate Fridays. In the early days of this arrangement Lady Lucan had seen her husband at these times, but in latter days the hand-over had been carried out through the nanny. He invariably returned the children to her early on Sunday evenings.

The inquest proceeded with questions from the Coroner and answers from Lady Lucan about her recent life with Lord Lucan. A Coroner's Court does not usually keep an exact note of its proceedings, but in the case of the Sandra Rivett inquest a verbatim report was made

by a skilled shorthand writer. I have quoted the exact
words spoken by everyone, even though they may on
occasions appear garbled and ungrammatical.

Q. When did you last see your husband?
A. To speak to or with my eyes? To speak to, it must have
    been about 18 July, on my son's sports day.
Q. When did you last see him without speaking to him?
A. On 24 October.
Q. Was this casually, in the street?
A. No, I looked out of the window and saw him.
Q. What was he doing then?
A. Sitting in his car. I noticed he was wearing dark glasses.
Q. Was this outside 46 Lower Belgrave Street?
A. Yes.
Q. Was he looking in any particular direction?
A. He was about to drive away.
Q. What sort of car was this?
A. A dark blue Mercedes-Benz.
Q. A car that you knew well?
A. Yes.

Dr Thurston continued his questions in this vein,
eliciting the information that Lord Lucan did possess a
key to number 46 and that, apart from one telephone
call about collecting the children, the Earl had not spoken
to his wife for several months before 7 November 1974.
Then the Coroner moved on to tackle the estranged
couple's financial arrangements.

Q. Were you receiving a regular allowance from your
    husband?
A. Yes, I was.
Q. Did he pay the rates and the telephone bill and water
    rates?
A. That was the arrangement, that he would do that.

Q. Was that fullfilled, do you know?
A. I imagine so because the water gets cut off otherwise, doesn't it?
Q. Could I ask how much you were allowed by your husband?
A. £40 per month.
Q. And that payment was always perfectly prompt?
A. It was erratic.
Q. Did you get the total in the end?
A. In the end.
Q. Do you know anything about your husband's financial situation?
A. I have read a bit about it.
Q. Did you know from personal knowledge whether he was in financial difficulties?
A. I did read an article which suggested it, in the *Daily Express*.
Q. But you didn't know from your personal knowledge?
A. No.

Lady Lucan, speaking in a clear but quiet voice, told Dr Thurston that her husband had owned power boats in the past but, as far as she knew, had never had any connections with the port of Newhaven. She said that one of her husband's boats had sunk, and another had been smashed when it was dropped on to a quayside. She believed that he had always raced his boats out of Hamble, near Southampton.

The Countess, who on each day of the inquest wore a hat or a headscarf to hide the still disfiguring scars on her head, confirmed that Lord Lucan had generally enjoyed good health with no serious illness. She then went on to answer the Coroner's questions about Sandra Rivett.

Q. Did your husband know Sandra Rivett?

A. He met her when he collected the children and brought them back.

Q. And that was all as far as you were aware?

A. Yes, as far as I am aware.

Q. If we could ask you about Sandra Rivett. You have had various nannies. How many nannies have you had in the last six months, until 7 November?

A. I had several, including temporaries.

Q. When did Sandra Rivett come to you?

A. I think she came early in September.

Q. From an advertisement, or recommendation?

A. One particular woman provided all the nannies I had.

Q. An agent?

A. Yes, a friend.

Q. Did you get on well with her?

A. With Sandra? Yes, I did.

Q. What sort of temperament?

A. Even temperament.

Q. Cheerful?

A. Yes.

Q. Do you know whether she had many boyfriends?

A. I know of two, she talked to two.

Q. And, of course, you knew she was separated from her husband?

A. Yes, I did.

Q. Had any men friends come to your house?

A. No.

Q. Had she asked if a man could come?

A. No.

Q. What was her usual night off?

A. Thursday night – Thursday was her day off.

Q. Could you say anything about her stature, would she be of similar height to yourself?

A. Her husband described her as 5 foot, 2 inches, and I am 5 foot 2 inches.

Q. Had she tried on any of your clothes, a coat or anything of that kind?

A. She had tried on a dress. It had been given me by another woman, but it was much too large, and I asked Sandra if she would like to try it on, and she kept it.

Q. Although the same height she was rather fuller built than you?

A. Yes.

Q. On the evening of 7 November 1974, this was a Thursday?

A. Yes, it was.

Q. Sandra's usual day off. Was she at home that evening?

A. She was.

Q. Why was that?

A. Because her current boyfriend had his day off on Wednesday, and she asked if she could change hers on Wednesday as well, so she could go out with him. [Lady Lucan's version of why Sandra changed her night off conflicts with that given by the nanny herself to her mother immediately before the murder. Sandra had told her mother that she was ill with suspected glandular fever and felt too unwell to go out. Although I have no way of knowing which account was genuine, I did discover that Sandra had visited her doctor just a few days before, who had confirmed the diagnosis of glandular fever.]

Q. And there would have been at home, yourself, the three children and Mrs Rivett?

A. Yes.

The jury, and indeed the entire courtroom audience, listened intently to Lady Lucan's answers as she went on to describe how her house was secured each evening. She said that at about 6 pm they usually put a chain on the front door. On this evening, however, they had forgotten to do so. There was a second door leading from the basement kitchen to outside the front of the house. This was used every day to take out the rubbish but was then always kept bolted.

The Countess then confirmed what my police inquiries had already shown, that escaping via the rear door into the garden would have been unlikely, if not impossible. She explained that there was a trellis on the wall with roses. 'It would have been a prickly business,' she said.

Having set the scene in the house, Dr Thurston asked about the specific events on the night that Sandra died. He continued:

Q. How did you spend the evening of 7 November from about eight o'clock?
A. Watching television.
Q. Where?
A. In my bedroom.
Q. Who was watching television at eight o'clock?
A. My daughter Frances.
Q. And Mrs Rivett?
A. She was not watching it with us.
Q. Just you and your daughter?
A. Yes.
Q. And what time did Mrs Rivett look into the room? Could you tell, approximately, the time?
A. At about five to nine.
Q. What did she say?
A. Would you like a cup of tea.
Q. This was quite a usual thing, was it?
A. I had the habit of getting myself a cup of tea at that time, but it wasn't a very usual thing for her to put her head round the door.
Q. When she offered to get some tea, did you accept?
A. Yes, indeed.
Q. Your bedroom is on the second floor in the front?
A. Yes, it is.
Q. Where were you when she said she would get you some tea?
A. I was lying on the bed.
Q. And your daughter also?
A. Also.

Q. You can place the time from the television programme at about five to nine?

A. Yes.

Q. Did Mrs Rivett take some crockery with her?

A. I don't know what she did.

Q. We have the crockery [Lady Lucan was shown the exhibits]. Do you recognize these cups?

A. Yes, I do.

Q. These were taken by Mrs Rivett?

A. I am told that.

Q. But had they been in your room?

A. They were taken from my room. She may have had them in her own room.

Q. And then you were watching the news at nine, was that it?

A. Yes.

Q. And when did you begin to wonder about the tea?

A. At about quarter past nine.

Q. Did you hear anything unusual during this time?

A. Nothing unusual.

Q. So what did you do then?

A. I decided to go downstairs and find what had happened to the tea.

Q. And how far did you descend the house?

A. To the ground floor.

Q. What did you do when you got there?

A. I looked down the stairs leading to the basement.

Q. Was there anything unusual?

A. There was no light on at all.

Q. Nowhere in the basement?

A. Nowhere.

Q. There is a two-way switch that you can switch the light on, from the top of the stairs, and the other way round?

A. I believe you can, it may be possible.

Q. Was the light usually left on?

A. No, you can stop at the door of the basement stairs.

Q. Did you try this switch?

A. No I didn't. I just saw it was dark, and so she couldn't be there.

Q. The light is switched on from the top of the basement stairs?

A. Yes.

Q. Did you call out?

A. I called her name.

Q. What happened then?

A. I heard a noise.

Q. What sort of noise?

A. Just a noise of somebody, or something, in the downstairs cloakroom.

Q. This is where there is a wash-basin and toilet?

A. Yes.

Q. What happened next?

A. I walked towards the sound, at any rate moved towards it.

Q. What happened then?

A. Somebody rushed out and hit me on the head.

Q. Did this happen in the area at the top of the stairs, approximately?

A. Approximately, yes.

Q. Was there more than one blow?

A. About four.

Q. Did you hear anybody speak at that time?

A. Not at the time I was being hit on the head, later.

Q. Then what?

A. The person said, 'Shut up.'

Q. Did you recognize the voice, who was it?

A. My husband.

Q. What did he do then, what happened to you?

A. He thrust three gloved fingers down my throat, and we started to fight.

Q. What happened during the fight?

A. It's difficult to remember, it was seven months ago, but during the course of it he attempted to strangle me.

Q. From behind or in front?

A. From in front, gouge out my eyes.

Q. And all this was at the top of the stairs, was it?

A. Yes.

Q. And you were on the ground by this time?

A. Yes.

Q. Do you remember sitting up somehow between his legs with your back to him or sideways?

A. I would say sideways.

Q. Then he desisted a little after that, did he?

A. He desisted, yes.

Q. There is a photograph of a top metal support on the balustrade of the stairs that has been disturbed. Can you explain that?

A. I would have dislodged it with my leg in the struggle.

There had been barely a sound in the courtroom during the entire period of Lady Lucan's gripping account of her life-or-death struggle. She stood impassively in the witness box, giving her terse answers to Dr Thurston's questions. Between each question there was a pause as the Coroner recorded Lady Lucan's answers in longhand, before moving on to the next question. Then he asked about the aftermath of the fight:

Q. Did you manage to persuade your husband to help you – first in the downstairs cloakroom?

A. I asked him if I could have a drink of water.

Q. And what did you do? Where did you go?

A. We went into the downstairs cloakroom, and I had a drink.

Q. I believe there was only hot water available. Is that right?

A. Yes.

Q. Was it dark in the downstairs cloakroom, or had the light been switched on?

A. It was dark.

Q. Following this you both went upstairs. Is that right?

A. Yes.

Q. Where did you go?

A. We went upstairs to my bedroom.

Q. Who was in there?

A. My daughter was in there.

Q. That's Frances, isn't it?
A. Yes.
Q. And the television was still on?
A. It was still on.
Q. What did you do when you got there?
A. I said something.
Q. You said you felt ill, is that right?
A. Yes.
Q. Did you lie on the bed?
A. I did.
Q. What did your husband say when you lay on the bed?
A. He didn't say anything. We went together into the bed-
   room, before I lay on the bed, and together we looked at
   my injuries.
Q. After you had done that?
A. After we had done that, I think I said I didn't feel very
   well, and he laid a towel on the bed, and I got on it.
   [This account directly contradicts what Lady Lucan told
   me immediately after the murder – that her husband
   instructed her to put a towel on the bed.]
Q. Would this towel have been laid on the pillow?
A. Yes.
Q. And your daughter, by this time?
A. She was sent upstairs as soon as we came into the bedroom.
   The television was switched off, and she was sent upstairs.
Q. And you were now lying on the bed – and did your
   husband say anything about helping you further?
A. Very vaguely I understood that he was going to get a cloth
   to clean up my face.
Q. For this he would have gone into the bathroom?
A. Yes.
Q. What did you do, while he was in the bathroom?
A. I heard the taps running, and I jumped to my feet and
   ran out of the room and down the stairs.
Q. Where did you go then?
A. I ran to the Plumbers Arms.
Q. That's only a matter of 30 yards from your house?
A. Yes.

Q. From there, assistance was sought – and then did you go to St George's Hospital?

A. Yes.

Q. How long were you in there?

A. Just under a week.

Q. Have you seen your husband since the time he went into the bathroom off the bedroom?

A. No, I haven't seen him.

Q. You have no doubt it was he?

A. No doubt at all.

Q. (Could Lady Lucan be shown the letters?) It is not the content, but the handwriting, Lady Lucan. Can you recognize it?

A. Yes, I would say it was his handwriting.

Q. Your husband's?

A. Yes.

Q. [Also the sack] Had you ever seen this before the evening of the 7th?

A. I do not recognize it from before.

Q. What was he wearing?

A. He was wearing a sweater of sorts, no tie and grey flannel trousers. That's the best I can do.

Q. And you have mentioned gloves. Did he take them off?

A. No, he took those off earlier.

Q. When you had gone to your bed?

A. He took them off before.

CORONER TO JURY: Is that clear, so far, ladies and gentlemen?

Q. There is just one small thing. I think that in the kitchen there is an electric kettle. Is there some defect by which, when it is switched on, the red light shows?

A. It does the opposite to what it should.

Q. The red light, then, is showing all the time?

A. Yes.

The Coroner knew that the seemingly irrelevant

question of the defective light could be important later in the hearing, when the entire issue of lights in the basement would be raised. For now, however, with this gentle question about her kitchen equipment, he brought his own questioning of the Countess to a close.

As Dr Thurston leant back in his imposing leather seat, there was sudden movement in the previously deathly still courtroom. Reporters working for the news agencies and the two London evening papers scurried for the telephones outside. The audience inside collectively let out its breath. I, along with the rest of the room, had been caught up in the drama of Lady Lucan's unfolding story. But more drama was to follow, as the Coroner invited the massed ranks of lawyers to question the Countess.

Mr Michael Eastham QC was the barrister retained by Lord Lucan's mother, the Dowager Countess of Lucan. He sailed straight to the defence of her son.

Eastham.   Lady Lucan, the separation was 7 January?
A.   7 January 1973.
Eastham.   And the position was that, even before the separation, you entertained feelings of hatred against your husband?

There was a sharp intake of breath among the fascinated spectators at this first hostile thrust of the hearing. Before the still calm Lady Lucan could respond, her own lawyer, Mr Bruce Coles, had jumped to his feet to object. In the ensuing legal tussle, some of it conducted in the absence of the jury, Mr Eastham strongly argued that understanding Lady Lucan's attitude to her husband was vital to the case. He explained:

'I don't enjoy my task, but you know in the two written accounts, especially the one written to Mr Shand-Kydd, the person really is saying in the terms that he was not the attacker, and Lady Lucan was making it look as though he was the attacker. The relationship must, therefore, be relevant as to whether this is an honest recollection, or purely fabrication.

'My instructions are as follows: By the beginning of 1973, this lady, quite definitely, hated her husband. I can prove that. Thereafter, there were long litigations, heard in camera, which exacerbated the situation. The Earl only wanted to look after the children, and you will know that a large number of doctors expressed conflict.

'What I would like to have in evidence, was [that] there was a suggestion made of paranoia, and I would like to have in evidence that the situation deteriorated, as a result of the long and protracted proceedings. It could be made to sound a great deal worse than that.'

The Coroner was quick to rule on the Dowager's lawyer's attempts to have the couple's past battles aired again in his court. He warned Mr Eastham that his observations would be entirely one-sided and continued:

'This is an inquiry and not a trial, although some aspects tend to get that way. I don't think evidence about a witness's mental state should be brought into it. I don't think this should come into it. There will be other evidence, quite a lot of scientific evidence, that might help the jury.'

Mr Eastham was still reluctant to give up his chance of introducing evidence favourable to Lord Lucan and detrimental to his wife. 'No scientific evidence will show she had feelings of hatred for her husband, or what her mental condition was in 1974,' he politely retorted.

Despite his protestations, Mr Eastham graciously accepted the Coroner's final ruling that questions of Lady Lucan's mental health or her attitude towards her husband could not be entered before the jury.

'In view of the ruling,' he said, 'I don't think I can assist the jury at all, and I shall ask the lady no further questions at all.'

In Lady Lucan's main evidence she had described how she had ended up between her husband's legs, and that he had then desisted from his attack. The reason for his giving up the struggle only became clear during cross-examination of the Countess from solicitor Michael Watling, who asked:

Q. Is it right that you grabbed hold of him during the course of the struggle?
A. Yes.
Q. By his private parts?
A. Yes.
Q. What effect, if any, did that seem to have on him?
A. He went back – he moved back.

After this exchange there was a sense of anticlimax as Dr Thurston returned to more mundane matters with his aristocratic witness. He tried to ascertain if any other person had been present.

Q. Lady Lucan, we are speaking of this struggle. You called Mrs Rivett's name, did you see anybody else at the time apart from your husband? Did anybody brush past you? Did you hear sounds?
A. I saw nobody else.
Q. Nor at any time during that evening?

A. Nor at any time during the evening.
Q. I am going to ask my officer to reiterate your evidence. Is there anything you wish to alter?
A. No, there is nothing.

CHAPTER 13

AN ORDEAL OF
CONCENTRATION

Lady Lucan's evidence had held the court enthralled.
The next witness, reading the words of the Countess's young daughter, was to have a similar effect.
Woman Detective Constable Sally Bower, the officer
whom I had sent to accompany Lady Lucan and her family
on their stay in the West Country, had taken a statement
from Lady Frances Bingham, the couple's elder daughter,
on 20 November 1974, 13 days after the murder.

WDC Bower said that she believed Lady Frances was
telling her the truth and had not been upset at the time she
made her statement. The Coroner overruled an objection
from lawyers representing the Lucan family, and the woman
police constable then read out the young child's words:

I live at 46 Lower Belgrave Street, London SW1, with
Mummy, my brother George and my sister Camilla, and

178

whoever is looking after us. Mummy and Daddy don't live together, but I usually see Daddy every other weekend. We stay the weekend with him at the Gibbs house in Northampton or with the Shand-Kydds, or with a friend of Daddy's, Lord Suffolk who lives in Wiltshire, at a place called Charlton Park.

George, Camilla and I spent the weekend of 2–3 November 1974 with Daddy at the Gibbs house in Northampton. Daddy took us home to Lower Belgrave Street at 5.30 pm on Sunday, 3 November 1974. The last time I saw Daddy was on Thursday, 7 November 1974. On that day I didn't go to school because the bus didn't come for me, so Mummy said I need not go. Camilla and George went to school as usual. I spent the day at home with Mummy and Sandra, our nanny. As far as I know nothing unusual happened that day, and nobody came to visit us at home.

On Thursday evening we, that is Mummy, George, Camilla and Sandra and I, all had our tea together. I think that was sometime around 5 pm or 5.30 pm. After tea I played with one of my games in the nursery. Then about 7.20 pm I watched *Top of the Pops* on the television in the nursery. Mummy, Camilla, George and Sandra were downstairs in Mummy's room. They were watching the *Six Million Dollar Man*. I went downstairs and joined them about 8.05 pm, and we all watched the television in Mummy's room.

When the programme finished at 8.30 pm, I went back upstairs to the nursery and played a little more with my game. Sandra brought George and Camilla upstairs and put them to bed. I had had a bath before I started watching television, and I was wearing my pyjamas after my bath.

I stayed in the nursery for about five minutes only, then I went downstairs again to Mummy's room. That would have been about 8.40 pm. I asked Mummy where Sandra was, and she said she was downstairs making some tea. I didn't see her go downstairs so I don't know if she took any empty cups with her. I didn't notice whether or not there were any empty cups in the room.

After a while Mummy said she wondered why Sandra was so long. I don't know what time this was, but it was before the news on the television at 9 pm. I said I would go downstairs to see what was keeping Sandra, but Mummy said, No, she would go. I said I would go with her, but she said, No, it was OK, she would go. Mummy left the room to go downstairs, and I stayed watching television. She left the bedroom door open, but there was no light in the hall because the light bulb is worn out, and it doesn't work.

Just after Mummy left the room, I heard a scream. It sounded as though it came from a long way away. I thought maybe the cat had scratched Mummy, and she had screamed. I wasn't frightened by the scream, and I just stayed in the room watching television. I went to the door of the room and called Mummy, but there was no answer so I just left it.

At about 9.05 pm, when the news was on television, Daddy and Mummy both walked into the room. Mummy had blood on her face and was crying. Mummy told me to go upstairs. Daddy didn't say anything to me, and I didn't say anything to either of them. I don't know how much blood was on Mummy's face, I only caught a glimpse of her.

As far as I can remember Daddy was wearing dark trousers and an overcoat, which was full length and was fawn coloured with brown check. I was sitting on the bed as they came in the door, and I couldn't see them very well. There were two lights on above Mummy's bed and one other side light on. I didn't hear any conversation between Mummy and Daddy. I couldn't see if Daddy's clothes had any blood on them. I wondered what had happened, but I didn't ask.

After Mummy told me to go upstairs I got straight up and went upstairs to my bedroom, which is on the top floor of the house. I got into bed and read my book.

I didn't hear anything from downstairs. After a little while, I don't know how long, because I don't have a clock in my room, I heard Daddy calling for Mummy. He was calling, 'Veronica, where are you?'

I got up and went to the banisters and looked down and saw Daddy coming out of the nursery on the floor below me. He then went into the bathroom on the same floor as the nursery. He came straight out, and then he went downstairs. That was the last I saw of him. He never came up to the top floor of the house that night, either to look for Mummy or to say goodnight to me. I didn't notice at any time whether or not Daddy was wearing gloves.

The last time I saw Sandra was when she took George and Camilla upstairs to bed. I was very surprised to see Daddy at home that Thursday night, but I never asked why he was there. During the last weekend we spent with Daddy on 2 and 3 November 1974, Camilla told Daddy that Sandra had boyfriends and went out with them. Daddy asked when Sandra went out with her boyfriends, and Camilla said Sandra went out with her boyfriends on her days off. Then Daddy asked me when Sandra had her days off. I said her day off was Thursday.

After the moving evidence from Lord Lucan's little girl, there was a total contrast in the court proceedings as the next witness, Arthur William Whitehouse, took the stand. Mr Whitehouse had been the head barman at the Plumbers Arms on the night of the murder. There had been eight people in the bar that evening when, at 9.50 pm, the door burst open and in ran Lady Lucan. Once again the witness was questioned by Dr Thurston:

Q. Did you know who she was then?
A. No. All I did was to give her assistance. I caught her before she fell on the floor. I laid her on a bench.

Q. What was her condition?
A. Head to toe in blood.
Q. Was she very hysterical, upset?
A. She was quite all right for a few minutes and then a state of shock took over. I covered her over, she then started shouting, 'Help me, help me, I've just escaped from being murdered,' and shouting, 'My children, my children, he's murdered my nanny.' But no name was mentioned.
Q. Did you telephone for the police?
A. Yes, it was my immediate reaction. Once I'd got Lady Lucan on the seat the immediate thing I did was to telephone for the police and ambulance.
Q. Were they there quickly?
A. No, they were quite delayed. They took about ten minutes, the ambulance came after about twenty minutes.

The next witness was Dr Michael John Smith, medical practitioner and divisional surgeon for the Metropolitan Police. He confirmed he had been called to the house at 10.45 pm and had been shown downstairs to the basement.

'On the floor I saw a large canvas bag, which appeared to contain a human body,' he said. 'I also noticed bloodstains on the floor. I didn't disturb the bag in any way. I was satisfied that the body was dead, and that death was not due to natural causes.' Dr Smith added that he thought that the death had occurred very recently, 'within an hour or so'.

The first two policemen on the scene on the night of the murder told how they had been called to the Plumbers Arms and had subsequently gone to 46 Lower Belgrave Street. Sergeant Donald Baker, attached to Gerald Road police station, described what he had found at the house:

Q. What was the position of the blind?
A. It was half-closed.
Q. Halfway down the window?
A. Fully down the window and the slats were at an angle of 45°.

The sergeant said that the only light inside the basement window had been a small red glow, and that the two officers had then kicked open the front door. The door had burst open very easily because, although four locks were fitted, only one of these had been engaged. Inside the officers had searched the premises, finding the children upstairs and the lifeless body of Sandra Rivett in the basement. Then Sergeant Baker had searched the backyard.

Q. Could you see anyone outside?
A. There was nobody outside, and we looked around the walls, and I was quite satisfied nobody had climbed over the walls.
Q. Why?
A. It was very high with a trellis round the top and creepers all the way round. There were no footprints, and no creepers had broken away.

Detective Sergeant Graham Forsyth described to the hushed court how he first examined the body of Sandra Rivett.

'I noticed a large canvas sack lying against the wall next to the kitchen door,' he said. There was a woman's arm hanging from the sack, and the rest of the body was enclosed by the sacking. Her flesh was warm to the touch, but I couldn't feel any pulse. There was a large pool of blood in front of the sack. The sack itself was bloodstained and in places seeping through. The blood appeared to me to be very fresh. There was also what appeared to be a footmark in the blood, which led to a room containing a central-heating boiler.'

Sgt. Forsyth said he had later met the Dowager Countess of Lucan and told her that her daughter-in-law had been attacked and was in hospital, and that the nanny had been killed. Lucan's mother explained that the couple were separated and added: 'The children are made wards of court, and Veronica was to continue with medical treatment for a mental condition.'

When the officer asked for further details, the Dowager replied: 'A manic depressive, not violent, except verbally. In the original court case it was thought she was a danger to the children. I knew something was wrong because John telephoned me a short while ago and told me to come here.'

Having managed simultaneously to slur Lady Lucan's name and totally distort the reality of the custody case, the Dowager proceeded to offer her son what protection she could. Sgt. Forsyth outlined the further conversation between himself and Lucan's mother.

Q. What time was this?
A. About 10.45.
Q. What did he say?
A. There has been a terrible catastrophe at 46. Ring Bill Shand-Kydd immediately. He said he was driving past the house, and he saw a fight going on in the basement between a man and Veronica. He went in and joined them. He said Veronica was shouting and screaming. He was very shocked. I said to him where are you going, and he said I don't know. He then just rang off.
Q. Did he say what was wrong?

A. No. I tried to find out but he just told me to get the children out as soon as possible.

At the rear of the small Westminster courtroom were two of Sandra's relatives. My thoughts went out to them as the dead woman's horrific injuries were outlined to the Coroner by pathologist Professor Keith Simpson. His clinical delivery of the medical findings seemed to emphasize the stark reality of the attack. This leading Home Office expert described how he had conducted a post-mortem examination on the morning after the killing:

> The body was clothed in a smock sort of dress, brassière, pants, all undisturbed, all heavily stained with blood from the wounds I am about to describe. I thought that death had clearly taken place before it had been encased in this bag. I found on medical examination the dead woman to have been a healthy person.
>
> There were three blunt injuries to the face, three areas of heavy bruising. One lay over the right eye, $1\frac{1}{2}$ inches; the second lay on the right corner of the mouth, $\frac{3}{4}$ inch, close to the end of the upper lip; and the third lay over the eyebrow.
>
> The first group consisted of three heavy bruises to the face; the second group were to the head above the right ear. There were four splits in the scalp on the right side of the head, on the right side of the head above the right ear. All these lay above the ear. The other two lay in front of the other two towards the right eyebrow in the hair margin. In no case did I find the skull fractured beneath these splits.
>
> On the back of the head there lay the fifth and sixth splits in the scalp. These lay above the nape of the neck, $2\frac{1}{2}$ inches apart. There were three blunt injuries to the face and six splits from heavy blunt injury to the scalp.

I found also heavy bruises on the top of both shoulders without splitting the skin.

On the back of the right hand was some superficial bruising, likely to result if the hand were placed between the blunt instrument and the body. These were protective injuries.

On the front of the right upper arm were a series of four-in-line bruises as if fingers had been gripping the arm heavily.

There was a great deal of blood, mainly from the nose and mouth into the air passages and the skull. This was not fractured, but there was a good deal of surface bruising of the brain, and these injuries must have caused the unconciousness. It was these injuries, together with the bruising of the brain, that had caused death.

I attribute death to blunt head injuries, inhalation of blood, and it was this that had made it clear that no further gain of consciousness had followed. This blood entering the air passages had itself precipitated a difficulty in breathing. I removed specimen samples of head hair, blood, urine, and these I handed to Det. Constable Morgan, the exhibits officer, together with the clothing and canvas bag.

Questioned by the Coroner, Professor Simpson said that he thought most of the injuries were entirely consistent with having been caused by the lead-piping weapon. There was, however, one slight discrepancy. The wounds to the left eye and the mouth did not fit infliction by this weapon so well. Astonishingly, in view of the injuries that Sandra had already suffered, the pathologist concluded that the dead girl had also been punched with a fist.

Susan Maxwell-Scott told the eager courtroom of the last time that Lord Lucan had been seen alive, or dead. She told how she had let him in and offered him a scotch and water. As before, she was questioned directly by Dr Thurston:

Q. How did he look?
A. He looked a little dishevelled, because when I had seen him, he was normally very tidy. His hair was a little ruffled.
Q. Were there any marks on his clothes?
A. I did notice, while he was sitting down, a damp patch on his trousers. It would have been the right side of the hip.
Q. What was the first conversation that passed between you?
A. I said, 'Is anything the matter?', and then he told me what had happened at his wife's house that evening.
Q. How did he describe this first of all?
A. I am going to do my very best, but it is difficult after seven months. He said he had been walking past Lady Lucan's home on his way to change for dinner.
Q. The word 'walking' is very important.
A. Well, I am almost certain. He could have said he was passing. He said he saw through the blinds of the basement what looked like a man attacking his wife, Veronica. He had been saying to me that it was all an unbelievable coincidence, and I knew, because he had told me on the previous occasion, that he was in the habit of walking past the house.

   He said he let himself in the front door, to which he had a key, and ran down to the basement. As he entered he slipped in a pool of blood as he got down to the bottom of the stairs. He wasn't, of course, telling it like a story. This is my best attempt at the narrative.

   The man he had seen attacking his wife ran off. Whether this was on hearing Lord Lucan running down the stairs, probably calling out, or whether it was on seeing Lord Lucan coming into the room, I don't know, but the man made off.

   Lord Lucan, perhaps unfortunately, rather than chasing the man went straight to his wife. He said the man made off. In my own imagination it was probably out of the back door. He went to his wife, who was covered in blood and very hysterical.

Q. Did he say anything further about what his wife had said?

A. Yes. That at first she was very hysterical, and she cried out to him that someone had killed the nanny. And then, almost in the same breath, she accused Lord Lucan of having hired the man to kill her, not Sandra. This, Lord Lucan told me, was a thing she frequently accused him of; having a contract to kill like in American television movies.

In response to Dr Thurston's questions, Susan Maxwell-Scott described Lucan's own account of helping his wife upstairs and tending to her wounds. Then, when asked how Lord Lucan had known about the nanny in the sack, she continued:

A. I am not very clear about that, but I think Lord Lucan said, 'Nanny's murdered.' I gathered he had seen the sack. He described this basement area as being horrific, and he did mention the sack, which Lady Lucan indicated to him, in which he assumed was the body. But I think he felt a bit squeamish about the blood and did not want to look too closely at it.

At the end of the lengthy hearing, Dr Thurston summed up the evidence in just 70 minutes and talked of the task now facing the jury.

'I do not, in this case, think I can ask you to consider the question of accidental death,' he said. 'The injuries were inflicted by some other person. If you are satisfied with what you have heard and satisfied on the evidence this was an attack by another person, then your verdict would have to be murder. I cannot see how I can offer you an alternative.

'The second point is that you have got to ascertain the persons, if any, to be charged with murder or manslaughter and, on the evidence you have got, to decide whether you feel you can name someone. You have got the evidence before you.

'There is the possibility of an intruder, and you have got to remember what a serious matter this is from the point of view of stigma. The responsibility is yours, and I am going to ask you to withdraw to the jury room. I will leave you now to your deliberations.'

With these words the jury retired, to emerge at 11.45 am with a verdict announced by the jury foreman: 'Murder by Lord Lucan.'

Dr Thurston, clearly relieved that this most difficult of cases was finally over, received the verdict with equanimity. Thanking the jury for their care he stated:

'I will record that Sandra Eleanor Rivett died by blunt head injuries, and that at 10.30 pm on Thursday, 7 November, was found dead at 46 Lower Belgrave Street with injuries to the head; and that the offence was committed by Richard John Bingham, Earl of Lucan.

'I must explain the position. This is a very rare procedure in a Coroner's Court. If a person is named then it is my duty to commit that person for trial to the Central Criminal Court. Now, in practice, what happens is, while one goes through the required procedure, invariably no evidence is offered at the inquest on your finding, and the person concerned is brought before the examining magistrates by indictment in the ordinary way.

'But, in this case there is nobody I can commit for trial, because Lord Lucan, at the moment, is not here, and there is no doubt if he turns up he will be charged before justices. So I will keep this on my file.

'I would like to thank you for your attendance. It has been an ordeal of concentration.'

The inquest verdict caused headlines around the world and once again brought the name of Lord Lucan to the forefront of public attention. It also led to an outcry from the family, friends and supporters of the missing Earl who complained bitterly that Lord Lucan had, in effect, been condemned as a murderer without the benefit of a trial.

Few of these people seemed to take any account of the fact that, if Lord Lucan had been so condemned, there had always been an instant remedy open to him. He had only then, or now, to walk into any Metropolitan police station and ask for me, and I would have been delighted to have given him the full trial that his supporters were demanding.

There was no doubt, however, that the necessity to hold an inquest before the criminal trial, and the Coroner's powers to name the killer and commit him for trial, had added immeasurably to the complexity of the case. This fact was recognized a few years later when the government introduced measures in the subsequent Criminal Justice Bill to remove for ever the powers of a coroner's jury to name a suspected killer. Lord Lucan thus has the dubious distinction of being the last man in British legal history to suffer this fate.

The fact that her son had been branded a murderer was to cast a shadow over his mother, the Dowager Countess of Lucan, for the rest of her life. Until her death on 19 November 1985 in a nursing home in Daventry, Northamptonshire, she never ceased defending her son and remained a fearsome opponent for anybody who believed in the correctness of the inquest jury's verdict.

In July 1978, three years after the inquest, the Dowager Countess was at the forefront of an attempt to clear Lord Lucan's name. Solicitors acting for Lucan's mother approached the then Director of Public Prosecutions, Tony Hetherington, asking that the subsequent changes in the law should be applied, retrospectively, to the case of Lord Lucan. They drew up a petition asking that the finding of the inquest jury be replaced by a finding that Sandra Rivett had been murdered 'by a person'. The petition was refused on the advice of the Attorney-General, Sam Silkin.

There was a second and more tragic postscript to the hearing at the Coroner's Court in Horseferry Road, when the same courtroom later housed the inquest into the death of Dominic Elwes, one of Lucan's closest and most loyal friends. For months before the killing, the pair had either lunched or dined together at the Clermont Club, and Lucan had been due to lunch with Elwes on the day of the murder. They also spent some time at Lord Suffolk's country residence, at Chorley Park, on the weekends when Lucan had access to his children.

After the murder, at the meeting of the Just Men, it had been Dominic who agreed to visit Lady Lucan at St George's Hospital to try and find out exactly what had occurred. He had become upset and tearful when he saw the extent of her injuries. From my inquiries, I formed the opinion that Dominic Elwes was highly emotional but was considered to be amusing, well liked and popular with Lucan and his group of friends. However, this acceptance by the group was to change, dramatically, over the months that followed.

Dominic was accused by his former wealthy friends of having helped a *Sunday Times* journalist write an uncomplimentary article about Lucan and the Lucan set. His denials fell on deaf ears, particularly since he had accepted a commission from the newspaper's magazine to paint a fictional group portrait of Lucan and his friends, supposedly in the Clermont Club.

Dominic was not only criticized for the painting. He was also wrongly accused of supplying private holiday photographs to the magazine. He claimed to be ostracized by some of Lucan's friends and barred from many London clubs that had previously formed the backbone of his social life. Dominic, who I considered to be a weak, sensitive and emotional character, committed suicide at his flat at Stewarts Grove, Chelsea, in September 1975.

At the subsequent inquest, also conducted by Dr Gavin Thurston, a verdict of suicide by taking an overdose of sleeping tablets was returned. He left an almost unreadable note, in which he gave instructions as to who should be invited to take part in his memorial service. In what I have always taken as a reference to James Goldsmith, his wife Annabel and London club owner Mark Birley, there was also the chilling message: 'Tell Jimmy, Annabel and Mark that I curse them from my grave.'

CHAPTER 14

THE FORGOTTEN VICTIM

The inquest into the death of Sandra Eleanor Rivett left a number of unhappy people in its wake. There was the Dowager Countess of Lucan, Lord Lucan's mother, who felt that the jury's verdict had branded her son as a killer without him having had any chance to put his side of the story. Many of Lucan's other relatives and friends were quick to voice their outrage at the murder verdict.

The other unhappy group were the relatives of Sandra Rivett herself, the forgotten victim of the Lucan case. Immediately after the Coroner's summing up and the jury's verdict, Sandra's aunt, Vera Ward, hit out at the lack of concern and consideration for the totally innocent girl who had lost her life. 'It's like the story of the prince and the showgirl,' she said. 'The entire inquest has been devoted to the life of Lord Lucan, and the life of poor Sandra has been almost ignored.'

I have always felt the greatest sympathy for Sandra's family and believed all along that their complaints of her being the forgotten victim were totally justified. In press reports of the original murder investigation and of the inquest Sandra's name was barely mentioned as other than a footnote to the story. For day after day in the Coroner's Court in Horseferry Road, Westminster, the lawyers and witnesses discussed the actions and motives of the Lucan family with barely a reference to the innocent girl who lost her life as a result of their family feud.

This lack of concern for the loss of a vivacious young girl, whose attractive personality lightened the lives of those who knew her, reached its peak in the weeks after the inquest. With the jury's murder verdict the newspaper now felt free to indulge in an orgy of speculation about the case and about the likely whereabouts of the missing Earl.

I was astonished to see an article in the *Evening News*, then London's biggest circulation newspaper, in which Sandra's death was relegated to the status of a competition entry. The newspaper gleefully recounted brief details of the murder and then offered a case of champagne for the reader who produced the best fictional version of Lucan's flight from justice. It was the very height of bad taste and deeply offensive to Sandra's still grieving family.

It was in June 1975 that the death of Sandra Eleanor Rivett was finally registered before the City of Westminster Registrar for a formal death certificate to be issued. The information for the certificate, issued on 21 June 1975, is usually provided by a relative of the deceased but, on this occasion, came from Dr Gavin Thurston, as Coroner for Inner West London.

Many years later I obtained a copy of the death certificate from the Public Search Room at the General Register Office, St Catherine's House in the Aldwych, London. The certificate records the fact that an inquest had been held and lists her details as a 'Children's nanny of 46 Lower Belgrave St, Westminster, SW1 – Wife of Roger Rivett, a Security Officer'. It is in section 8 of the standard death-certificate form, headed 'Cause of death', that Sandra's entry stands out as unusual. The certificate reads: 'Blunt head injuries inflicted by a named person'. Centred on a line of its own after the cause of death is the stark word, 'Murder'.

The certificate is also interesting for the fact it omits. Nowhere on the official record does it mention Lord Lucan as the 'named person' responsible for the crime.

The bare paper records do no sort of justice to the character of Sandra Rivett, a girl about whom everybody that I spoke to in the course of the murder inquiry had nothing but good to say. She was born on 16 September 1945 in Basingstoke, the daughter of Albert David Hensby and his wife, Eunice. Albert was then private number 60980265 in the Royal West Kent Regiment, although he listed his former civilian occupation as bank manager on the birth certificate.

The couple had been married for more than eight years and were to have a total of four children, all girls. Sandra had two elder sisters, Pamela and Theresa, and a younger sister Charmaine who was born in 1953. When Sandra was just 2 years old the family emigrated to

Application Number G 011019

QDX 125324

CERTIFIED COPY   **OF AN ENTRY**

DEATH	Entry No. **211**

Registration district *Westminster* Administrative area

Sub-district *Westminster* *City of Westminster*

1. Date and place of death *Seventh November 1974.*
46, Lower Belgrave Street, S.w.1.

2. Name and surname *Sandra Eleanor RIVETT*

3. Sex *Female*

4. Maiden surname of woman who has married *HENSBY*

5. Date and place of birth *16.9.1945. Basingstoke*

6. Occupation and usual address *Childrens Nanny*
46, Lower Belgrave Street, Westminster, S.w.1.
Wife of Roger Rivett, a Security Officer

7.(a) Name and surname of informant
Certificate received from G. Thurston coroner for Inner West London. Inquest held 16th June 1975.
(c) Usual address

8. Cause of death
Blunt head injuries Inflicted by a named person.
Murder.

9. I certify that the particulars given by me above are true to the best of my knowledge and belief .... Signature of informant

10. Date of registration *Twenty First June 1975*

11. Signature of registrar *D. Littleton Registrar*

Sandra Rivett's death certificate.

Australia but returned to England seven years later in December 1955. She started school at the local Caterham-on-the-Hill secondary school where she was to stay until the age of 14.

At school Sandra was described as 'intelligent, although she does not excel academically' but was a highly popular girl with her schoolfriends. She left school to start work as an apprentice hairdresser near her home in Woodville Close, Caterham, but lasted in the job only six months before taking a job as a secretary with a drug packing company in Purley Way, Croydon.

A broken romance at the age of 18 broke Sandra's heart, and she was deeply depressed for many months. Eventually her family encouraged her to seek medical help, and in 1963 she was admitted as a voluntary patient suffering from depression to a mental hospital near Redhill. It was there that she met a boy named John, two years older than herself and working as a builder in the hospital where she was being treated. They fell deeply in love and upon Sandra's discharge from hospital continued to see each other regularly. They eventually announced their engagement.

Sandra became pregnant by John and on 13 March 1964 gave birth to a baby son named Stephen in the local Mayday Hospital, Croydon. Neither Sandra nor her fiancé was ready for the commitment of getting married, let alone bringing up a baby boy. Sandra was devastated when, even before her son was born, the father visited Albert and Eunice Hensby and told them that he was not ready for marriage and was having second thoughts about the planned wedding to their daughter.

At the time of the birth Sandra had been working

as a children's nanny for a Croydon doctor who agreed to become her baby's godfather. Afterwards she went back to live with her parents and admitted to them that she was considering giving the baby away for adoption, as she could see no way of coping financially and bringing the child up on her own.

However, Albert and Eunice could not bear the thought of giving away the newborn baby. They offered to look after the child themselves, and Sandra, who never wanted to lose touch with her baby, agreed that Stephen's grandparents could bring him up as their own son. The boy was legally adopted by the Hensbys on 26 May 1965.

Sandra continued to live with her parents and lost touch with John after she started working in a local old folks' home. Then, in the summer of 1966, Sandra left home to stay with her elder sister, Theresa, at her home in Portsmouth. There she met Able Seaman Roger Rivett, a friend of Theresa's husband, David Stevens. Roger, a year and five days older than Sandra, swept the 21-year-old girl off her feet. The young seaman fitted in dates with his new girlfriend between intense practice for his role with the Portsmouth Command Fieldgun Crew who were appearing at that year's Royal Tournament.

The couple married on 10 June 1967 in a register office ceremony in Croydon, ten months after their first meeting. Their circumstances were a world apart from the wealthy life of Belgravia and the Lucan family with whom Sandra's destiny was later to be entwined. The working-class background of them both was clearly reflected in the details recorded on their marriage certificate.

At the time Sandra gave her occupation as a

The marriage certificates of Roger Rivett and Sandra Hensby (above) and the Lucans (below).

'domestic' in an old people's home in nearby Caterham. Her husband was a Royal Navy able seaman who was then living with his parents at the Surrey village of Coulsdon. The simple ceremony was witnessed by both fathers, Thomas Rivett, a gardener, and Albert Hensby, who was then working as a porter.

Sandra and Roger set up home in a furnished flat in Kenley, Surrey, but just four months later Roger was posted to join HMS *Caprice* and spent the next eleven months away from his wife at sea. Roger was later to say that his new wife wrote almost every day for the first six months of his tour of duty, but then the letters began to tail off, and he grew suspicious that she could be involved with another man.

In 1969, desperate to save their marriage, Roger and Sandra agreed that a drastic change had to be made in their lives. Roger decided to buy himself out of the Royal Navy and take a job on land. He started work as a loader for British Road Services, near their flat in Kenley, while Sandra had a part-time job at Reedham Orphanage in Purley. She was only employed as a domestic cleaner but began working more and more with the orphanage children and told her friends and family that working with children was the job that she loved.

For some years the change in the couple's circumstances worked wonders. But by early 1973 Sandra and Roger began arguing regularly and drifted more and more apart. By the July of that year Roger decided to leave and go back to sea. He joined the Esso company as an able merchant seaman on one of their tankers, leaving Sandra alone in their flat. A few months later on a short leave, Roger visited his wife who was then working at Palmers Harvey, a wholesale cigarette company in Tamworth Road, Croydon.

'I started to take her out again, and things seemed to be all right between us,' said Roger, but shortly he was sent back to sea, and again the letters became sporadic.

By April 1974 Roger was back living with Sandra after being paid off sick from his tanker job, but the enforced togetherness simply increased the passion of their arguments. In particular, Roger became deeply suspicious that Sandra was finding other company in his spells away at sea, and in May 1974, after a furious row, he left their flat for good and went back to live with his parents.

Sandra kept on the flat in Valley Road, Kenley, even though she was by now on the books of a domestic agency in London's posh Belgravia district and had a regular job looking after an elderly couple in Belgravia. Sandra had got the job with the assistance of a recommendation by the house mistress of Reedham School, Rosemary Jordan.

Rosemary was just three years older than Sandra and had met her a couple of years before when Sandra had worked as a cleaner at Reedham School. Despite the difference in their work positions, the pair had become firm friends, before Sandra moved on and their friendship drifted apart. Now they met again, for the first time in three years, for a drink. At that time in mid-1974 Sandra was happy, but complaining that she was overworked. The two girls began seeing each other regularly, and Sandra confided to her friend the details of her several different boyfriends.

Among these was Australian John Hankins, born in Sydney, then living in London and working as a relief manager for a London chain of pubs. The two women often went to nightspots in and around London, such as Tiffany's Dance Hall in Piccadilly, or Scarlet's in Purley, Croydon. Sandra was a vivacious and outgoing girl, never shy, and was a popular dance partner.

Just six weeks before she died Sandra was sent by her

agency for a job at Lady Lucan's home in Lower Belgrave Street. She was paid only £25 per week to look after the three young Lucan children, but told all her friends and family how happy she was in her job. On both the Tuesday and Wednesday nights of the week she was murdered, Sandra spoke on the telephone to her mum Eunice at her caravan home in Basingstoke.

She talked of going home to see the family at Christmas and said how much she already loved the children and how very fond she had become of Lady Lucan. Sandra told her mum that Veronica Lucan treated her as a friend, not as an employee, and always as an equal. The two women were on first-name terms.

Veronica clearly returned the friendship that Sandra felt. Years after the murder Veronica told a newspaper reporter that she had found Sandra to be the ideal 'mother's help' and added, 'Sandra and I got on very well. She was small like me, just 5ft 2ins, and like me was rather lonely. She was working to pay off a pile of debts, and I really thought she would stay with me for a long time to come.'

Veronica revealed that the tiny stature of both women caused them some problems in their day-to-day life in the large Belgravia home that they shared with the children. They were both unable to reach up to the light fittings in the tall stairways of the building, so that when the bulbs blew they waited for ages to replace them. 'We were used to the dark, and we walked around like cats or used torches,' said Veronica.

Sandra's mother, Eunice, was not surprised to hear how friendly they had become. Sandra was an easygoing girl who always impressed everybody she met with her happy disposition. Said her mother: 'She made other people happy when they were in her company. She could make a joke out of anything, and I don't think she could make an enemy of anyone.'

Sandra also told Rosemary Jordan how happy she was to be working at the Lucan household – but there was one cloud on the horizon in the shape of the absent Lord Lucan.

Sandra said she had met him only occasionally, when Lord Lucan arrived to collect the children for his every other weekend access visits. At those times it would be Sandra who had to meet the aristocratic earl in the hallway of Lower Belgrave Street and hand over the children. Lady Lucan was invariably upset by his visits, to the point where she would rather keep out of the way in her bedroom while he was in the building.

The only other time that Sandra met with Lucan was when he occasionally let himself into the house with his own key to collect any mail. On the surface Lord Lucan was always polite and courteous to the children's nanny. He remarked that he was pleased that she seemed to be a well-mannered and sensible girl, and that the children had given him good reports of her work.

There was, however, another hidden side to the Earl's presence. Sandra told her friends that both she and Lady Lucan were being constantly pestered by nuisance telephone calls at all hours of the day and night. On occasions the phone would ring more than a dozen times in a single hour, and when answering the call they would be met with just heavy breathing or total silence. Lady Lucan insisted to Sandra that the calls had to originate with her estranged husband.

Although Sandra had a number of boyfriends during the summer of 1974, including at least one married man whose involvement with the murdered nanny was later to cause him great embarrassment, she was thinking of settling down with her Australian barman friend, John Hankins.

Shortly after meeting John, Sandra telephoned her estranged husband, Roger, and said that she felt she would like a rapid divorce. She told him that she had met somebody else with whom marriage was a possibility. Roger, who admitted that when the marriage broke up both parties were relieved to end the years of bickering, told her he was happy to go through with the divorce as fast as possible, but that they would have to wait for at least two years of separation for an uncontested divorce hearing. In a genuine attempt to help her Roger did suggest that he would be willing to divorce Sandra if she would provide evidence for grounds of adultery, but she never replied to his offer.

For John Hankins, meeting Sandra was the start of an intense and passionate relationship, which may well have ended in marriage. John, then aged 26, had been in Britain for two years, working as a barman at the Grange Pub in Ealing before joining St George Taverns as a relief manager, working week by week at different pubs around West London.

It was in the Plumbers Arms, the public house to which Lady Lucan ran seeking refuge on the night of the killing, that John first met Sandra while he was working as relief manager. He was introduced by a regular customer who knew Sandra well, and they began dating regularly almost immediately. Sandra would call in at whichever pub he happened to be working that night, or they would go out on the town on his infrequent nights off.

John told the police that Sandra had appeared to be on very good terms with Lady Lucan but had talked of the friction between her and her husband and wanted to have as little as possible to do with Lord Lucan. Their short relationship was passionate but stormy. Sandra sometimes stayed the night with him in the pubs where he was working, but they also had frequent rows.

Just the Sunday before she died Sandra had stormed out of his room, only returning the next day to make up a silly argument. Patching up their row brought the couple even closer together. Although they had known each other for only six weeks, Sandra and John discussed the possibility of marriage, and Sandra offered to go back to Australia with her new boyfriend the following year if her divorce from Roger could be settled by then.

On the night of her death, John was one of the last people to whom Sandra ever spoke. He had telephoned her that evening about 8 pm for a five-minute chat to make plans for their next date. He said little, publicly, about his lost girlfriend in the weeks after the killing but did tell one newspaper: 'One thing I want to make clear is that Sandra was a very nice girl. We might have got married and had talked about her returning to Australia with me.'

The couple would normally have been going out together on a Thursday night, but Sandra had decided to change her night off because she was feeling unwell. She told her mother Eunice the day before that she had been suffering from a sore throat and that a doctor had warned her she could be suffering from glandular fever. She felt it better for her health to stay in on the night of 7 November. It was both sad and ironic that Sandra's concern for her own health was to lead directly to her death in the basement kitchen in Lower Belgrave Street.

As the murder inquiry began, there was a further hardship to be faced by Sandra's parents. As is normal in murder cases it was not possible for Sandra's body to be released from the mortuary immediately for burial or cremation. On many occasions a legal team acting for the defence in a murder case will want to make their own independent post-mortem examination of the body. In the case of Sandra Rivett, as the days turned into weeks with no sign that Lord Lucan would ever come forward to answer questions, let alone mount a defence and seek a second post-mortem, the Coroner finally decided that Sandra's remains had to be given back into the care of her family.

Sandra was cremated at a service in Croydon crematorium on 18 December 1974. Neither Veronica nor any other member of the Lucan family attended the ceremony, and a police spokesman explained that Veronica had stayed away to avoid further upsetting the family.

There was a floral tribute from the detectives involved in the murder investigation and from her estranged husband Roger. From her parents came a heart-shaped wreath carrying the message: 'To our darling daughter, Sandra – Mum and Dad.' There was also a sheaf of deep pink chrysanthemums and white carnations from Veronica and the children. Perhaps the consideration that went into the gesture by Veronica is in part summed up by a misspelling of the names of one of the children, George, Frances and Camilla, for whom Sandra had cared. Veronica had ordered the flowers by telephone, but the wording somehow became garbled in the process. The card attached to Veronica's flowers was finally to read: 'To Sandra with Love from Veronica, Frances, George and Pamela'.

The cremation was not the last service that I attended to mark poor Sandra's passing. On 7 November 1975, the first anniversary of the murder, I went with Dave Gerring to Westminster Cathedral for a requiem mass in memory of Sandra. The service had been requested by one of Sandra's friends and was conducted by a cathedral chaplain. At the time the newspapers suggested that we were attending the ceremony in the hopes of catching a repentant Lord Lucan lurking among the congregation. The reality was, of course, that we simply felt it fitting that we should pay our respects along with the brave family of the murdered girl.

The unpalatable truth is that, in the years since the tragic events of 1974, the legend of Lord Lucan, the happy-go-lucky gambling peer who has stayed one step ahead of the law, has grown, while the memory of Sandra Rivett, his most unfortunate victim, has been all but forgotten.

On the seventh anniversary of Sandra's death, her mother Eunice was interviewed by one of the national newspapers and revealed that she traditionally placed flowers on Sandra's memorial stone in Croydon crematorium on the dead girl's birthday and on the anniversary of her death. She said that every single night of her life when she went to bed, she still saw Sandra's face – the pretty girl with thick auburn hair and vivid blue laughing eyes. As her mother remarked, 'She was such a happy child – this has all been so very unfair.'

CHAPTER 15

INNOCENT OR GUILTY?

The Sandra Rivett inquest was criticized at length by friends and family of the seventh Earl of Lucan because it gave, as they claimed, only one side of the story. The sole version of the events that occurred at 46 Lower Belgrave Street on the night of 7 November 1974 came from the Countess of Lucan, who had her own, self-admitted, reasons for wishing Lucan ill. From the outset I believed Lady Lucan's account, but there has always been another, totally different version of what happened that night. It was given by Lord Lucan himself, in the several communications from him, both orally and in writing, in the hours immediately after the event.

So could Lucky Lucan be innocent? That was one question that I and my colleagues in the incident room at Gerald Road police station obviously had to examine in the greatest of detail. What was Lord Lucan's account?

How did he explain the dead body of Sandra Rivett encased in her canvas shroud in the basement, the blood-stained and tape-wrapped bludgeon lying on the floor and his own bloodstained and dishevelled flight from the scene?

The answers to these questions came initially from Lucky Lucan's own lips. After fleeing from the Belgravia house, he had telephoned his mother, the widowed Dowager Countess of Lucan, to give the first hurried explanation of the tragedy that had befallen the family.

Lucan's mother was a highly intelligent woman who in her earlier life had helped her husband to run a highly successful political career and had built her own formidable reputation as a determined politician. From the very first contact that I had with the Dowager, I realized that her love of her son was the overwhelming motivation in her life at that time. For such a bright woman, she proved remarkably vague about the exact contents of that all-important telephone call from her elder son.

Her very first version of the contents of the call came on the night of the murder itself, when she appeared, unannounced, at 46 Lower Belgrave Street. In later interviews and in her account to the inquest, the Dowager Countess was to make small but significant changes to her evidence.

The basic facts of her story, however, remained roughly the same. She said her son had been passing the house when he had seen a fight and had interrupted that fight in the basement. He had made no detailed explanation of what had happened but had muttered incoherently about blood and mess. She had taken this as a general expression of horror and disgust and had formed the impression that her son had said he 'couldn't take it'.

There was another person to whom Lord Lucan personally told his own version of events. This was Susan Maxwell-Scott, the wife of his close friend and gambling companion, Ian Maxwell-Scott. He had visited Susan at her home in Uckfield, Sussex, on the night of 7 November, just a couple of hours after the murder.

Susan spent a considerable amount of time with Lord Lucan at her home that night. She was to make a number of separate statements to police over the next few months, each time covering a different detail of what had occurred. Again, her account of Lucan's words followed a similar line.

Lucan told Mrs Maxwell-Scott that he had been walking past his family home on his way back to Elizabeth Street to change for dinner. Through the blinds in the basement window he had seen a man attacking Veronica. He let himself into the house with his key and went down to the basement where he saw a horrifying sight. Lucan claimed he had slipped in a pool of blood and that the man had run off.

Veronica, the Countess of Lucan, was in an appalling state with blood all over. He claimed to have tried to calm her down as she was in a state of hysteria. Veronica had then shouted that Lucan had paid a man to murder her.

Lucan had taken his wife upstairs, where he found his daughter Frances was still up and had sent her to bed. He went to the bathroom for towels to clean up his wife's injuries, but when he emerged, Veronica had disappeared and left the house.

Lucan had told Susan Maxwell-Scott that, when he first entered the basement, Veronica told him that the man had killed their nanny and put her in a sack. Susan thought that she recalled Lucan telling her that he had not gone near the body. Lucan claimed that he had then realized that he was now in the house, with blood on him. He knew that his wife Veronica would do anything to incriminate him and had panicked and fled from the house to get away from it all.

There were two further communications from the seventh Earl of Lucan, in which he tried to shed light on what had happened and convince his friends that he was innocent of any crime.

The first, and slightly more detailed tale, came in the letter that he wrote in front of Susan Maxwell-Scott on that night in Uckfield. The letter was sent to his brother-in-law, Bill Shand-Kydd, and mentioned, once again, that he had interrupted a fight between a man and Veronica. The man had left. Lucan had taken Veronica upstairs, sent Frances to bed and tried to clean his wife up.

Lucan explained that Veronica 'lay doggo' on the bed and had left the house while he was in the bathroom. He claimed that the circumstantial evidence against him was strong because Veronica had demonstrated her hatred for him in the past and would do anything to see him accused.

A subsequent letter to friend Michael Stoop, the man who had loaned him the Ford Corsair car, in which he had fled from the scene, added no new information. The only point of relevance to his defence was that Lucan had given his opinion of what had occurred.

He called the events, 'a traumatic night of unbelievable coincidences'.

In summary, therefore, within a few minutes of the killing, Lucan had come up with an account that sought to explain away some of the most damning evidence against him. I believe, however, that it is an account that he will come to regret should he ever stand before a British jury. For although it is superficially attractive as a form of defence, it fails to stand up to the sort of rigorous questioning and detailed examination that he would have to undergo as a murder-case defendant.

The defence fails to offer any explanation for some most inconvenient facts, such as the discovery of the near identical lead piping in the boot of the abandoned Ford Corsair, or Lucan's previous threats to murder his wife.

However, the first major problem for the Lord Lucan defence barrister will be to account for the invisible man. The Earl claims to have interrupted a fight with a man in the basement – and yet no trace of this mystery assailant has ever been found. There was not the slightest shred of forensic-science evidence that could be uncovered at the house in Lower Belgrave Street to suggest that another man had been present.

The only description available from Lucan's story is that the assailant was a male and was large. He is supposed to have murdered the nanny and violently assaulted Veronica, and yet Lord Lucan's wife saw no other person in the house except her husband. The Countess of Lucan has stated clearly, persistently and without hesitation that it was her husband who attacked her with a bludgeon, stuck his fingers down her throat, clawed at her eyes and attempted to strangle her.

In the aftermath of the killing, the entire area around the Belgravia home was covered by a series of police searches and house-to-house inquiries. Among the scores of local residents who were questioned, not one single person could be found who had seen this large and bloodstained man loitering or running from the scene at the material times.

Despite all the attendant publicity for year after year, nobody has ever come forward to back up Lucan's story. The sole exception was a punch-drunk boxer who claimed to have known of the mystery second man. He later admitted making up the entire story, from start to finish, and was convicted of wasting police time.

If our invisible man did exist, it was hard to see how he had escaped. Lord Lucan just said he had 'left' – but in what manner? He certainly had not fled up the stairs past Lord and Lady Lucan to reach the front door and out into Lower Belgrave Street.

He had not escaped through the front basement door. That had been firmly locked on the night of the murder. A second basement door led out to the back garden. It was closed but unlocked. If our mystery man had fled by that route then he would quickly have found an insuperable problem. The rear garden was enclosed by a six-foot brick wall, which was covered in moss.

I ordered the closest possible examination of this wall, but not a single sign or mark could be found to suggest that any assailant could have scaled such an obstacle. He would, in any event, have had to have been a climber of considerable skill to surmount the wall and then the three-foot wooden trellis, partly covered by bushes and roses, on top. In what I consider to be the final nail in the coffin for this back-door escape route, I had the area searched by police dogs. They failed to pick up on any trace of a scent.

One of the problems facing any investigation of Lord Lucan's story is that his account remains short on detail. Even so there are a number of vital points, which, I believe, can be irrefutably proved to be untrue. Such proof makes it hard for any sensible person seriously to consider his story. One of the most important issues to be tackled is the question of how the mystery man, whom Lucan saw attacking his wife in the basement, ever got into the house. There was no evidence of forcible entry to the premises. So how did he get in? Did he have a key? If so, from where did he get it?

The next point involves Lucan's supposed sighting of the basement fight while passing the family home. It was clearly a matter that I needed to investigate fully in the early stages of the 1974 murder inquiry. To that end, I and several other officers carried out a series of experiments at the house to ascertain the veracity of what Lord Lucan had told his mother and Susan Maxwell-Scott.

Taking into account that the venetian blinds in the basement breakfast room were set at about 45°, I thought it unlikely that Lucan would have seen a fight there, while driving, or walking, past the house.

Two days after the murder, at about 10 pm on a cold and overcast November evening, I went with some of my team to the address. I sat in the front passenger seat of a car and was driven past the address. From my seat it was impossible to see the basement window in question, and the driver could see even less. We were about seven to eight feet from the front of the building because, as on the night of the crime, there were cars parked alongside the kerb.

The Dowager Countess of Lucan had initially talked of Lucan driving past Veronica's home. But, after hearing that this would have made it impossible for him to see a fight, her memory improved a little, and she then recalled his words as just 'passing' the house. It may well have been on foot.

I asked one of my detectives to enter the house; go to the basement; switch on the breakfast-room light and stand at the foot of the stairs. In company with another officer, I then stood outside the building to see what was visible from the pavement. We could distinguish no more than the faint outline of the officer inside – and that was only possible when we stooped down low on the paving stones.

The policeman inside the house then switched on the light in the kitchen. Again, it was only by bending low that I could see him clearly. He was standing at the foot of the basement stairs, and it was impossible, under any circumstances, to see more than the bottom three or four steps of that staircase. When I walked past the house, standing up straight in a normal walking position, I could see into the kitchen – but had no view at all of the breakfast room where the murder had occurred.

The experiments proved to our total satisfaction that Lucan's story of passing by and seeing an attack on his wife was impossible to believe. The street lights turned on in the road outside were nowhere near enough to light up the inside of the house. Without an interior light turned on in the basement, nobody could have seen such a thing.

But could there have been such a light? Lady Lucan was certain that there had been no light on in the basement area when she was attacked at the top of the stairs leading down to the breakfast room and kitchen. Undoubtedly, there were no lights on when police arrived at the scene. So who could have turned off the lights? And why should this have been done midway through a murderous attack?

The ordinary switch controlling the light at the bottom of the basement stairs could be switched on or off from both the top and the foot of the stairs. When Lady Lucan came down to see what was delaying Sandra Rivett from bringing her tea, the basement was in darkness, and the switch at the head of the stairs did not work.

This is hardly surprising. When police officers arrived, they found the basement was in darkness because somebody had removed the bulb from its holder and left it lying on a nearby chair.

Giving Lord Lucan's story the benefit of every possible doubt, one should rightly ask if the mystery assailant could have removed the light bulb himself. This would, of course, have to take place after Lucan had seen a fight through the window – but before the attacker had fled from his approach. The idea of a blood-crazed killer taking time out from his flight for freedom to pop out the light bulb and leave it neatly on the chair has always been a concept that I have had the greatest difficulty in accepting.

Finally, could there have been some form of electrical problem with the all-important basement light? When I arrived at the murder scene, I waited until the bulb had been fingerprinted and then replaced it in its holder at the bottom of the stairs. I feared it could have fused. Once back in its socket – it worked perfectly.

I believe that the practical experiments I and my colleagues conducted 20 years ago in Lower Belgrave Street completely destroyed Lord Lucan's defence case. His claim to have witnessed a mystery assailant attacking his wife inside the darkened basement is directly contradicted by the known facts. The sight-lines from the pavement and the light levels at the foot of the stairs make the Earl's version impossible to believe.

Let us for a moment, however, set aside the facts and consider the situation IF Lucan had, by some unexplained means, truly seen a fight as he 'passed by' the premises. Even then, his defence fails to answer one vital question: Who was the woman whom he saw being assaulted that night?

It most certainly was not his wife. Lady Lucan stated, from the very first moment of the inquiry, that she had never set foot in the basement. She insisted that she had been battered around the head and half-strangled on the ground floor, at the head of the stairway leading down to the kitchen. It was an area that Lord Lucan could never have seen from the street, however low he had stooped to the pavement. Lady Lucan has remained steadfast in her account through many police interviews and published accounts of her story over the past 20 years.

Even more convincing, though, is the mass of forensic-science evidence that confirms the Countess's report. In particular, examination of the blood splashes and stains at the scene confirmed every word that Lady Lucan had said. Dr Margaret Pereira is known to be one of the country's foremost blood experts. She personally conducted the investigation, and I have retained the utmost confidence in its findings.

Dr Pereira took a series of swabs at the top of the stairs where Lady Lucan had been attacked. She collected samples from the heavily bloodstained carpet, walls, the door and the ceiling at this spot. Even the lampshade had been splattered with blood. Her laboratory examination revealed that each and every sample was group A – the blood group of the Countess of Lucan. Both assaulted women had, of course, bled profusely from the severe wounds to their heads. The subsequent investigation was helped enormously by the fact that Veronica and Sandra had different blood groups.

Numerous other swabs were taken by Dr Pereira in the kitchen, breakfast room and from the walls and ceiling in the area at the foot of the stairs. With just six exceptions, these basement samples matched the blood that soaked the United States mailbag containing the victim's lifeless body. Laboratory tests identified all these samples as group B – the blood of Sandra Rivett.

Much has been made, by amateur theorists over the intervening years, of the six swabs that proved the exception to the rule. One sample was taken from a small bloodstain in the centre of the kitchen floor. This proved to be Lady Lucan's group A blood. If the Countess had never set foot in the basement, how could this blood spot have been found on the floor?

The answer, I am convinced, lies in the many movements of police officers, police dogs, scientists, fingerprint experts and undertakers at the scene in the hours after the murder. Given the number of people who had to walk in and out of the rooms, stepping over the bloodstained carpet at the top of the stairs, then the only surprising finding is that not more of Lady Lucan's blood group was discovered spread around the basement area.

The two most controversial swabs were both taken from the mailbag shroud. Each tested positive for Sandra's group B blood and yet also gave some reaction to Lady Lucan's group A. I believe that the mailbag, still containing Sandra Rivett's body, was contaminated when it was removed on a stretcher from the basement.

The body was loaded on to a stretcher, to be carried by undertakers up the stairs and transferred to the nearby Westminster mortuary. The unfortunate victim had been doubled up in the sack, and the resultant bulky shape on the stretcher had proved difficult to manoeuvre up the narrow staircase and round the 180° turn at the top of the stairs. Once again, given the fact that the walls and door in this area were heavily soaked in Lady Lucan's blood, it would have been surprising not to find traces of her blood grouping rubbing off on the mailbag.

The fourth and fifth swabs revealed faint traces of Sandra Rivett's group B blood on Lady Lucan's dress. Heavier staining of the same group was found on Lady Lucan's right shoe. In my view this could well have been transferred to the Countess in the course of the fierce battle with her husband, while she was fighting for her life at the top of the stairs. Lord Lucan's clothing would undoubtedly by that stage have been soaked in the dead nanny's blood.

The last group B swab was found on some leaves in the back garden. I am convinced that this blood was transferred from the shoes of the police officers, or the pads of the police dogs, as the rear of the premises was searched for any possible escape route.

The overwhelming weight of forensic-science evidence totally supports Lady Lucan's statement that she never descended to the basement area of the house. The Countess could not, therefore, have been the woman victim who Lucan allegedly saw through the basement-kitchen window. There was only one other adult woman in the Lucan home that night, the unfortunate nanny, Sandra Rivett. She and Veronica were of a similar size. So could it not have been poor Sandra that Lord Lucan caught sight of through the window as she fought for her life?

Once again the theory folds, almost as soon as the defence has been uttered. Having seen the attack taking place, Lord Lucan, by his own account, intervened straightaway. In his words, he 'interrupted the fight'. It could have taken him no more than seconds to let himself in with his key and rush down the basement steps.

If it were Sandra whom Lucan had seen through the window, then the killer must have been a rapid worker indeed. He needed to have struck the nine or ten fatal blows to Sandra's head and body; waited the minute or so that it took her to die; manhandled her dead weight into the mailsack; folded the top over; begun washing his hands in the ground-floor cloakroom; rushed out and bludgeoned Lady Lucan; and all within the time that Lord Lucan had taken to open one door.

Considered as a whole the forensic-science evidence forms a damning indictment of Lord Lucan's story. The numerous holes in his hasty excuses can be opened with ease. However, were he to have offered a different explanation on the night, perhaps denied any visit to the house, or simply said nothing at all, then his defence would have been an easier task. We had no fingerprint or forensic-science evidence to place him at the scene.

It is his own words and writings that most clearly implicate Lord Lucan in the vicious attack on the nanny and Veronica. Lady Lucan's account would have been just her word against his. She would have been prevented, anyway, by law, from giving evidence at his trial for the murder of Sandra Rivett. The evidence of his own daughter Frances, then just 10 years old, was always slightly muddled, and, even in the unlikely event that she would be called for the prosecution, any competent defence lawyer could have handled that problem with ease.

Unfortunately for the missing Earl, his defence is now one he is stuck with. As many a politician has found to his cost, it is often the cover-ups rather than the original sin that causes most problems. Were Lucan to return for his trial, he could hardly disown all he had said and written, suddenly to produce a new and more convenient defence.

It is ironic that Lucan's own attempts to cover up his crimes will cause his greatest troubles in the dock at the Old Bailey. Together with his mother's ready adaptation of inconvenient facts and the determination of some friends to bolster his story, Lucan's own words may still yet, metaphorically, place a silken noose round his neck.

CHAPTER 16

DEATH BEFORE DISHONOUR?

There are a number of uniquely British institutions that sail on serenely through the generations, unruffled by the activities and scandals of individuals. One such is *Debrett's Peerage and Baronetage*, the annually published guide to the upper classes, which lists the family history of all the British aristocracy. Those who are within its pages – and many who wish they were – have been known to refer to *Debrett's* as the 'stud book' of the British peerage.

Debrett's makes no moral judgements about the people who are to be found within its covers. If you are a lord of the realm, then there is an entry for you. It is no surprise therefore that the history of the Lucan family can still be found there to this day. You will find no mention of dead nannies, nor arrest warrants for murder. Instead the learned guide satisfies itself with the simplest of entries about Richard John Bingham. It records: 'The seventh Earl has been missing since the night of 7 November 1974.'

Debrett's is, of course, for once in serious error. The seventh Earl has actually been missing only since 8 November 1974 – a whole day less than they calculate. He did not leave the Uckfield home of Susan Maxwell-Scott until around 1.15 am on the Friday morning following the murder. The last confirmed sighting of the Earl was as he drove down the driveway of Grants Hill House and out through the gates that led into Church Road, Uckfield. From that moment on his whereabouts have remained one of the great crime mysteries of our time.

Did he drive the car onwards to Newhaven? Or was he spirited away by rich and powerful friends and into a lifetime of hiding? Could the Corsair car have been driven down to the nearest coastal port as a so-far successful decoy operation?

Since the finding of the vehicle in Norman Road, the seventh Earl has apparently vanished from the face of the earth. This disappearing trick, worthy of Houdini in his prime, has prompted many to suggest that he may have chosen the ultimate escape route and taken his own life, rather than face the wrath of British justice. Certainly Lucan held no religious beliefs, which might have deterred a more God-fearing man from the path of suicide. Like his parents before him, he had been a committed agnostic for all of his adult life. He had no fears of hell-fire and damnation.

I have been asked about this life-or-death issue on very many occasions over the 20 years that I have been closely identified with the case. Until now I have kept my real opinions only to myself. In a series of newspaper interviews I have been reported as believing that Lucan was dead – but my statements were a carefully calculated ploy, to further the police investigation and to help in the capture of the wanted Earl.

The necessity for such subterfuge arose from the great changes that have taken place, over the past few decades, in the way in which newspapers report crime. In my early days with the Metropolitan Police Force, murders were of sufficient rarity to warrant considerable attention from Fleet Street. For weeks, and sometimes for months, the newspapers would maintain reporting teams on the case, and stories would continue to rumble on.

By the time of the Sandra Rivett murder, however, a great deal had changed. This most serious of crimes was, by then, not such a rarity at all. Some murder investigations would warrant barely a paragraph or two, on the inside pages, after the initial burst of publicity had passed.

Every experienced detective knows that the right form of publicity can be a vital weapon in the fight against crime. The investigating officers' task can be made a lot easier if they can enlist the help of the public. In this manner, vital witnesses can be encouraged to come forward and help build up the jigsaw of information that can lead to a successful conclusion.

In the case of Lord Lucan, we were initially swamped by the activities of the national newspapers' band of crime reporters. The case made headline news for several days, not only in Britain but also around the world. As a news story it was rivalled only by the November 1974 search for a mainland team of IRA bombers. The terrorists had set off a device in a Woolwich pub on the same night, at about the same time that nanny Sandra Rivett was dying at the hands of her killer.

Yet, after the first few days of headlines, I realized that something new would need to be done to keep the name of Lord Lucan, and the search for his whereabouts, at the forefront of the public's mind. The question of whether Lucan was alive or dead was of overwhelming importance to the popular press. Both I and my deputy, Detective Chief-Inspector David Gerring, were repeatedly asked our opinions. It seemed a golden opportunity to keep the publicity ball rolling and to keep public interest alive.

Accordingly, I hit on the ploy of taking a stance about the likelihood of Lucan having 'done the honourable thing' and fallen on his own sword. I decided on the option of death, and I told reporters that suicide was clearly the favoured course. Over the years, I became stuck with my chosen publicity-seeking option.

Many of Lucan's friends have also, publicly, stated that they believe him to be dead and gone. It would, of course, be a most convenient end to the saga for all concerned. No Lord – no body – no suspect – no trial. The truth is that I have always had considerable difficulty in accepting not only that Lucan would ever have committed suicide but also that he could commit the act in such a way that his body would never be found.

Around 30 to 40 unidentified dead bodies are found in Britain each year. They are buried in a paupers' grave, at public expense. Their only record of having passed from this life is a listing in the 'Unknown' section of the

Register of Births, Deaths and Marriages at St Catherine's House in London.

Many of the unidentifiable bodies are those of new-born babies, where no clue is ever found to the identity of the unfortunate mother; a number are down-and-outs from the streets of our major cities, long cut off from their families and known by only a first name to their fellow citizens of the streets; there are usually more men than women on the list each year.

Intensive efforts are made to put a name to every unknown corpse. Adult bodies are checked against the police records of those who are missing. The one thing of which we can be certain about this unfortunate flotsam and jetsam of modern-day life is that none of them has ever proved to be Richard John Bingham, the seventh Earl of Lucan.

The case for Lord Lucan having killed himself therefore rests on no more than guesswork and circumstantial evidence. Supporters of the suicide theory advance a number of arguments as to why the fugitive Lucan would have preferred to die. They point to the final letter that Lucan wrote in the few hours after his disappearance from Uckfield. The letter was posted, unstamped and from an unknown location, to his close friend, Michael Stoop. It was, in part, written in the past tense.

He told Stoop: 'When you come across my children, which I hope you will, please tell them that you knew me and that all I cared about was them.' A later section of the same letter continued: 'and I no longer care except that my children should be protected.'

It is entirely possible to read the Stoop letter as

the last words of a man determined to die. But death is by no means the only reason why he should have written such words. Lord Lucan was an intelligent man, who knew that the police would never close the file on the hunt for the killer of Mrs Rivett. He must, by then, have calculated that his only way of avoiding life imprisonment in a British jail was to run . . . and keep on running.

Even before the night of 7 November, Lucan had already failed to win custody of the children. They were in the care of their mother. Lucan must have known that, as a convicted killer, he had little chance of ever being allowed to see them again. For him, the children were already in the past tense – a part of his life he must abandon for ever in order to stay out of the hands of the law.

English law does make provision for cases in which a person has gone missing without any body ever being found. After seven years the closest relatives are entitled to apply for a High Court ruling that the missing person must now be presumed dead and his affairs wound up. It has thus been open to the Lucan family to apply for such a declaration of death at any time since the seventh anniversary in November 1981. They did not do so then and have never done so at any time in the 20 years since the Earl of Lucan's disappearance.

In the absence of any confirmed sighting of the Earl, any High Court ruling would certainly succeed, and the missing Lord's tangled estates could then be properly and completely wound up. Perhaps more importantly from the family's point of view, a presumption of death would make it possible for the heir to the earldom, Lucan's merchant-banker son Lord Bingham, to inherit his rightful title and take his seat in the House of Lords as the eighth Earl of Lucan. It is hard to understand why Lady Lucan or her children have not made such an application if they truly believe Lord Lucan to be dead.

Lucan's own friends and family appear evenly divided on whether or not his character would have led him to suicide. Many have claimed that he was an honourable man, from a family with a long history of honourable service to this country. They believe that, when facing these most extreme of circumstances, Lucky Lucan would have done 'the right thing'.

Others point to Lucan's behaviour in the months since he lost the custody battle for his children. He exhibited clear signs of depression, he drank more, he chain-smoked cigarettes, and his whole character became more subdued, introspective and unhappy. Surely, they say, good grounds for believing that despair would have led him to give up his life.

Yet another school of thought accepts Lord Lucan's guilt in the death of Sandra Rivett. He had set out to murder his wife but had found himself, unwittingly, responsible for the death of a totally innocent young girl. With the realization of what he had done, an honourable man like Lucan may well have felt he had no other choice but death before dishonour. Unfortunately, Lord Lucan was not an honourable man. Indeed, in all my years of studying Lord Lucan's character, I can think of no single fact that could ever support such a character reference. In every facet of his life, from school days onwards, any sensible observer would have to conclude that 'dishonourable' was a far more fitting description.

In his school days at Eton he let down his family and teachers by failing to live up to their genuine expectations of this intelligent young man. His lack of effort was even criticized by his own mother in later life. He wasted his silver-spoon opportunities with a gambling obsession, taking profits from the pockets of his schoolfriends. In his banking career, a pattern of deceit and dishonour continued unchecked. He lied to his employers, his colleagues, his friends and his family about his continuing gambling obsession. He lied about his losses. He even lied about his reasons for finally quitting the bank.

In the last few months before the events of November 1974 Lucan behaved dishonourably to his closest and dearest friends. On many occasions he called on their friendship to extract loans that he knew in his heart he could never have hoped to repay. And there was the woman who told me how she had felt abused by Lord Lucan, after an evening of flattery led to a request for more money. His own widowed mother opened her purse-strings to help finance his continuing lifestyle of indulgence and laziness. To all and sundry Lucan spoke of repaying his loans by the sale of the family silver. In truth he knew that the heirlooms he was selling would fetch less than a quarter of the money he owed.

Even in his married life, Lucan lied from the earliest days to his young and vulnerable wife Veronica. The lies were about money. When, as her children grew older, Veronica began to question his financial activities, he turned on her with a vicious and unrelenting campaign to brand her insane. In the end he turned to murder.

There have been times when I have been moved to anger at the platitudes and praise heaped upon Lucan by the very friends and relations whom he treated so badly. They have not, as I have, had to face the consequences of Lucan's murderous attack. Nobody who had ever seen the battered face and body of poor Sandra Rivett, laid out on a mortuary slab, could for one moment have thought of her killer as 'an honourable man'.

The suggestion that Lucan, having murdered the wrong woman, would kill himself from his own feelings of guilt and remorse fails to withstand close scrutiny. On the contrary, everything he did was calculated to keep him from justice, rather than carry him down the path of confession and sorrow.

When Lady Lucan appeared on the murder scene, her husband at once attacked her, landing blow after blow on her head with a length of lead piping. When she fought him to a standstill, his talk was not of the guilt at what he had done, but of ways of escaping retribution.

Lady Lucan recognized his character well when, in a desperate bid to save her own life, she gave her estranged husband the impression that she could help him. It was only upon this quick-thinking suggestion that Lord Lucan attempted, half-heartedly, to tend the terrible injuries he had already inflicted upon her. I believe the Earl would have killed her even then, and that Lady Lucan only saved her own life by seizing the first opportunity to flee from his clutches.

Lucan's subsequent flight from the house revealed a streak of self-preservation that overrode any other emotion. He abandoned his children, knowing full well that in the basement breakfast room was the terrible sight of the murdered nanny's body, bloodstained and dangling grotesquely from a sack. The basement staircase and the ground-floor walls were splattered and splashed with the blood of both Sandra and the Countess of Lucan.

In the top-floor bedroom were his three young children. Lord Lucan knew that the eldest child, Frances, was awake and had already faced the traumatic sight of her own mother covered in blood and crying with pain. What father, who professed to have risked all for the love of his children, could possibly have abandoned the youngsters alone in such a place? Surely, any 'honourable' man would have faced up to the consequences of his actions, rather than run the risk of his 10-year-old daughter, wandering downstairs in search of her mummy, coming across that terrible sight in the basement. What honour could there be in such an action?

The Earl's self-preservation instinct remained to the fore as he fled out of London to Uckfield. His telephone conversations with his mother, if her account is to be believed, revealed no trace of remorse. Instead, there was a garbled and incomplete account of a mystery assailant. At Grants Hill House, the lies were embroidered, with not the slightest hint that suicide was even an option. Why should it have been when Lucan was denying his guilt?

We have the assurance of Susan Maxwell-Scott that Lord Lucan was calm and controlled within hours of the murder. A little dishevelled, a little bloodstained, not quite his normal immaculately dressed self, but undoubtedly not a man on the verge of suicide through guilt and remorse. Indeed, having dealt quite quickly with the events at number 46, Lucan proceeded to drink up his whisky and chat for a while – about old times and mutual friends. Then: 'I must get back and sort this all out,' he told her.

In the letters to Bill Shand-Kydd, written on the night of the murder, Lucan once more trots out his alternative story, again with no hint of confession, nor apology. The correspondence reveals a man more worried for himself, and his financial future, than for the two women whom he knew had been desperately hurt. The second Shand-Kydd letter, in fact, concerned nothing other than money. It dealt with the repayment of his four demanding bank managers, pausing only to dismiss the dear friends and relations to whom he owed cash. 'The other creditors can get lost for the time being,' he said.

This letter, headed by Lucan 'Financial Matters', has always seemed to me yet another pointer that Lucan was very far from contemplating suicide. He specifically asked for the proceeds of the family silver sale to be used to repay his outstanding bank overdrafts. Lucan knew that the banks were losing patience with his debts and that he could face bankruptcy if action were not taken.

I believe that, if he had planned to take his own life, the last thing on his mind would be repaying the banks. A man on the edge of the precipice may think of many things – but not the NatWest and Midland banks! Would he not have left this final legacy to repay the personal loans to close and trusted friends, or to help the children he would be leaving behind?

A second factor comes into the equation when considering Lucan's fate. How could he have killed himself in such a way as to ensure that his body would never be found?

The first and most obvious answer is by drowning at sea. He had previously described how he had intended to murder his wife and dispose of her body in the busy shipping lanes of the Solent. 'I would never be caught,' he boasted.

Perhaps he did have access to a boat on the night he disappeared. Perhaps he did take it out to sea and jump off, having weighted himself down so that his body would never resurface. Perhaps he occupied the watery grave once intended for Veronica. Poetic justice indeed.

The drowning theory is, certainly, the chosen solution for many of Lucan's former friends and even for his wife, Lady Lucan. In a letter written to me in the spring of 1994, Lady Lucan explained that she now felt that his body rested at the bottom of the English Channel. 'My husband was a nobleman,' she said. 'Having failed to do what he set out to do, he would have taken his own life.'

The Countess's views are shared by some close friends, such as zoo owner and former casino boss, John Aspinall. In one of his rare interviews about the mystery, Aspinall was quoted in the *Sunday Independent* newspaper in January 1990 as being certain that Lucan was dead: 'Of course he's dead, he's at the bottom of the English Channel.'

Neither Lady Lucan nor John Aspinall are, of course, experts in the currents and vagaries of the English Channel and therein lies the problem with their theory. While the old adage, 'The sea gives up its dead,' may not be universally true, it is undoubtedly true for the

English Channel off the coast around Newhaven.

To establish the true likelihood of Lady Lucan's suggestion I went to the real experts, to men who have spent their entire lives dealing with the sea – and in particular the sea near Newhaven where Lucan's car was abandoned. I found universal scepticism about the possibility that the Earl could have met his end in that way.

Bob Domin knows the sea better than anybody. He also has the strongest qualifications for knowing exactly how bodies behave in the water – because he acts as an undertaker for people who wish to be buried at sea. He has been working on his tug for more than 21 years, since before Lord Lucan disappeared, and in each of those years has been involved in an average of five sea burials a year. He told me that the demand for burials at sea was far higher than that figure, but that the practice was actively discouraged by the Ministry of Agriculture, Fisheries and Food and was also an expensive form of funeral.

In the English Channel, not far off the coast of Newhaven, is one of several maritime areas where such funerals take place. Twenty years after the Lucan disappearance I went out to sea with Bob Domin to try and solve, once and for all, the mystery of whether he could be resting in a watery grave. Bob Domin's description of the practical mechanics of burial at sea appeared to rule out that possibility.

The popular Lucan suicide myth is that he had a boat waiting to dispose of Veronica's body, or hopped on the cross-Channel ferry and jumped off unseen. In either case the scenario requires him to have had some convenient way of weighting himself down to sink below the waves.

The first revelation from Bob was to make nonsense of such suggestions. He told me of the amount of weight that Lucan would have needed to secure to his body, in order to ensure that he sank beneath the waves of the Channel. Bob revealed that as much as three hundred-weight of ballast needs to be securely attached to a corpse to be certain that it sinks to the bottom. Anything less, and, sooner or later, that body will rise up to the surface.

Further research revealed that in recent years there have indeed been been a number of unfortunate cases where weights in the burial shrouds of bodies committed to the deep have become detached or proved insufficient to keep the body down. With the growth in popularity of burials at sea, such incidents of corpses floating along the English Channel have given rise to protests about this bizarre form of environmental pollution.

As Bob pointed out: 'For Lucan to have drowned, without his body washing ashore or being found floating at sea, he would have needed a massive amount of weight.

'Such weights would have been too heavy for the man to walk to the edge of a ferry and throw himself off. And even on his own small boat, how would he have fixed such weights to his body in such a way that they stayed secure for long enough to anchor the body to the bottom?

'In this part of the Channel the tides and currents push the body eastwards, that's up the Channel, and this means that in 99 cases out of 100 the body will be washed up somewhere.

'The likelihood of Lord Lucan throwing himself over the side of a ferry or another boat and disappearing would be very remote. It doesn't make any difference how far out to sea he did it, he would still go east and be washed up on a beach.

'With our burials at sea, we go to extraordinary lengths to ensure that the body is safely buried and stays on the seabed until nature completes its work.'

Mr Domin was equally sceptical about another Lucan myth – that, had Lucan chosen to end his life in this way, crabs and other marine life would have disposed of the remains within days. He confirmed that bodies were disposed of in this way – but only if they are securely anchored to the seabed. Otherwise they float to the surface, and decomposition is a far lengthier process.

'Someone who's thrown himself into the water would float,' he said. 'Crabs, prawns, all crustaceans, are bottom feeders. They are not free swimming, and there's no way that a crab would attack a body that's free floating on the surface or some way below the surface. Fish would not do the same job either – the body comes ashore, and the sea does always give up its dead.'

It was hard to see how Lucan, running from the scene of a murder, could have produced, from nowhere, the convenient weights to solve his burial problem and keep him on the bottom. Even then, his resting-place would, most likely, have been disturbed. The entire area is also heavily trawled by local fishermen, whose equipment would be liable to disturb any weighted corpse. For that very reason specified areas of the seabed are designated as burial grounds to warn fishermen away.

In 1974, at the time of the murder, I had been

told by local fishermen that corpses were sometimes trawled up in their nets. They claimed then that, to avoid their catch being condemned, a body would sometimes be punctured and sent back to the bottom. This myth, too, was dismissed by the man I was to meet in Newhaven 20 years later.

Mr Domin told me that fishermen were so superstitious that they would have nothing whatsoever to do with any body found at sea. Rather than have any contact they would simply note the position in which the body had been found and invariably report it to the coastguard for recovery.

Putting aside for the moment the problems of burial at sea, I turned to the practicalities of how Lucan would have got himself into the water. Simply walking into the sea, or jumping from the sea front, would never have worked. Certainly, Lucan could have drowned himself in this way, swimming outwards until he could swim no more, but his body would never have sunk. Local experts were convinced that any person drowned in this manner would have been washed ashore within days.

The currents in the area are such that the coastline below Beachy Head is a favoured resting-point. Considering that I had arranged a detailed and thorough search of the entire coastline in 1974, and that this is a heavily populated and popularly walked stretch of the coast of southern England, the idea of the body being undiscovered seemed implausible. Even Robert Maxwell's corpse had turned up, floating serenely along in the Atlantic, several days after he jumped off his boat near the Canary Islands in the 1990s.

That left two sensible options. The ferry, or a

private boat. Both seemed unlikely. To believe in the idea of drowning from the ferry you have to stretch possibilities to the utmost. First, Lucan had to board the ferry in Newhaven Docks, unseen.

He was a distinctive, tall and haughty man of aristocratic bearing. He had a most noticeable, brown and ginger-flecked moustache, and, even if he had somehow shaved in the few hours since leaving Susan Maxwell-Scott's home, the mark of the moustache would have remained lily-white on his face. He had, after all, worn the moustache for his entire adult life. On top of all this, there is no indication that Lucan had anything other than light, casual clothes, which left him ridiculously dressed for the terrible weather. Susan Maxwell-Scott confirmed that he was dressed in this way when he arrived at her home and denied completely that she had helped him with any change of clothing.

Despite the most extensive inquiries, nobody was ever found who had seen a man dressed in this manner anywhere near the docks on the morning that the car was abandoned in nearby Norman Road. It was hardly as if he could have slipped abroad, unnoticed in a crowd of day-trippers. The first morning sailing to Dieppe on a wet and windy November morning does not attract a holiday crowd. Lucan would have stuck out like a sore thumb.

The small boat theory is no more attractive. In all the original inquiries I had come across no suggestion that Lucan owned, or had the legitimate use of, any boat whatsoever. No boats were missing along the south coast, and, despite the extensive publicity, nobody ever came forward to report that their craft had been taken, or tampered with, that night.

But what if Lucan had been lent a boat by a friend? Leaving aside the intriguing thought of a murder accomplice, could he have sailed such a boat out to sea? The answer is almost certainly, No. Just after the murder I obtained a most detailed weather report from the Newhaven coastguards. Their operational logbook for the morning of 8 November 1974 read:

> Wind varied from south to south-west, force 4 but at times varying to force 7/8. Moderate swell, visibility fairly good, overcast with mist and drizzle at times.

The coastguards told me that the strongest, force seven and eight, winds that night were considered to be 'gale conditions'. They believed that the weather was too severe for any small boat. The coastguard station officer said: 'We would have been most concerned if any motorcraft had left the harbour in winds like this, of force four or more.'

Years later Mr Dobbin looked up his own logbook to confirm the weather of that day. He told me: 'It was very bad weather, in fact the cargo ferry the *Capitain de Gough* actually cancelled her sailing. The weather was foul.' He was convinced that there was no chance that Lord Lucan could have left the shore that night in any small boat.

These later inquiries also made it clear that, even in the early hours of the Friday morning, the fugitive Earl would not have been able to slip out to sea in any craft. A spokesman for the harbour authorities told me that all shipping movements are faithfully recorded at the Newhaven West Pier, and that no small craft could have slipped out unnoticed in these severe weather conditions.

His view was backed up by Domin who told me: 'At Newhaven in particular all of the regulations have always been very strictly followed. The West Pier is manned 24 hours a day and 7 days a week by very experienced and responsible people. Every movement is logged – both in and out of this harbour.'

The more I looked into the matter, the more I found the drowning theory impossible to credit. If Lucan is not at the bottom of the English Channel, as so many of his family and friends have told me, how could he have killed himself in such a way that his body has never been found?

In the aftermath of his disappearance there were newspaper suggestions that the suicide could have been committed with Lord Lucan's own matching pair of expensive shotguns. Unfortunately for this theory the guns were discovered stored at Lucan's London gun-smiths and were later purchased from the bankruptcy trustee by the Earl's brother-in-law, Bill Shand-Kydd.

Again, at the time of the murder, it had been suggested that Lucan could have concealed his body by crawling into one of the substantial gorse patches that grow across the nearby Downs. As time has gone by, it has become less and less likely that such a hiding-place could have concealed his dead body for almost 20 years.

My conviction that Lucan would have found it impossible to commit suicide in such a way that his body could never be found was strengthened in the summer of 1994, when I discussed the case with one of Britain's leading pathologists, Professor Peter Vanezis, the man who runs Britain's busiest pathology department, based in Glasgow. Professor Vanezis, acknowledged by his peers as one of the greatest experts in his field, was as sceptical as I am about the suicide theories.

He told me: 'In salt water, such as the English Channel, it is hard to conceive of any situation in which a body would not be washed ashore on one of the Channel beaches within a relatively short time of entering the water. The gases created by the decomposition of the body would most certainly cause the remains to float.

'It is possible that if he had tied something around his arms or his legs, then those individual limbs could have become detached from the torso, but the bulk of the remains would inevitably come to the surface. Once there they float until being washed ashore.'

Professor Vanezis, with a lifetime of experience in investigating many thousands of suspicious and unusual deaths, told me that disposing of the human body is an immensely difficult task. In time only a skeleton will be left, and the bones themselves will always remain. There are often cases where foxes or other animals will have disturbed the bones, so that they can be found some distance away from other remains.

'Bodies are just so hard to get rid of,' he said. 'Short of grinding the bones into dust, there is very little that can successfully hide them away.'

There was a time in the 1970s when the suicide theory could have been believed. After meeting with the marine experts and coastguards of Newhaven, and finally with Peter Vanezis, I now firmly believe that suggestions of Lucan's death have simply provided a convenient full stop to the mystery for the very many people who would wish Lucan an undisturbed, secret and secluded future life.

CHAPTER 17

SIGHTINGS, HOAXES AND PSYCHICS

If Lord Lucan was, as I now believe, alive after his car was found in November 1974, where could he possibly have hidden from the massive worldwide search? Surely his distinctive features would have marked him out and led to an immediate capture? There were, indeed, many hundreds of sightings of the missing Earl. The problem was that there never really was the accompanying 'world-wide hunt' to follow them up. Lack of resources meant that the incident room was soon swamped with scores of potential Lucan locations. The team became dependent upon officers from other forces, and sometimes even outside agencies such as journalists, to follow up many leads.

In the weeks after the murder, information flooded into my office from all over the world. I received letters, often anonymous, from clairvoyants, mediums, diviners, dowsers, people who believed they had extraordinary sensory perception and cranks of every description. Very many were not worth bothering with, such as the anonymous note revealing that Lucan could be found 'near a railway line in Canada'! Or the Scottish medium who repeatedly boasted of knowing his whereabouts, and then came out with the dire – and thankfully erroneous – warning that I had terminal cancer and should seek immediate medical aid. That was ten years ago, and she never wrote again.

Others, from more reliable sources, had to be checked out as best we could. The information I received from Interpol, in June 1975, fell into this category and suggested that our wanted man could have been staying in France. A female hotelier in Cherbourg had reported to local police that a man answering the description of Lord Lucan had stayed at her hotel several times in recent months. One of the visits had been but a few weeks before. Because of the possibility, however slender, that Lucan could have escaped on a cross-Channel ferry, I knew it was essential to follow up this fresh lead fully as soon as I could.

Arrangements needed to be made, through diplomatic channels, for British police officers to carry out investigations abroad but, eventually, Dave Gerring and I set sail from Southampton to Cherbourg. Accompanied by a woman interpreter, we went to the local police station, where we were welcomed with almost too open arms and introduced to everybody from the office cleaner to the chief of police. Then followed an invitation we could not refuse, to celebrate the retirement of one of the Cherbourg force. At the party there was yet another round of introductions, this time to the mayor and assorted local dignitaries.

At last, with the formalities concluded, we booked into the Grand Hotel, where Lucan was reported to have stayed. We were still not permitted to interview the hotelier, Mme Guilpan, or her staff, until all of the paperwork had been completed to authorize our investigations on French soil. The following day we went to court and, after not a little difficulty, were allocated a French detective inspector as our minder. Local law required that the unfortunate officer had to carry a portable typewriter around with him everywhere we went, to take statements from anyone who might be able to assist our inquiry.

Madame Guilpan and members of her staff were interviewed and identified our various photographs of Lucan as the man who had stayed at the hotel on several occasions. I worried, however, that they described the suspect as speaking fluent French, while Lucan's grasp of the language was poor. We examined room 22 in which he had stayed, although in such a public place there was little hope of obtaining fingerprints or any other conclusive evidence.

Everywhere we went we were followed by newspaper journalists and television crews. Many of the local hoteliers saw this as a good opportunity to get some free publicity, so other reports of Lucan soon came flooding in.

While in Cherbourg, the ocean liner *Queen Elizabeth 2* docked in the port, and we took the opportunity of extending our investigation on board. We were given a conducted tour of the ship and replenished our stock of cigarettes and whisky to thank the French police who were helping us. The visit also gained us some publicity in the luxury liner's own newspaper. Because we still had further inquiries to make, we were reluctantly forced to decline the Captain's offer of a fast lift back to Southampton.

There had been other reported sightings of Lucan in nearby St Malo, and, in view of Lucan's gambling reputation, we interviewed staff at the local casino. Once again the effort proved fruitless. No trace could be found of our missing Lord. After a week abroad, Dave Gerring and I returned to England, satisfied that the Lucan look-alike in Normandy was unlikely to have been our lordship.

Another notable sighting, that was clearly worthy of further investigation, was one of many I received from prisoners in British jails. In November 1975, a Spanish national, who was remanded in a London prison for assault with intent to rob, contacted police and asked to see the officer in charge of the Lucan inquiry. He told me that, in April of that year, he had been in Colombia, South America, and believed he had met Lucan.

With a friend, he was driving between Villavicencio and San Martín, about 100 kilometres from Bogotá, when they met three people stranded with a broken-down car. His friend recognized one of the men as an American he knew, while the others were a Spaniard and a well-spoken Englishman. They all had a meal together and then offered the stranded group a lift to a nearby hacienda. In the house, situated off the main highway in an area known as San Lucia, they all had drinks, except for the Englishman.

My informant may best be described as an international thief, who took the view that in life he should miss no opportunity to make money. He was curious as to the true identity of the Englishman, whom he described as being as out of place as 'an eskimo in Piccadilly Circus'. He guessed that the Englishman was probably a man on the run.

It was another credible tale, but the problem remained of how to check out the information. I knew that corruption was rife in Colombia and had been warned that the American had considerable local influence. Via the Foreign and Commonwealth Office, a report was forwarded to the Colombian authorities, but nothing came back.

I knew that Scotland Yard resources would never stretch to sending me out to Colombia to conduct my own inquiries, but it was worthy of investigation. The answer was to leak the story to a friendly journalist, in this case Owen Summers of the *Daily Express*, in the hope that he could take the matter further. At great personal risk Owen duly visited Colombia and spent a hair-raising few days checking out information supplied by the Spanish informant. Owen identified the man as a 'Mr John' and eventually tracked him down to his own home in Colombia. Disappointingly, 'Mr John' turned out to be an innocent American businessman, who bore a startling resemblance to Lord Lucan. The *Daily Express* got a good story from the escapade, but it took me no nearer to finding the missing Earl.

Among other sightings were two notable leads from Australia. One resulted in the arrest and detention of an innocent English boilermaker who had emigrated down under from his home in Essex. The other caught a totally different fish. This was John Stonehouse, the British former parliamentary minister, who faked his own suicide from an Australian beach and fled to escape fraud charges building up against him in Britain.

Stonehouse made good his escape but left behind him not only his clothes on the beach but also a large number of suspicious creditors and police investigators. Their suspicions were confirmed when a keen Australian policeman arrested a man whom he thought resembled the missing Lord Lucan. Once again, I was disappointed when the suspect turned out to be not my Earl but the back-from-the-dead politician.

Over the years since Lucan disappeared, the police have had to contend with deliberate hoaxes, as well as the many cases of mistaken identity. The hoaxes have ranged from small-time joke telephone calls, through to major attempts fraudulently to extract money by false pretences.

On the night of 26 January 1975, Susan Maxwell-Scott was herself the victim of a fraudster when she received a hoax telegram purporting to come from Lord Lucan. It had been read to her over the telephone by somebody claiming to be a General Post Office operator. The supposed message read: TELL MOTHER ALL WENT AS PLANNED. I AM SAFE HERE, JOHN. The following day the telegraph office at Brighton was unable to confirm that such a telegram had ever existed, and my own inquiries showed this to have been yet another hoax.

A more serious case happened in early September 1982, while I was working as an investigator with the BBC. News came in alleging that the missing Earl had been found, in South America, by the notorious British adventurer and bounty hunter, John Miller. What made this story different was that the man claiming to have tracked down Lucan did have a track record of capturing fugitives from British justice.

Two years earlier, he had led an expedition of mercenaries to Brazil, where he succeeded in kidnapping the Great Train Robber, Ronnie Biggs. After being on the run for many years, Biggs was spirited off to Barbados, where his captor, Miller, planned to have him extradited back to Britain to serve out the remainder of his 30-year jail sentence.

Biggs, however, won a legal battle against extradition and, once again, defeated police efforts to return him to his prison cell. He eventually won the right to return to Brazil, where he is still at liberty.

Despite his failure to get Biggs back to Britain, John Miller, an ex-soldier who claimed to have been trained with the Special Air Service (SAS), made a substantial sum out of selling his story. He revealed how he had kidnapped Biggs from a Rio de Janeiro restaurant, flown him across Brazil in a chartered jet and sailed the captive robber to Barbados on a private yacht.

Miller was the boss of a private security agency based in London, and, at the time of the Biggs kidnapping, he boasted to reporters that Lucan would be his next bounty-hunting target.

The news editors of Fleet Street knew that Miller was a Walter Mitty character but, having once been proved wrong by doubting the truth of the Biggs story, they could not afford to miss out on the finding of Lord Lucan. When Miller, a Scotsman, telephoned a reporter on a Scottish newspaper claiming he had captured Lord Lucan, word soon leaked out and the world's press descended on his Trinidad hotel.

Within hours, I was telephoned by reporters seeking my opinion on the case. I told them immediately that I had not the slightest doubt that the story was a fake. As I pointed out at the time, you could see Lord Lucan's look-alikes on any street in London, and nothing about this particular story rang true to me.

Despite my protestations, and an official denial of any involvement from my colleagues at Scotland Yard, Miller played out his part to the full for days to come. Gradually he released more details of Lucan's supposed existence during eight years on the run.

The Earl was allegedly living in relative poverty, in a small shack in a small South American village. He had adopted the persona of an upper-class German and was using a forged German passport. Lucan was lonely, frightened and fed up with running. He wanted to go home and face trial. Perhaps most startlingly of all, Lucan claimed to be both innocent of the murder of Sandra Rivett and to know who the real killer was – a hired hit man who had himself died a few years before. I was amused to see that, perhaps not surprisingly, there was no explanation as to why anybody would have wanted to hire a hit man to kill Sandra Rivett.

More nonsense followed as Miller insisted that Lucan was under armed guard in a Venezuelan village. He insisted that he had sent pictures of the runaway to 'establishment sources' in London. They would soon confirm Lord Lucan's identity. At his Port of Spain hotel Miller received telex messages back from London and showed them to eager journalists as proof that his story was true.

Even the most gullible reporters began to smell a rat, however, when it was revealed that Miller had been dictating telex messages to himself. The forms had been given to hotel staff, with instructions to deliver the messages at the most dramatic and public moments. Miller finally flew off to Florida leaving the unsolved mystery behind him and with no financial reward for his efforts. Once there, he teamed up with another eccentric British exile to make one last attempt at convincing the world that he knew of Lucan's whereabouts. This time his chosen victims were from the world of television.

The man with whom Miller now joined forces in Florida was Colin Harrington, also known as Colin Levy. He was the former husband of Norma Levy, the prostitute at the centre of the sex scandal, which, many years before, had forced Tory minister Lord Lambton to resign.

The two adventurers now plotted a hoax that was to find its way on to British television screens. ITN reporter John Suchet, despite his own healthy scepticism, was persuaded to take a boat trip with Miller for a supposed rendezvous with Lucan at the deserted jungle island of Pumpkin Key, 30 miles off the coast of Miami. In front of the television camera Miller and his accomplices then played out an elaborate charade. A boat, allegedly carrying Lucan, arrived on the beach. A man got out and walked towards the cameras.

Suddenly, before 'Lucky' drew near enough for positive identification, all hell broke loose on the darkened foreshore. Bullets began to fly, people started running in all directions, and everybody fled for cover. Miller, the man who had set up the operation, was convincingly shot and claimed to have survived only because he was wearing a bullet-proof jacket.

Suchet and ITN maintained all along that they had never believed in the Miller story but had simply wanted to settle the matter one way or the other. They did, however, admit that they had paid out $4000 'expenses' to Miller for arranging the Lucan meeting.

It was just days after the action-packed film was shown on British television screens that reporter Trevor Kempson exposed the entire episode as a hoax. In the *News of the World* newspaper he revealed that the fake Lucan had been a former drugs dealer, paid a few hundred dollars to act out the part.

Even Miller's shooting had been just another stunt to lend authenticity to the sting. The con man had worn a flak jacket, into which a bullet had previously been fired at close range. Then, at the right dramatic moment in the farce on the beach, he had faked the shooting, to be duly saved by the much damaged jacket. Yet another Lucan myth had been exposed.

A far more intriguing and, I believe, genuine story did remain among my personal notes for many years, the details of which had been known to me since 1974. This time it was not a sighting, but more of a sounding. Like so many other minor facts, however, it was not recognized as significant until two decades later, when I at last linked up everything I knew about Lucan with the aid of a computer.

The story originated with the owner of a small

guest-house in Sussex. Just a few nights after the murder, she received a call from a 'posh'-sounding man seeking accommodation. The house was at Henfield, just a few miles away from Newhaven, and the call came on the weekend that Lucan's getaway car was found abandoned in the town.

Something indefinable, but odd, about the man's manner made the woman owner remember their conversation. When she later saw publicity about the possibility of Lucan having escaped via the south coast, she called her local police. She reported that the caller had spoken with a mature and cultured voice. He explained that he had found her number from Yellow Pages. He gave his name as 'Mr Charles' and asked if she had any vacancies for that night.

The owner apologized and said that her house was full but offered to recommend the name of a good local hotel. Mr Charles declined. He definitely did not want a hotel, just something small and quiet – like her guest-house. She then recommended another similar establishment in the locality and asked where he was, so that she might offer him directions. At this point, Mr Charles became vague and ended the conversation by saying only that he was, 'near Brighton', some eight miles away.

There was, on the face of it, nothing to distinguish this report from any of the hundreds of others I received at that time. It was not until many years later that my computer program picked out the one potentially important link that could not have been known at the time by either the woman owner, or the policeman who investigated her story.

For the connection was the name of the guest-house

concerned – Horton Hall. It was the same name as the country estate owned by the Shand-Kydd family; the house where Lucan had often sought refuge, and where he had spent most weekends for the past year, playing happily with his children on their access visits. An odd coincidence, yet again? Or could it be that the mystery caller was Lord Lucan, perhaps alone, and seeking a quiet resting-place to consider his next move? What more natural for a man, hunting through the Yellow Pages, than to be attracted by the advertisement with a name so reminiscent of his recent, and far happier, past.

Another 'sound sighting' – perhaps the most frustrating of all – came from Norman Road, Newhaven, where the Corsair car was abandoned with its treasure trove of clues still locked in the boot. The vehicle had been parked almost directly opposite a house owned by local resident Reginald Sims. He and his wife Phyllis had helped me greatly, in November 1974, by remembering the time that they first noticed the Corsair in the street.

I recall that Mr Sims, a shipping clerk, had later investigated the car further. He noticed that the interior was dirty and that the tax disc had fallen off on to the floor. Trying the car doors and the boot, he had found them to be locked. It was not until 1994 that I spoke to Reginald again and found that he still remembered the weekend well, from 20 years ago.

'There was one thing I never did think to mention to you at the time,' he said. 'Earlier that morning I was half-woken up by a noise from the road outside. I don't know what time it was – but I do know it was earlier than I would normally have woken.

'I remember thinking it was odd, but then it could have been the milkman. I almost got out of bed and went to the window to look; but in the end I slipped off back to sleep. I wish I had looked now – I might have seen Lord Lucan.'

Despite my promptings Reginald could, understandably, give me no further details of his early-morning alarm. We mused together on what it might have been. A curious peep from his window would have given me the answer to one of the central mysteries of the Lucan inquiry. Was it Lucan who parked the car in Norman Road? Was he alone? Or with companions and a second car to whisk him to safety? Or was it a friend planting a decoy? So near to the answers – and yet so far.

CHAPTER 18

THE RUNAWAY EARL

Of all the baffling mysteries that surround the Lucan case, none is so intriguing as the central question of 'Where Is He Now?' I believe Lord Lucan to be alive; I believe him to be guilty of murder; and I believe that I now know where he could have been for much of the two decades since he drove out through the gates of Grants Hill House in Uckfield.

It was nearly 20 years after the murder that I once again began a serious investigation into the likely whereabouts of the seventh Earl of Lucan. My first step was to re-examine my original inquiry and relate the moves I made then to the mass of further evidence, collected over the intervening years.

Thinking back to 1974, I recognized that Scotland Yard had never been able to provide the resources that would have been needed for Lord Lucan to be found.

The Lucan inquiry was an important case for the London police force. It was not, however, one upon which the powers-that-be really were able to spend much extra time or money. From the start my superiors accepted my interpretation of the case – that Lord Lucan was the perpetrator of the crime. They also knew just how much work would be required to bring him to justice.

It was clear that, having failed to murder his wife, Lord Lucan would be most unlikely to murder again. When I sought extra manpower, or the resources to check out properly the hundreds of sightings that had poured in about the missing Earl, I came up against an establishment brick wall. It was not that there was any political pressure to slow down on the case – but nobody was going to invest in the lavish resources necessary to catch one non-dangerous killer, however aristocratic and important he might be.

In theory, no unsolved murder case is ever closed by Scotland Yard. The file remains open, passing from hand to hand through the years until such time as the killer is caught, or any possible participants must surely be dead. In practice, however, it is rarely long before the files are consigned to the archives. There the case lives on in little but name alone.

So it was with the Lucan investigation. Within weeks, or certainly months, of the murder I was required to transfer much of my time back to the normal, heavy workload of a senior London detective. Crime elsewhere in my 'A' division had not ceased because of the Lucan case, and it all remained my responsibility.

Before too long the Lucan office was reduced to a few junior officers, logging potential sightings or any new evidence, but with no resources to search out the executor of this deadly attack. I was determined to keep the case active for as long as possible, and indeed I stayed on beyond my normal retirement target because of the case – but no senior officer could expect to be allowed the time or the money to go and travel the world looking for Lucan.

Perhaps the official police attitude to the Lucan inquiry in 1994 is best summed up by their reaction to the press and public interest stirred up once again by its twentieth anniversary. No senior Scotland Yard officer, even the Detective Chief-Superintendent nominally in charge, was willing to meet with reporters inquiring into the case. The Metropolitan Police press bureau, responsible among other things for generating publicity that might help police inquiries, was anxious to play down the matter of Lucan.

In the absence of any official police effort to track down a man whom I have always regarded as a vicious and cold-blooded killer, I set out on an investigation of my own. In years gone by, the media had eagerly portrayed the Lucan search as a massive 'world-wide manhunt' and talked of 'Interpol Red Alerts'. In truth there had been an Interpol Red Alert – but the reality is a little less glamorous than the phraseology would suggest.

The Interpol offices in Paris employ no investigators of their own. They act simply as a clearing-house for information, passing on messages and requests for help from member police forces.

The message about Lucan was, for a while, of paramount importance and would have reached the offices of police forces in member states all over the world. Such despatches are, however, released every day from Interpol, with each quickly superseding the last. While Lucan may at first have sat on the top of an Interpol pile, his picture and description fell quickly to the bottom of a dusty heap of paper.

It seemed to me that the first priority was to retrace my steps and discover what clues might have been missed all those many years ago. Computers are now the life-blood of any modern murder inquiry but were unknown in the police murder incident rooms of the early 1970s. Perhaps computer technology would, even now, offer a lead I could follow?

The power now at hand in the modern, desktop computer dwarfs even that of the few networked systems that would have been available within the British police service at the time of the murder. Over a period of many months I set out to feed every fact that I knew about Lucan into just such a computer. Details from my own memory, from recent interviews with witnesses in the case and from the hundreds of thousands of printed words in newspapers of the past two decades, all found a place in my database system.

The computer program was then asked to cross-reference the thousands of names, descriptions and facts that were stored in its memory. The results were startling. An astonishing number of coincidences were revealed for the first time by linking up such disparate information from hundreds of sources. Names that, at first, had meant little in isolation now jumped out from the pages of the computer print-out as it unfolded before me.

Patterns of people and places and behaviour began to emerge. In particular, a significant number of otherwise unrelated incidents focused my attention on one tiny spot on the map in a remote and distant African country. Remarkably, reports from diverse sources, separated in both distance and time from each other, all appeared to lead inexorably back to this area. Excited by the prospect of uncovering something new, I reached out for my atlas and eagerly turned to the relevant map. Could Lucan really be there? Or rather, had he been there in past years, as my computer program now appeared to reveal?

The Lord Lucan murder inquiry had taken statements from hundreds of people and collected tens-of-thousands of facts. My own personal notes had covered many hundreds of pages. My library of newspaper cuttings had more than 500 entries. Now I began reviewing the interconnections that my computer had uncovered.

It was a journey of discovery that was to take me many thousands of miles, through several different countries, over the months to come. It started, however, far closer to home, with the long-forgotten story of a prisoner I had met in a British jail cell.

The name of which the computer had reminded me was that of Dr Brian Sandford Hill. He had been a doctor, a general practitioner, who had fallen foul of the law on charges of false representation in a mortgage fraud. While on remand in Cardiff jail, the doctor approached another medical man, the senior orderly in the small prison hospital, to seek his advice. Dr Hill said he knew the whereabouts of the missing Lord Lucan but was agonizing over whether he should report this to the police. Lucan was clearly a professional gentleman, and it did not feel right for one professional to report on another.

Hill had very little choice in the matter, for his story was reported, at once, by the hospital orderly to the governor of Cardiff prison. In June 1975, a few days after the inquest into the death of Sandra Rivett, I received a report from the governor, David Morrison. He told me that prisoner Hill, Brian Sandford, had recently been in Africa and believed he had met Lord Lucan there.

I was soon on my way to the prison. At my meeting with Dr Hill I was impressed to find that he was seeking no favours from me. He firmly believed, wrongly as it was to turn out, that he would be cleared at his forthcoming trial and had no need of my help.

Despite this, Hill recounted how, until April 1975, he had been working on a 12-month contract in Swaziland in southern Africa. For his return journey to Britain he travelled by land-rover, from Swaziland to Lourenço Marques, now Maputo, in Mozambique, where he intended to catch a boat back to the United Kingdom.

When he reached the Mozambique border, Hill was stopped at gunpoint by Front for the Liberation of Mozambique (FRELIMO) troops, who searched his baggage. He had his bulldog with him who did not like the soldiers, and Hill was naturally scared when he saw their fingers tighten on the triggers. The doctor got out his stethoscope to show them that he was a medical man. In all, he was stopped 17 times between the border and Lourenço Marques but each time got through safely with the help of his medical mime.

Hill reached Lourenco Marques at about midday in a shocked and exhausted state. He planned to book into the Polono Hotel, the best accommodation in town. Wanting to exercise his dog and have a drink, he walked into the town centre, where he then sat at a table in the Pereri restaurant and ordered some wine. He was joined, almost immediately, by an English man and a Portuguese woman. The man said how delighted he was to hear an English voice, and they talked about a wide range of subjects, including the tense political pre-Independence state of Lourenço Marques.

The stranger gave his own name as James and introduced the woman as Maria. The couple had a frightening story to tell. The previous night FRELIMO troops had searched the flat above their own accommodation, whose occupants had been arrested and taken away. They admitted they were frightened and were planning to leave Mozambique within a few days. James asked Dr Hill if, meanwhile, he would book Maria into the Polono as his wife. He was prepared to sleep on the floor and even hinted that Maria would have sex with the doctor in return for his help.

Dr Hill did book himself and Maria into the hotel, as Mr and Mrs Brian Hill, and avoided producing his passport. James and Maria went out all afternoon, while Hill caught up with some much needed sleep. In the evening James suggested that he and the doctor should go out for a drink. Maria pleaded tiredness and said she did not want to join them.

The two men set off on a drinking spree around the dingy clubs and bars of Lourenço Marques. As they moved from bar to bar, they gradually became more and more drunk. Dr Hill was speaking of how glad he was to be going back to Britain, when his drinking companion suddenly burst into tears. James said he had three children but could never return to England and see them. Taken aback by the outburst, Dr Hill suggested that James could come back to England with him. He was unprepared for the answer. 'I can't – I'm Lord Lucan,' his companion replied.

This declaration meant little to Dr Hill. 'So what?' he retorted. 'I'm Brian Hill. What's stopping you?'

The tearful James explained that he had tried to kill his own wife and was wanted for murdering his children's nanny. He was surprised that Hill had never seen the worldwide publicity but accepted that the doctor had seen no English papers during his entire year in Africa.

Over more drinks the fugitive explained that he had escaped from Britain to Lisbon and had then travelled on to Lourenço Marques.

Both men eventually walked back to the hotel and the next morning Maria asked Hill to drive her, alone, to the airport. That same afternoon he and James walked into town and went into a barber-shop for a haircut. Dr Hill remembered that the shop had about seven barbers. They then had a few drinks and went back to the Polono Hotel in the mid-afternoon.

From that point onwards James became more jittery and said that he was expecting an important telephone call, which would arrive in Hill's name. Shortly afterwards the hotel receptionist paged Hill to the phone, where he spoke briefly to a caller who sounded as though he were an educated African. The man asked for James, who then spent 20 minutes talking on the phone.

That evening Hill and James again went out for

drinks, but at 11 pm James asked if they could go back to the hotel. He explained that he was expecting to be picked up from there around midnight. Back at the Polono, Hill took his dog for a walk and, on returning to the foyer at around 11.45 pm, saw James in the company of a young woman. Hill told me that, by now, he was fascinated with James's mysterious life and began chatting to the woman, hoping to learn more about the situation. Introduced as Mary, she revealed that she had met James in England, where she was studying at the London School of Economics.

Before Hill could find out more, a black Mercedes drew up outside. The driver of the car was a black man, and Maria, the woman whom Hill had first met with James, was sitting in the passenger seat. Explaining that he had to leave because Mary was his passport through various border controls, James said goodbye to Hill, giving him a last piece of advice: Dr Hill should book out of the Polona Hotel. Hill duly moved to a three-star hotel some 400 yards away.

I was impressed by the detail that Hill was able to recall in telling his story and showed him a number of photographs of the missing Lord Lucan. Hill was adamant that James and Lord Lucan were one and the same man.

At the end of my visit Dr Hill said he did not want to tell me anything about Lord Lucan's intended final destination. I was unable to persuade him to change his mind about this central point. I thanked him, anyway, for the help he had given and said my goodbyes. When I reached the front gate of Cardiff prison, there was a message asking me to return and speak further to Hill.

I found that Hill had decided to tell me all he knew.

'Take my word as a gentleman,' he said. 'No, I'm sorry, I can't expect you to do that. Take my word as a doctor; that man I saw in Lourenço Marques was Lord Lucan.

'I really want to help you all I can. James was taken in the Mercedes car through Tanganyika [Tanzania] and into Kenya, where he went to a farm. That's all I know.'

I left the prison thinking Dr Hill's story worthy of further investigation, and messages were sent to police in both Tanganyika and Kenya. I could not hold out much hope that they would find any trace of an improper border crossing so long after the event, and such proved to be the case.

The alleged facts seemed feasible, but confirming the story, without massive resources, was virtually impossible. To compound the problem of gaining any helpful leads from the Dr Hill sighting, I discovered that the United Kingdom had no diplomatic relations with Mozambique at that time. It was therefore impossible to check out even the simplest details of his claim. As with so much of the Lucan evidence, the papers were filed away.

In 1994 I tried once again to contact Dr Hill to discuss his sighting. After so long the only clue I had to his whereabouts was my recollection of him being a general practitioner in the Cardiff area. After drawing a blank with the records of the British Medical Association, I turned for help to British Telecom who gave me access to their archives department at Blackfriars in London, where I was able to discover the doctor's old address from the telephone books of the early 1970s.

From his 20-year-old address I tracked down neighbours who had known him and followed his trail through the years. I was finally given what I was assured was a current address for Dr Hill in Twickenham, Middlesex. It was with high hopes that I telephoned the number, believing that at last I would get the chance to go over with him in more detail the exact circumstances of Lucan's Mozambique visit. My hopes, however, were to be dashed with the discovery that the unfortunate Dr Hill, still a comparatively young man, had died of cancer just a few months before. I was forced back on the resources of my own memory and my personal notes from the time.

Armed with these notes and memories, the computer once again turned up a number of previously unlinked facts, which proved worthy of deeper investigation. Two interesting points had jumped to mind from my recall of the Dr Hill conversation: his reference to Lord Lucan's reported escape route via Portugal and his links with the Portuguese woman, Maria. According to the computer, it appeared that Portugal had cropped up time and again in my Lucan case files.

The first entry concerned a conversation that had taken place just a few days before the Lower Belgrave Street killing. On the Monday of that week Lucky had spoken of his desire to return to Portugal to a senior official of the Portland Club, the London contract bridge centre, where he regularly played bridge and backgammon. Lucan said he was planning to buy another power boat, which he wanted to berth in the Portuguese Algarve.

A further computer file related to a summer

holiday, barely three months before the murder, on which Lord Lucan took all three of his children to a villa in the sun. Because he was separated from his wife, Lucan had needed someone suitable to help him care for the children on this visit to Portugal in 1974. A student from Cambridge University, Yvonne Drewry, was recruited by Lord Lucan as a temporary nanny for the trip. She was just 19 and had been introduced to the Earl by their mutual friend, Stephen Raphael.

This holiday, in the July and August of 1974, was by no means the first time that Lucan had holidayed in Portugal. Among Lucan's personal correspondence in the bankruptcy files were a number of bills for Portuguese holiday homes. It seemed apparent that he had a great love for the country. Could it have been to there that he fled after escaping from Britain?

I realized that the student nanny Yvonne's knowledge of this Portuguese trip could be of immense value. She would know where they stayed and which friends Lucan had in that country. But how could I find her, 20 years on?

CHAPTER 19

A LUCAN LEGACY

I had, by now, become used to the problems of tracking down long-forgotten witnesses, two decades after the event. I knew that Yvonne Drewry had been a college student, and with the help of university authorities, friends and relatives I finally traced her telephone number in Los Angeles, where she now lives and works.

Our conversation, in the summer of 1994, did not get off to the brightest of starts. In my eagerness to contact Yvonne, I had miscalculated the time difference from London. When I telephoned, a sleepy-voiced woman seemed happy to help with her recollections of Lucan, but gently complained that I had woken her up at 5.30 am to discuss something that had already waited 20 long years.

From Yvonne I learnt that she, Lucan and one of his children had flown to Portugal from Heathrow on

19 July 1974 and had driven to a private villa in Estoril. She believed that Lucan had been lent the villa through a friend called 'Peter', whom she thought was an Englishman who lived permanently in Portugal. During the holiday, which ended on 15 August 1974 with a flight back to Heathrow, Lucan had visited a German family, living some 50 miles away, with whom he seemed to be great friends.

Yvonne's most interesting observations, however, related to visits back to England, which Lord Lucan had undertaken in the very first week of the holiday. It transpired that two of his children had been suffering from chicken-pox at the time of the trip. Because of this they had been too ill to leave the care of Lady Lucan for their flight to the sun. Yvonne confirmed that Lord Lucan had been forced to make two separate trips back to England, returning with one child on each occasion.

The nanny's story tied in with something that Lady Lucan had said during the inquest into the death of Sandra Rivett. The Countess told the court that one of the very few conversations between herself and her husband, over the summer of 1974, had been about her children's illness and the arrangements for their holiday.

In the course of the original inquiry, I had learnt of the missing Earl's habit of chartering light aircraft to take private parties of friends on trips to the Continent. He had often flown by this means to racecourses around Britain and to France when one of his thoroughbreds was running. This was, of course, an area I had investigated fully in the immediate aftermath of the murder, when all the ways in which Lucan could have escaped from Britain were under intense scrutiny. Each wealthy friend and witness had been closely questioned about their ownership of boats or planes to which Lucan could have had access.

Those investigations had shown, however, that Lord Lucan did not hold a pilot's licence and had always rented his planes from commercial charter companies. Like many of his earlier extravagances, Lucan had abandoned the habit in recent years, as his money began to run out. All of the charter companies that he had ever used for this purpose had been checked out, and I was confident that Lucan had never been spirited out of the country by this means. Now, however, an informant who did not wish to be named had given me the very first clues to suggest that he could have had access to private air travel, just a few months before the murder. But whose plane had he used?

Yet again, the computer was to make an interesting link from a previously insignificant detail. It highlighted the fact that one of Lucan's close friends in the year or two before the murder had been the renowned British racing driver, Graham Hill. Although Hill recognized Lucky Lucan was an incorrigible gambler, he found him excellent company, and they became close friends and dining companions.

Among the Lucan correspondence, which I was shown by bankruptcy trustee Dennis Gilson in 1994, were letters from Graham Hill to the seventh Earl. The correspondence, dealing with a car that Lucky was thinking of buying, was interspersed with private jokes, and clearly indicated that the two enjoyed the closest of friendships.

Any friend of Lucan with access to his own private plane was now of interest in my inquiry. I already knew that Hill had lost his own life in a tragic aircraft accident just one year after the murder of Sandra Rivett. He, and five members of his racing team, died instantly when their twin-engined Piper Aztec plane crashed into trees and exploded on the approach to his home airfield at Elstree, Hertfordshire, in October 1976.

On that night Graham Hill had been returning from a flight to Marseilles and had apparently decided to risk continuing his approach, despite clear warnings of deteriorating weather conditions. What now linked this tragic event to Lord Lucan was a single comment in an otherwise unimportant conversation with my police investigators after the murder. Hill had, it seems, spoken of the Portuguese holiday trip that Lord Lucan had taken with his children in 1974. He told of a favour that Lord Lucan had asked of him, and which he had been happy to fulfil for a friend.

The year before, in 1973, Graham Hill had formed his own motor-racing team to further his career as Britain's leading motor-racing star. To help his gambler friend, he had asked members of the team to arrange for the transport of Lucky Lucan's Mercedes from Britain to Portugal. On his instructions the car was driven down through Europe and delivered to the Estoril villa for Lucan and the children to use during their holidays.

It was a kindness for a very good friend. But could Graham Hill ever have performed an even greater and more controversial favour for the seventh Earl of Lucan? I clearly needed to know more about the planes to which the racing driver had access.

An in-depth investigation of Hill's aviation career and credentials had been conducted after his fatal crash by the much respected Air Accident Investigation branch of the Department of Trade and Industry. Its subsequent report revealed that Graham Hill was a highly experienced pilot who constantly flew himself and his team all over Europe for both business and pleasure.

Had he lived, however, he would have faced prosecution on a number of counts of breaking aviation laws on the night that he crashed. His twin-engined Piper, fully capable of flights deep into Europe, had originally been registered in the United States. Hill had failed to realize that the original US registration had been cancelled a year earlier, and that its certificate of airworthiness had expired some 15 months earlier. Despite this, the plane had been well maintained and was safe to fly.

In addition there were further serious legal infringements by the pilot himself. Hill's American licence to fly on instruments had lapsed, and his British private pilot's licence did not permit him to fly, on instruments, in the sort of weather conditions that he experienced that night. Even worse, he was found to have broken the law by carrying passengers, at below 3000 feet, in low visibility conditions, when he did not hold the correct licence rating. The report concluded that the precise reason for the aircraft crashing short of the runway could not be established but added: 'Hill may have expected too much of his abilities.'

Graham's grieving widow, Bette, later revealed that Hill had loved flying his aircraft even more than driving his car. She said he was a careful pilot, but that they spoke of his flying as 'Hilarious Airways'. She said that the plane was often used to take her and her children abroad on holidays and almost daily on business trips.

Hill had never been a daredevil on the racing track and had not appeared so in the air. But he clearly had a disregard for the niceties of Britain's aviation laws, had been a close contact of Lucan's and had proved willing to help out a friend.

When I met with Lucan's close friend Charles Benson in the summer of 1994, he stressed to me that both he and Lucan had been 'very, very close friends' of Graham Hill. Indeed just days before his own death Hill had invited Benson to stay with him for the weekend at his Hertfordshire home. The visit never took place because of Hill's subsequent fatal crash. Another interesting fact to emerge, all these years later, was that on the very night before the murder, on Wednesday, 6 November 1974, Lucan had dined as usual at the Clermont Club with one of his closest friends – the racing driver Graham Hill.

Is it conceivable that Hill could have considered helping Lucan out of his biggest scrape of all? The answer may never be known, but it remains an intriguing possibility that might explain how the seventh Earl could have first set off on his foreign adventures.

Reviewing my notes, it now appeared entirely possible to me that, even following a 20-year-old trail, some new facts could be uncovered or new connections made to pinpoint the escape route of Lord Lucan. From the basis of the previous account from Dr Brian Hill, I had uncovered substantial facts to back up his assertion that

Lisbon had been Lucan's first port of call on his flight from British justice.

But the mystery appeared to be running round in circles. How could I move it forward again? What was the link between Lord Lucan's likely jumping-off point in Portugal and Dr Brian Hill's sighting in Africa? The answer was to come from the most unlikely of sources – a car crash on an Essex road that led the trail straight back again to strife-torn Mozambique.

The car crash in question caused the unexpected death of former Grenadier Guards officer David Hardy, who was knocked down and killed in an Essex road accident just before Christmas 1980. Conducting routine inquiries after the death, a police constable found an address book among the dead man's possessions. Flicking through the pages, the officer found a most remarkable entry, reproduced below. It read: 'Lord Lucan, c/o Hotel Les Ambassadeurs, Beira, Mozambique.'

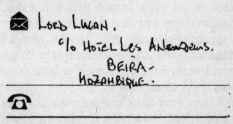

Was this an old address for the lucky Lord – perhaps a holiday destination that he could have visited well before the 1974 murder? Or was it a more up-to-date address, tucked away in a book that its owner never expected others to see? David Hardy could hardly have foreseen the tragic circumstances by which his address-book entry would end up in the hands of Scotland Yard.

I had, by then, retired from the police service and was working at the London headquarters of the BBC. Despite my departure, the murder file remained open, and local police officers quickly reported the matter to the Metropolitan Police detective who had replaced me in command of the Lord Lucan inquiry.

The story of how the address book had been found came to the ears of Fleet Street journalist Chester Stern, who decided to investigate further. Chester, who was on the public relations staff of the Metropolitan Police before becoming crime reporter of the *Mail on Sunday* newspaper, began to look into the background of the unlucky David Hardy.

He discovered that Hardy was a former army officer, a little down on his luck but still able to live in a Chelsea flat because he received a small income from a family trust. He did have a reputation as a heavy drinker and, in the years immediately before his death, had needed frequent financial help from his friends to maintain an upper-class lifestyle. He was also a regular client at the Clermont Club, where he would undoubtedly have known Lucan, although there was little evidence to suggest they were close friends.

The former Foot Guards officer did, however, have one very close friend among the Clermont regulars. This was business consultant Peter West, frequently seen at the club playing *chemin de fer* and known to be an acquaintance of Lord Lucan. This link with the missing Earl was strong enough to send Chester Stern flying off to check out the story in Mozambique.

At the Mozambique hotel that had been named in Hardy's address book, staff recognized pictures of Lord Lucan. They were certain that the suspect had stayed in their hotel 'many years ago' but had subsequently transferred to a second hotel, near the beach.

At this next location the reporter made another, startling discovery. A search of past hotel registers failed to find any trace of Lord Lucan – but did uncover the names of John and Davina Maxwell-Scott. The couple, listed in the register as British, had stayed at the hotel for more than a week in the April of 1975 – five months after the disappearance of Lord Lucan.

As Chester explained in his subsequent newspaper story, Susan Maxwell-Scott had been the last person in England to see Lucan alive. Coming across such an unusual surname while looking for Lucan abroad was yet another of those all-too-frequent coincidences. Back in England, reporters asked Susan Maxwell-Scott about the hotel register. She was adamant that neither she nor her husband Ian had ever visited Mozambique – and she knew of no family members with the names of John and Davina.

One fact that had not been known to police, or to the reporters at the time of this original story, was the additional coincidence that my overworked computer had now identified. This revealed further links between Peter West, the eventful 1974 holiday in Estoril and Lord Lucky Lucan.

I knew that West had been in the headlines before. In the 1950s he had married Miss Davina Portman, a model who had the reputation then of being the most beautiful woman in London. The marriage almost immediately ran into trouble and finally ended in a headline-making divorce case in 1965. Now, a few simple checks convinced me that Lucan and West were perhaps more closely linked than I had previously thought.

For West, it seems, was yet another friend who had done Lucky a favour. He had arranged the purchase of the hard-up Earl's air tickets for the Portuguese holiday in the summer of 1974.

Through a contact in the travel business, West had arranged for Lucan to buy the five return tickets he needed from London Heathrow to Lisbon. The Earl had paid by cheque for the tickets for himself, nanny Yvonne and the children George, Camilla and Frances.

In March 1973 Lucan had been invited on holiday to the estate of the industrialist and financier Sir James Goldsmith in Acapulco, Mexico. The seventh Earl, who had separated from his Countess wife just a few weeks before, had enjoyed the holiday immensely. Years later, among correspondence shown to me by the bankruptcy trustee Dennis Gilson, I unearthed a copy of the letter written by Lucan after his return from Acapulco. The typewritten note on Lucan's personal notepaper was full of private jokes about his lazy lifestyle and racist comments about 'greasers and dagoes'. Dated 26 March 1973, the letter read in part:

> Dear Jimmy and Annabel,
> I have been so involved since Mexico that I have had all the time in the world to write and thank you for the holiday in the land of the greasers – never do today what can be put off until tomorrow. I loved Mexico not the countryside or the climate or the alleged indigenous population or Eric's filthy messed up foreign food; but the

world of BJ's and AP's that was opened to me, not orifically, to use a piece of Aspinalia, but orally via what bankers might call 'your good-selves'.

After further jokes about 'flying aerodagoe', the letter concluded:

I love you both and wish life could always be like that.

West, a close friend and business contact of Sir James, had been on that same Acapulco holiday with Lucan and a few other close friends, such as Dominic Elwes. Holiday snapshots taken of the group had subsequently appeared in the unflattering *Sunday Times* magazine article about the Lucan set. Yet another picture, actually painted by Elwes for that same article, also showed Lucan and Peter West together. They and other gamblers were shown in their natural habitat at the Clermont Club.

As a founder-member of the Clermont Club, West, 49 years old at the time of Lucan's disappearance, had known the Earl for ten years or more. He himself told me that, although they had been close friends for years, he had seen even more of Lucan from 1973 onwards. Now Peter West – the man who had married Davina, the man who had helped with Lucan's air tickets – had popped up once again in this latter-day tale from Mozambique.

When I recently met Chester Stern in London he had one further nugget of information about the mystery of the Lucan legacy. Chester had been given the Hardy address book, as a memento, by the dead man's widow. She also revealed to him that the Lucan entry could not have been made until after the Earl's disappearance. It transpired that David Hardy's wife had given her late husband the notebook, herself, as a present in 1975 – nearly a year after Lord Lucan had apparently vanished from the face of the earth. Was this puzzling entry, involving yet more of Lucan's friends and acquaintances, truly a contact for the missing Earl? Or simply a joke from a Walter Mitty character who wished to appear 'in the know' about the fate of Lord Lucan?

My computer-generated inquiries had set my thoughts off on a grand and circular trip. From Britain to Mozambique – to Portugal – to Britain – to Mozambique yet again. It seemed entirely possible that Lucan had fled by air from Britain to the Portugal he knew so well. And now, I had the added possibility that he could have flown that same route, by light aircraft, before.

There was one further, odd postcript to this story from Mozambique. The second hotel, to which Lucan allegedly moved, and where the Maxwell-Scotts appeared in the register, was named the Hotel Estoril. It is plausible that, with memories of his last happy holiday with the children still fresh in his mind, Lucan was drawn towards a familiar place-name, to somewhere he had once been so content. To my mind the episode had echoes of an earlier, just as peculiar, coincidence – the mysterious Mr Charles who had telephoned the Horton Hall guest-house in far-away Sussex just a couple of days after the brutal killing of poor Sandra Rivett.

One thing was certain. If Lucan had rested awhile in Portugal after fleeing from Britain, his onward route to Mozambique would have presented few problems. The East African country is a former Portuguese colony and consequently has excellent and long-established transport links with Lisbon.

Even more importantly, at the time of Lucan's flight the country had been torn apart by years of civil war. Diplomatic relations with Britain were non-existent, and any idea of extradition would have been out of the question. In the Lourenço Marques of the 1970s there were few authorities to ask questions, and even fewer border controls that could not be passed with the help of a few dollars bribe. Mozambique had many enticing qualifications, as a temporary home, for a lord on the run.

Evidence that Lucan had been in both Portugal and Mozambique was entirely circumstantial – but it was beginning to build to impressive dimensions. All a coincidence? Of course it could be. But perhaps one coincidence too many for comfort.

CHAPTER 20

INTO AFRICA

Encouraged by the interconnections overlooked for almost 20 years, I delved deeper into every possible African link. Another prison visit had stuck in my mind for a very long time. In January 1977 I had received a further call to visit a prison, this time in Leeds, and to interview a second man who had information to offer about the Lucan case. This was Trevor Walton, a British citizen who had fled the country two years before when facing trial for a number of motoring offences.

Although the charges, which included drink-driving, were relatively minor, Walton had been told by his solicitor that he could receive three months in jail. Fearing imprisonment, Walton decided to 'skip off to southern Africa' for a while. He fled to Rhodesia where, after working in a cotton factory in a place called Grandmervan, he joined the Rhodesian Light

Infantry as a private soldier.

Hoping to hide completely from the charges awaiting him back in London, the new recruit joined up with the infantry under the fake name of Terry Walters, and he was allocated the army number 728025. He was to meet so many New Zealanders, Australians and Americans who had served in Vietnam that Walton compared the unit in which he served to the French Foreign Legion.

He eventually was granted leave and in what Walton remembered as being the August of 1976 went to Gaborone in nearby Botswana, a frequent rest and recreation destination for the soldiers because of the availability of alcohol, gambling and girls. Walton recalled it as the weekend of a final rugby test between the New Zealand All Blacks and South Africa's Springboks. The town was crowded and in celebratory mood.

Trying to check on Walton's story I made inquiries about that particular rugby tour and discovered that my informant's memory had been relatively reliable. The rugby test to which he referred actually took place not in August 1976 but in the following month of September. The records show that the final match, on 18 September 1976, was won by South Africa with a score of 15–14, giving them a 3–1 final victory over the All Blacks touring team.

Under his real name the runaway soldier checked into the Holiday Inn complex in Gaborone and went out on the town. That evening he met the owner of a Botswana construction company, and the two men fell to talking about the politics of southern Africa and the 'strange people' to be found out there. To demonstrate his point, the Botswanan pointed out a man at the bar and assured his companion that this was Lord Lucan.

Walton, who later saw the man playing at the craps table in the Holiday Inn casino, described him as around 40 years old, very fit, six foot tall and with dark hair that was going grey. He was clean-shaven and spoke with a cultured accent. Walton was told that the man lived in the nearby town of Palapye, had something to do with mining and had not been there long. I showed photographs of Lucan to Walton, and he readily identifed him as the man he had seen in Botswana.

Not long after the Holiday Inn incident Walton grew tired of life in the Rhodesian Army. Eventually he came back to Britain to 'face the music', receiving the prison sentence he had tried to avoid.

Once again the story was interesting, and I had left the prison where Walton was housed wishing that it were possible to do more than add the notes to my growing collection of sightings. Attempts were made to contact the local police in Botswana in order to check out this man's story, but no effective inquiries were ever made.

There was a tiny postscript to the tale that Trevor Walton had to tell me, when a batch of letters was forwarded to Scotland Yard from a national newspaper. Every paper receives its fair share of crank mail, and the letters sent on to us were those that in some way or other mentioned Lord Lucan.

Among these was a letter written by Trevor Walton some time after his meeting with me. By then he had been moved to a Nottingham jail, and the reason for his letter to the newspaper was to ask for a job. He stressed that, despite his criminal record, he had the intelligence and motivation to make a good journalist and, by way of inducement for him to be given a job, repeated part of the tale about meeting Lucan in southern Africa. The newspaper letter and the original statement were not married up in police files for many years after the event. However, when I did see the second letter I was interested to note that he had stuck, unerringly, to his original story.

There was, however, one fact that had jarred in Walton's account and had cast doubt in my mind when I first heard his tale. He reported that Lucan had been playing craps, the American dice game, when he saw him in Gaborone. At that time I had not known that Lucan played the game of craps, and it was only many years later that I discovered that he had become addicted to this dice game in the months just before his disappearance. It was a fact that Walton could not possibly have known, and therefore it added to the credibility of his tale. It was another small pointer to me that this story was worthy of investigation.

By now I was closely studying maps of southern Africa to identify clearly the town of Palapye in Botswana, which Walton had claimed was a refuge for Lucan. I realized immediately that there were very close links between this tiny spot on the map and another, equally fascinating report, which I was able to follow up only in 1994.

This second sighting had originated some ten years earlier, from an employee of the Botswana Development Corporation named Don Thomson. He had reported a sighting of Lord Lucan in the Tuli Block in Botswana, a wealthy and sparsely populated area of large game and hunting ranches, many of which are owned by rich expatriates.

The information came to him originally from a game-park warden who travelled through the Tuli Block, escorting wealthy patrons on hunting and photographic safaris. The district is far removed from the popular image of a poor southern Africa. Some ranches stretch for dozens of miles in every direction, and the ranch houses may only be reached down lengthy and strictly private roads.

Because of the many wealthy southern Africans and foreigners who own homes in the Tuli Block, the local police force were, in the early 1980s, when the sighting was reported, hostile to all outsiders. Strangers were liable to close questioning and a clear suggestion to 'get out of town'.

Anxious to cash in on his news, Don Thomson approached a local South African newspaper reporter, Norman Chandler, and the Johannesburg correspondent of the London *Sunday Times*, Eric Marsden. Together the three men went off on safari, posing as potential buyers of a Tuli Block estate in order to gain free access to the area that they wanted to search.

Over lunch at a London restaurant in 1994 Eric Marsden told me of his safari adventures, and the frustrations they felt at being unable to ask direct questions of the hostile local population. With little progress to report, the team moved south to the Botswana town of Gaborone. It was there that their persistence finally began to pay dividends. At the Holiday Inn, the same location mentioned by Trevor Walton to me some years before, the staff responded instantly to the pictures of Lord Lucan.

With increasing excitement the hunters found more and more hotel employees who confidently agreed that the Lucan picture was the spitting image of a regular visitor to the hotel who was based in Johannesburg.

The man in question was reputed to be the boss of a South African clothing company. He made frequent visits to the Holiday Inn, usually staying in the very best rooms reserved for VIP guests. One booking earlier that year had been cancelled by the mysterious guest at short notice. On checking further it was discovered that the weekend of the cancellation was also the weekend of a Zambia/South African summit, which meant that the hotel and the town itself were filled with journalists reporting the event.

Back in Johannesburg two addresses were traced for the suspect. One was his home apartment and the other a business address in the centre of the city. For several days there was no trace of the man himself, although when Marsden called at the apartment and peeped through a window he saw that the room was clearly occupied and fully furnished. He finally got through to him on the phone and asked to meet to 'clear up a case of mistaken identity'. The man agreed to a meeting but warned that he was about to leave on an urgent trip to Cape Town, and the meeting could not take place for a couple of days. He was never to return.

When the journalists called at his Johannesburg flat, the caretaker reported that the tenant had given up the rental. When they called at the office, they found it had been closed down, literally overnight, and the staff had been given a single month's pay. Astonishingly, the reporters involved were never given the chance to follow up their quarry. Despite having evidence that their man had left the country, they had other journalistic tasks to perform.

'I really thought that this was a serious story which needed further investigation,' Eric Marsden told me. 'However, my job in South Africa was always to report on the political situation in that country, and my superiors in London were anxious for me to return to my normal role. I have always wished that it could have been taken further. It may well have been him.'

The coincidences between these two events, once again separated by many years and originating from two completely different sources, were too much to ignore. Walton had named the town of Palapye; Thomson had pinpointed the Tuli Block, just a few miles away. Walton had spoken of Lucan at the Holiday Inn casino in Gaborone; Thomson's inquiries led directly to the same hotel.

Was it truly possible that the two most authoritative sightings I had investigated in 20 years of following the Lucan case could really have led by coincidence to this one tiny dot on the African map? I had to find out.

I flew into Johannesburg, South Africa, on 9 May 1994. It was a city in some turmoil. Scrutineers were still counting the votes in the troubled country's most historic election – the first in which every South African of any creed and colour had been entitled to vote. The former Labour leader Neil Kinnock was a fellow passenger on the flight, and Jan Smuts Airport was packed with arriving dignitaries from all over the world, who were crowd-

ing into the city for the election result and the inaugura-
tion of President Nelson Mandela.

After settling into my hotel I went to meet one of
the men whose previous stories about Lord Lucan had
fitted into all the other information that had led me
towards southern Africa. This was Norman Chandler, a
highly respected South African journalist who was then
working as the Bureau Chief of the *Star* newspaper.

Chandler told me that at one stage he believed that
they had missed Lucan on one of the massive estates by
a matter of just 18 hours. In the end they were defeated
by the vast distances involved, the wariness and hostility
of the local wealthy white residents and the remote nature
of so many of the households that they would have liked
to have visited.

In addition to checking out the Tuli Block sighting,
there was one other reason for stopping off at Johannesburg. I tried without success to trace and interview Lord
Lucan's brother, Hugh Bingham, whom I had last met
nearly 20 years before.

In the aftermath of the murder I had talked with
Hugh Bingham and had been impressed by him as a
decent and honest man. He had clearly loved his brother
dearly and had lunched with him regularly, but the two
brothers moved in separate worlds. Just six months after
the killing, Hugh had told me that he had been offered
a job in South Africa and would shortly be leaving
Britain. I had no reason to ask him to stay, although
his departure fuelled some newspaper speculation that
he could be meeting Lord Lucan abroad.

There had been few clues to his whereabouts in
the intervening years, just one or two old newspaper

articles reporting him as working in the mining industry in various parts of southern Africa. To my surprise I found Hugh now working in Johannesburg and very much at the centre of local political life. He was employed with the government body overseeing the first free elections in the spring of 1994.

With my hopes raised I telephoned his home without getting a reply. I went to the address on the outskirts of the city to find that he occupied a first-floor flat in a detached house. The door was opened by a friendly woman who confirmed Hugh Bingham lived there but was out.

She allowed me into his home to leave a note asking him to telephone me at the hotel. Unfortunately when he finally did call it was to refuse my offer of a meeting, and I could elicit no reason why not. It was a disappointing response from one of the few members of the Lucan family and friends who had ever seemed willing sensibly to discuss his brother's role in the Sandra Rivett murder.

However, armed with Norman's and Eric's full account of their travels in Botswana, I decided to head in that direction in my continuing search for news of the long-lost seventh Earl. I had always planned that Johannesburg should be no more than a stopping-off point along my way. I boarded a small ten-seater Cropscraft plane and flew into the tiny Seretse Khama Airport in Gaborone, Botswana.

I booked into the Gaborone Sun Hotel, a casino and conference centre, that used to be called the Holiday Inn Hotel up until the late 1980s. It was the building where British prisoner Trevor Walton had sworn he had seen Lord Lucan, and despite the change in ownership the hotel seemed much as Walton had described it.

I had barely settled in to my room when I received a telephone call from a person from my Metropolitan Police past. Russell Allen, an ex-Detective Superintendent of the Fraud Squad, was working in Gaborone and had already heard on the grapevine that I was in town. He was working with another former London officer, ex-Commander Graham Cresswell, to set up an anti-corruption unit within Botswana.

Over dinner the two former colleagues proved to be a mine of information to help me in my search. I learnt that Botswana was an interesting location for anybody seeking a remote, yet civilized spot in which to disappear. The country has an area greater than France – but a population of only just over a million.

I was particularly interested in the Tuli Block, and my new contacts explained that this was an area, on the border between Botswana and South Africa, that stretched for hundreds of miles along the banks of the Limpopo river. There were numerous border posts between the two countries, some only open in the daylight hours.

Such border checkpoints are only manned by police between 8 am and 4 pm, and at all other times it is a simple matter to slip over the border unnoticed and unrecorded by any official. These official border posts are many dozens of miles apart, and crossings can easily be made between the two countries by traversing the arid river-bed during the dry season. Animal poachers frequently cross the borders, and beautifully carved ivory objects were still readily available in souvenir shops in both countries.

The following morning I looked in at the casino, which offered some 50 or more fruit machines, *chemin de fer* and blackjack tables, but no longer had the craps table on which Lucan allegedly played many years before. I discovered that the hotel register and other written records from the time in which I was interested had been destroyed when computers were introduced into the hotel.

I went to see Senior Superintendent Russell Allen at the Anti-Corruption Unit offices and there examined maps and photographs of the Tuli Block. Local officers explained that the land was split into large sections, owned privately by wealthy, white individuals as estates, game reserves and farms. The great majority of such estates were heavily protected by fences, large gates and security staff.

We discussed the possibility of Lucan visiting the area, or even living on one of the properties. I learnt that the houses are often built some 15 to 20 kilometres down rough tracks leading through dried-up river-beds, rocks and hills away from the main dirt roads. Everybody who knew the area agreed that, with the right sort of help, it would have been entirely possible for Lucan to have lived in this remote district with little fear of discovery. Clearly I had to see the area for myself. Back at the hotel I found a white Botswanan, Abraham 'Brumpy' Malan, waiting for my return. The unlikely named Brumpy insisted that he had seen Lucan many years ago, but at first he wanted to be paid for his information. After considerable haggling Brumpy reluctantly gave me his story of seeing Lucan in the very casino in which we were meeting. He boasted of his connections within

Botswana and of his friendship with the late president, Sir Seretse Khama.

Brumpy pointed out the very spot where he alleged Lucan had been gambling in the Holiday Inn casino. He claimed that he had also heard that the missing Earl had stayed for a while in Bulawayo in Zimbabwe but could produce no evidence to substantiate his claims. He clearly was not a reliable character and, despite his aggressive insistence that Lucan had been seen, I was by no means convinced.

A few days later I flew into the Tuli Block, about which I had now learnt so much. It was an hour's flight to the privately owned airstrip called Tuli Lodge, some miles away from the Mashatu Game Reserve. It was immediately clear how easy movement would be in or out of this country for Lord Lucan or any other fugitive from justice. The airstrip was deserted, and the corrugated hut, which served as both immigration headquarters and customs post, was unmanned.

Although there were no people in sight, there was certainly no shortage of animals. In a subsequent drive into the game reserve I travelled through scrubland for over an hour, seeing elephants, zebras, ostriches and a huge variety of beautiful birds.

The local police force consisted of one sergeant and a constable who, as Norman Chandler had warned me, were uncooperative if not openly hostile. They warmed up after a while and told me that arson and housebreaking were the most prevalent local crimes. They claimed never to have heard of my quarry. Other inquiries among local white residents and the local African population produced no better results and, somewhat dispirited, I flew out to the nearby town of Maun, where I was to interview a woman who had hunted for Lucan in the Tuli Block a decade before.

I drove for some hours to a crocodile farm on the banks of the River Limpopo where I had arranged to meet the woman, named Janice Main. She was very well spoken and moved in the upper social circles of the white residents of Botswana. She proved to have an interesting tale to relate.

Janice had helped to organize the Chandler and Marsden safari in search of Lucan and related how the group had come to grief in the Tuli Block. They had camped in a dried-up river-bed, but in the night the camp was charged by a herd of angry, wild elephants. Escaping from the tents the expedition had sought refuge for the night in a nearby estate, but on returning in the morning they had found that the elephants had destroyed the camp and all their equipment.

On the safari Janice had been embarrassed by their visits to wealthy estates, where they had not been made welcome, and she had formed the opinion that the search for Lucan was a waste of time. However, her view was to change dramatically just a few weeks later, after she had returned to Gaborone.

In Gaborone, known to all the local population as 'Gabs', Janice went to a hairdresser's salon on the ground floor of one of the town's major office blocks. She told me: 'The office block is called Debswana House, the top floor of which, in those days, was where the De Beers company used to sort their diamonds. Anyway, it was on the ground floor of that, and I walked out of my hairdressers. It was very quiet on a Saturday afternoon. Then I heard these footsteps echoing behind me on the marble floors, and it was a very confident footstep, so instinctively I looked behind to see who it was. I looked straight at him – I mean, I got cold sweats and, I thought, it's him. I'd been looking for him all over the Tuli Block, and here he is.

'I was sort of stunned and didn't know what to do, so I turned around and looked in the window of a travel agency or something else that was on the ground floor. But I had another good look at him as he walked past me and thought – What do I do now? I wanted to say, "Hello – are you Lord Lucan? I've been looking for you," but it all seemed so stupid, so I just followed him out of Debswana House.

He went down the stairs, into the car park, got into a Toyota Land Cruiser and drove off. I stood there for about half an hour not sure what to do. I'm convinced it was him.'

Janice described the man as middle-aged, of military bearing with very good posture and immense self-confidence.

'I think the overwhelming impression is a presence, an aura, like a magnetism. It's like sometimes in the bush you get a sort of connection with something that has an aura about it – almost a danger. I'd been studying pictures of Lord Lucan for days before on this Tuli trip, and I'm absolutely certain that it was him that I saw that day.'

Janice's story was both credible and convincing. I asked her why she had taken no action after seeing a man whom she knew was wanted for murder. She told me she felt that someone in his position was entitled to survive in this unpopulated area, living as a hermit for the rest of his life, if he wished. She believed she had no right to interfere. I felt sure that if, at the time, she had known the full horrific facts of the killing of Sandra Rivett, her answer might well have been different.

The sighting that Janice reported to me in Gaborone was certainly one of the more convincing accounts that I have come across in 20 years of searching for Lucan. I felt that her absolute conviction that she had met the seventh Earl may well have been true. In a way her recollections had taken me closer to Lucan than any other report in the past two decades.

But the path I was following, one that had taken me from the genteel world of Belgravia to this crocodile farm in a remote southern African town, was clearly an old and cold trail. Lucan might well have passed this way a decade before, but I knew I would now need to look elsewhere for a solution to this mystery of the missing Earl.

CHAPTER 21

THE SEARCH CONTINUES

RICHARD JOHN BINGHAM, EARL OF LUCAN.

Born:	London 18.12.34. Height: 6ft 2ins.
Complexion:	Ruddy.
Hair:	Dark brown, brown and ginger-flecked moustache.
Eyes:	Blue.
Teeth:	Gold fillings.
Wearing:	Light-coloured jumper, dark-coloured trousers.
Habits:	Smoker of Peter Stuyvesant cigarettes; drinks vodka; frequents race meetings, gambling clubs, may travel abroad.

This original police description of Richard John Bingham, aged 39, was likely to be of little use in my continuing quest for Lord Lucan. However, upon my return to England I learnt of a new computer program, developed by the FBI in America, which had enjoyed startling success in tracing missing persons or fugitives who had been on the run for years.

The program works by computer-ageing the last-known photographs of the missing person to produce a picture, as scientifically accurate as possible, of how they would appear today. The method is basically very simple. The operator feeds the last-known portrait of the missing person into the computer and adds additional pictures of their mother and father, at an age as close as possible to the target figure. The pictures are blended together to mix mother, father and offspring into a new composite image that can be astonishingly accurate.

When I saw the results of some of the program's work I realized that this could be an invaluable tool in the search for Lord Lucan. The last picture that I had of the missing Earl was 20 years old and showed him as a man of just 39. In reality he was now fast approaching his sixtieth birthday.

Although in my days at Scotland Yard I had requested police artists to provide me with 'aged' pictures of the fugitive, they had always before had nothing other than guesswork with which to work. Now there was the chance of a portrait that had every chance of providing a realistic image of the wanted man.

The computer program requires more than just an input of the relevant photographs. The manner in which the ageing process develops in each individual is a complex combination of heredity, lifestyle, fitness, muscle tone and so on. The skill of the operator is of vital importance in obtaining the best possible result. When

I tracked down a copy of the program in Britain, I discovered the most skilled operator possible was at its controls.

The programmer was a former police officer, Peter Bennett, whom I had known during my days at Scotland Yard, where he had managed the Metropolitan Police visual identification bureau. I was delighted to renew our acquaintance and knew that my task was in the safest of hands. Together we set about the task of creating a 60-year-old seventh Earl of Lucan.

Pictures of his mother and father were scanned into the computer and gradually a new image emerged on the screen. The experts predicted that Lord Lucan's hairline was most likely to recede in the same way as that of the sixth Earl. On the other hand his facial features and lines were likely to age more in the manner of his mother, the late Dowager Countess of Lucan.

When the computer had completed its work, the finished colour picture required just a little freehand artwork to smooth out the lines. Finally, looking out at me from the screen was the 60-year-old seventh Earl of Lucan, the man I had been hunting for 20 years since that fateful night of 7 November 1974. It was an eerie sensation to stare into the eyes of the man I believe to have been responsible for such a vicious crime and yet who has continued to evade the justice he most richly deserves.

It is ironic that had Lord Lucan surrendered to the police on the night of the murder, been tried and convicted, and sentenced to life imprisonment, he would have served no more than perhaps ten years in a British jail. Although a life prisoner is technically never free from his sentence and liable to recall to prison at any time, the reality is that few such prisoners serve more than a decade in jail.

Were Lucan now to be found, or to return voluntarily to the United Kingdom, he would still find himself in the dock at the Old Bailey on those charges from which I obtained arrest warrants so many years ago. In separate trials he would stand accused of the murder of Mrs Sandra Eleanor Rivett and the attempted murder of his wife, Lady Veronica, the Countess of Lucan.

Many people have suggested that he has nothing to fear from the British legal system. That so much time has slipped by that he would be able to return with impunity. However, both the forensic and witness evidence available against Lord Lucan is still compelling. It remains in the archive files of New Scotland Yard and in the mind of Lady Lucan. I believe that the inevitable result would be: 'Guilty'.

The equally inevitable sentence of life imprisonment is something that Lucan will continue to evade at all costs. Human beings are infinitely adaptable animals, and the Earl will have adapted, as would we all, to a new life abroad.

For many of the years that he has been missing, I believe that Lord Lucan has been able to live in relative comfort in the warmth of southern Africa. Probably with a little help from, as yet, unidentified friends he has built a reasonable life; conceivably even a more useful life than his wastrel twilight existence as a gambler in the London he left so abruptly behind.

Now he appears to have moved on. I have never given up on my search. Since my new computer-produced portrait of Lord Lucan was created, new steps have been taken to track down the missing Earl. Quietly, and with no attendant publicity, a series of small notices has been appearing in newspapers around the world.

In places as diverse as Manila and Toronto, Gaborone and Acapulco, the new face of Lord Lucan has looked out from the pages at tens of thousands of readers. The advertisements give no clue as to the nature of the inquiry, simply showing his photograph and the words:

MISSING PERSON

RICHARD HAS BEEN MISSING FROM HIS HOME IN THE UNITED KINGDOM FOR THE PAST TWENTY YEARS. IF YOU THINK THAT YOU KNOW THE MAN IN THIS PICTURE THEN PLEASE CONTACT THE BOX NUMBER BELOW.

To date there has been no single response that has led me further towards my goal of finding Richard John Bingham. But the advertisements will continue to appear. Sooner or later an acquaintance, a neighbour, a servant, a newspaper reader, simply the woman who sells him his cigarettes – or a reader, of this book – will spot a resemblance. Take a look now at the man sitting next to you as you read these lines. Could he be Lord Lucan? If so, then please let me know.

The Earl's mother, the late Dowager Countess Kaitilin, once returned from a walking holiday in Turkey to be asked by an eager reporter if she had met with her son. Her reply was sarcastic: 'Do you seriously think I would say if I had?'

Hugh Bingham also once spoke of his missing brother. At his South African home he said that he believed that his brother still lived but added: 'The world is a very big place. There are plenty of hidey-holes still to be found.'

I believe that one of those hidey-holes still holds Lord Lucan, and, wherever he may be, I have my own personal message for the missing Earl.

'Do not relax, my Lord. Keep a watchful eye over your shoulder. There will always be someone looking for Lucan.'

Warner now offers an exciting range of quality titles by both established and new authors. All of the books in this series are available from:
Little, Brown and Company (UK),
P.O. Box 11,
Falmouth,
Cornwall TR10 9EN.

Alternatively you may fax your order to the above address. Fax No. 0326 376423.

Payments can be made as follows: Cheque, postal order (payable to Little, Brown and Company) or by credit cards, Visa/Access. Do not send cash or currency. UK customers: and B.F.P.O.: please send a cheque or postal order (no currency) and allow £1.00 for postage and packing for the first book, plus 50p for the second book, plus 30p for each additional book up to a maximum charge of £3.00 (7 books plus).

Overseas customers including Ireland, please allow £2.00 for postage and packing for the first book, plus £1.00 for the second book, plus 50p for each additional book.

NAME (Block Letters) ....

ADDRESS..

....

☐ I enclose my remittance for _____

☐ I wish to pay by Access/Visa Card

Number ☐☐☐☐☐☐☐☐☐☐☐☐☐☐☐☐☐☐

Card Expiry Date ☐☐☐☐